THE DARDANELLES DISASTER

THE DARDANELLES DISASTER

Winston Churchill's
Greatest Failure

DAN VAN DER VAT

Duckworth Overlook

This edition first published in 2010

First published in the UK and in the US in 2009 by
Duckworth Overlook

LONDON
90-93 Cowcross Street
London EC1M 6BF
info@duckworth-publishers.co.uk
www.ducknet.co.uk

NEW YORK
141 Wooster Street
New York, NY 10012
for bulk or special sales contact sales@overlookny.com

A catalogue record for this book is available
from the British Library

ISBN 978-0-7156-3779-1 (UK)
ISBN 978-1-59020-339-2 (US)

Typeset by Ray Davies
Printed and bound in the UK by
JF Print Ltd, Sparkford, Somerset

Contents

For James and Katie
from their grandfather

List of Illustrations

List of Illustrations

French soldiers from the Colonial Regiment inspect a smashed searchlight. *Imperial War Museum*

The Kaiser and Enver Pasha converse on the deck of the *Goeben*. *Imperial War Museum*

The commanders and chiefs of staff on HMS *Triad*: (L to R) Commodore Roger Keyes; Vice-Admiral John de Robeck; General Sir Ian Hamilton; Major-General W.P. Braithwaite. *Imperial War Museum*

The man who answered the 'Turkish Question', Mustafa Kemal Atatürk. *akg-images*

The undoing of the Allied fleet. The Turkish minelayer *Nusret* – the modern copy at Çannakale. *Author's photograph*

Atatürk's verdict on the Dardanelles and Gallipoli campaigns. *Author's photograph*

Preface
Blunder upon Blunder

The official biographer of Winston Churchill, central figure in the Dardanelles disaster of 1915, writes that '[Admiral of the Fleet Lord] Fisher's return to the Admiralty coincided with Britain's only serious naval defeat of the war'. Fisher had been recalled from retirement to his old post as First Sea Lord on 30 October 1914: the reference is to the Battle of Coronel on 1 November, when Vice-Admiral Graf Spee's German cruisers crushed a British squadron off Chile. Yet much of the same third volume of Sir Martin Gilbert's biography is necessarily devoted to Churchill's leading role, as First Lord of the Admiralty, in the Royal Navy's abortive effort to reopen the Dardanelles after Turkey had closed them in August 1914.

As the political head of the navy Churchill personally presided over this unique fiasco, which led to his dismissal and almost destroyed his career. Since his style of administration could hardly have been more 'hands on', he did not merely preside over the disaster but intervened, if not interfered, in almost every operational and political aspect of it, large or small, often acting beyond his powers and presenting his Cabinet colleagues with *faits accomplis*. Yet his proposal to outflank the Central Powers – Germany, Austria-Hungary and their allies, including Turkey – by attacking the latter as the weakest link in a front deadlocked from Belgium to the Balkans – is now widely accepted as the boldest strategic concept of the First World War. However, as with so many other failed British military enterprises, it was undermined by appalling incompetence in execution. Churchill's great error was to go ahead with the navy alone after Kitchener, the Secretary of State for War, insisted that there were no troops available for the combined operation which contemporary informed opinion (including Churchill and Kitchener) had long since agreed was necessary to force the Dardanelles.

The Dardanelles disaster swelled the rising tide of complaints in Britain about 'bungling in high places'. After the navy's failure was bloodily redoubled by the army's at Gallipoli, heads eventually rolled, including

Fisher's and Churchill's; and to survive as Prime Minister, Asquith was forced to replace his Liberal administration with a coalition Cabinet.

The Royal Navy's abortive solo attempt to reopen the Dardanelles was prompted by another naval failure: the ineptly missed opportunity to deploy immensely superior forces to stop and destroy the Mediterranean Division of the German Imperial Navy in the first week of the First World War. Rear-Admiral Wilhelm Souchon was allowed to take his two ships, a battlecruiser and a light cruiser, over 1,000 miles from Sicily across the eastern basin of the Mediterranean to the Dardanelles. He eluded both the bulk of the French fleet and the British Mediterranean Fleet, which by itself was much his superior in firepower and numbers of ships, even though he could so easily have been trapped in the Strait of Messina between two groups of British ships each endowed with firepower superior to his. This incident was the subject of one of my earlier books, *The Ship That Changed the World* (1985), to which this volume forms a sequel.

The consequences of Souchon's escape to Turkish waters, enabling the Germans to activate their secret alliance with Ottoman Turkey by provoking Tsarist Russia into a war against the Turks, were recognised by both British and German leaders as worth two extra years to the Germans and their allies in a war that lasted just over four. The Dardanelles strait was closed to the Entente powers – Britain, France and Russia – and the latter was effectively cut off, unable to export grain to the other two, who likewise were prevented from delivering much-needed munitions in return. The British were prompted to try to reverse this, not only to reopen the link but also to turn the eastern flank of the Central Powers by passing through the Dardanelles strait into the Sea of Marmara, knocking Turkey out of the war by threatening Constantinople, passing through the Bosporus into the Black Sea, joining hands with the Russians and going up the Danube to attack Austria-Hungary from the rear.

The failure of the great seaborne bombardment of the Dardanelles forts in March 1915, a leisurely seven months later, in a bid to reverse the Germans' diplomatic and strategic coup, only served to compound its results exponentially. Compared with the consequences of the Royal Navy's double failure – Souchon's escape and the rebuff at the Dardanelles – the defeat at Coronel, handsomely avenged within weeks at the Battle of the Falkland Islands, where Spee's squadron was all but wiped out, was a marginal skirmish of minor strategic significance. The abortive attempt to reopen the Dardanelles by naval gunpower alone, judged by its consequences, may therefore stand as the Royal Navy's most significant failure, certainly in the First World War, probably in the twentieth century and possibly in all the 500 years of its existence. A victory for the Spanish Armada in 1588 or for Napoleon's navy at Trafalgar in 1805 would have been rather worse, but neither came to pass, becoming instead the Royal Navy's most important victories. A British failure to overcome the U-boat blockade imposed by the Germans in each world war would surely have surpassed the Dardanelles fiasco in gravity but was narrowly averted in each case.

This gives the Dardanelles campaign – Turkey's only military triumph in 1914–18 – pride of place in the brief list of Britain's strategic maritime failures. Chronologically, and also in terms of suffering and loss, the ensuing Allied failure to seize the Gallipoli peninsula by military force in order to outflank the Dardanelles defences takes first place among the results. This was intended to help the fleet and its supply ships to get to Constantinople without being shelled from the shore. The bloody slaughter in the Gallipoli campaign, a smaller-scale but sometimes even more intense extension of the stalemate on the Western Front, understandably draws the general reader's eye from the naval failure of which it was the first *consequence*. This book however focuses on the primary role of the Royal Navy in these extraordinary events.

It does so without footnotes. I have managed to rub along without them in nine previous forays into naval history, convinced as ever of my belief that general readers, for whom this and all its predecessors are intended, are not interested in them. If they have anything in common with me, they may actually be irritated by having to interrupt what I hope is a good read by going to the back of the book, only to see such immortal notations as 'op. cit.' or 'ibid.'.

The Note on Sources, and the Select Bibliography at the end reveal the material and earlier works on which I drew to assemble this story.

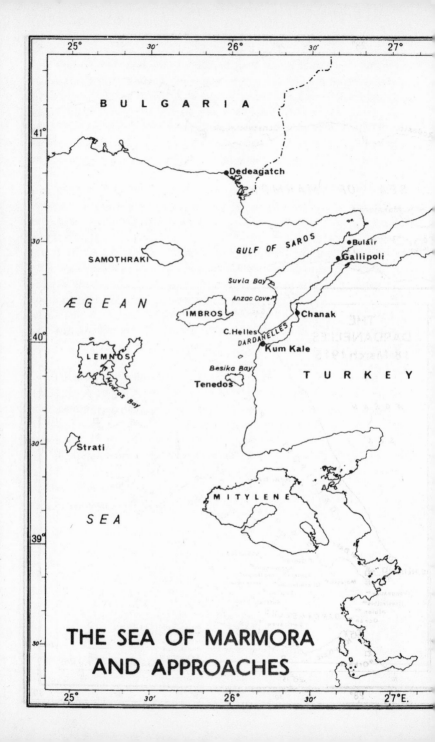

THE SEA OF MARMORA
AND APPROACHES

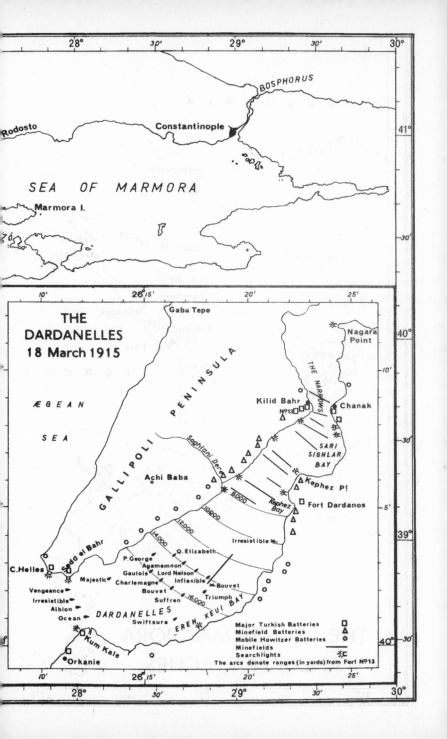

Acknowledgements

I should like to thank the following for the support and assistance I have received over the many years I have explored the Dardanelles story, taking on other projects but always returning for another look at a subject which has fascinated me ever since I first took an interest in naval history 30 years ago.

The staffs of the British Library, the London Library and the libraries of the London Borough of Richmond upon Thames; the staffs of the British National Archives (known as the Public Record Office when I started), and the German Federal Military Archives in Freiburg-im-Breisgau; the Turkish Naval and Army Museums in Istanbul and the Naval Museum at Çannakale.

I am no less grateful to Annette Boon for help with my non-existent Turkish; Rezan Muir and the Turkish Area Study Group; Dr Kenan Çelik, formerly of Çannakale Onsekiz Mart University and latterly battlefield guide, who took me on an invaluable personal tour of the Dardanelles and Gallipoli.

I could not have finished this book without the support through many vicissitudes of my former agent, Jonathan Pegg, late of Curtis Brown, and his successor, Shaheeda Sabir; and of Peter Mayer and especially Mary Morris of Duckworth Publishers. Further acknowledgements are in the note on sources.

None of these is responsible for any error, for which I alone am to blame.

Introduction

The Voyage of the *Nusret*

The modest Turkish harbour of Nagara, on the Asian shore of the Dardanelles, lies less than four miles north of the Narrows, the most constricted section of the strait between the Sea of Marmara and the Mediterranean. It was from there that the minelayer *Nusret* set sail half an hour before midnight on 7 March 1915, under the command of Yuzbashi (Lieutenant) Hakki Bey of the Ottoman Navy. Alongside him on the open bridge stood Birindji-Yuzbashi (Lieutenant-Commander) Hafiz Nazmi Bey, leader of the naval minelaying specialists who had sown the Dardanelles minefields. He was accompanied by a German mine specialist called Bettaque; another German naval officer, Engineer Reeder, was in charge of the engines below. He had checked them and the boilers to enable the vessel to achieve silent running with minimal smoke output. Their unspectacular afterthought of a mission would change the course of the First World War and of world history: it was to be the most effective and devastating minelaying operation ever undertaken, and was to engender the turning-point of the Dardanelles naval campaign.

The 364-tonne vessel was that rarest of objects in the Turkish fleet of the period – a modern, purpose-built craft, ordered in 1910 from the Germaniawerft shipyard in Kiel in the far north of Germany and commissioned into the mostly decrepit Ottoman Navy in 1913. She was 40 metres long with a draught of 3.4 metres and capable of 15 knots. Her twin shafts, driven by two coal-fired, triple-expansion engines, made her suitably manoeuvrable, and she was armed with a pair of 47-millimetre quick-firing guns forward plus two parallel racks on her long, open afterdeck with a capacity of twenty mines each. Her single tall smokestack loomed abaft the bridge. Although the *Nusret* rated two inconspicuous lines in the 1914 edition of *Jane's Fighting Ships*, she was not even noticed by Mr James Stewart, who was leading the regeneration work on the Ottoman Navy on behalf of Armstrong and Vickers until forced to stop when Turkey and Britain went to war. At the behest of the Royal Navy in October 1914, he had compiled an exhaustive, ship-by-ship report on the Turkish fleet, right down to tugs and motor launches, without bothering to mention Turkey's sole up-to-date minelayer.

The modern naval mine was first used by the Russians in the Crimean War (1854–6) to protect their harbours. The earliest types did not contain enough explosive to sink a ship: two British gunboats struck them but were only moderately damaged and did not sink. Essentially, until more sophisticated varieties were developed before and during the Second World War, the sea-mine was a moored, floating bomb, held in place just below the surface by a cable attached to a weight lying on the seabed and set off when a vessel struck one of its detonator 'horns' – the contact mine.

Initially used defensively to protect harbours, mines were sown offensively for the first time by both sides in the Russo-Japanese War of 1904–5. In April 1904 the Imperial Japanese Navy used mines to blockade the Russian Pacific Fleet in its Manchurian base of Port Arthur. When the Russians came out, two heavily armoured battleships struck mines: one, the flagship *Petropavlovsk*, sank within minutes; the other, *Pobeda*, was badly damaged and towed away. The rest returned to harbour and stayed there. Among the dead on the flagship was Admiral Makarov, Russia's best contemporary naval commander. A month later the Russians laid a minefield in their turn in the waters outside Port Arthur. Two out of six modern Japanese battleships hit mines: the *Yashima* succumbed in a few minutes while the *Hatsuse* sank a few hours later while under tow. None the less Admiral Togo's four remaining capital ships managed to defeat eight badly led Russian battleships in the decisive Battle of Tsushima at the end of May 1905. The unprecedented and spectacular success of a cheap and simple weapon against some of the period's most powerful ships, the strategic armaments of the day, shocked the world's leading navies, most of which had observers on both sides during the conflict. Whereas the transverse lines of mines in the Dardanelles can be seen as purely defensive, the *Nusret*'s postscript of an eleventh line, in a separate area known to be used for manoeuvre by enemy battleships, was unmistakably offensive in character.

International conventions required mines to be constructed so as to defuse themselves if they broke free of their cables, and the use of free-floating mines was prohibited. These rules were soon broken in the opening months of the First World War. The humble contact mine as used in that

2

war proved capable of embarrassing the world's most powerful fleet, the US Navy, as recently as the late 1980s when Iran sowed them in the Strait of Hormuz: the Americans had no minesweepers in commission and had to rely on allies to provide some.

By 1914 mines were much more powerful than 60 years earlier, capable, as we have seen, of mortally wounding mighty battleships by exploding under their hulls, undermining the main belt of armour around a heavy ship's vitals. A typical German 'Carbonit' mine contained 80 kilograms of explosive. Thousands of mines were sown by both sides in 1914, not only defensively to protect ports but also offensively, to inhibit enemy fleets and shipping. Mines were usually laid by fast purpose-built or converted ships, destroyers and also, a little later in the war, by submarines. Aircraft were not yet strong enough for the task.

The Turks and their German allies predictably began laying mines, ultimately in ten lines, across the Dardanelles, mostly south and west of the Narrows, on 3 August 1914. There is some confusion in the records about whose inspired idea it was to lay an eleventh line of mines *parallel* to the shore of Erenkeui Bay, on the Asian side of the Dardanelles and about two miles south of the last of the ten transverse lines – the mission of the *Nusret* on 7–8 March. Credit for the decisive idea is usually given to a Lieutenant-Colonel Geehl, described as a Turkish mining expert. Research for this book established that Geehl, whose name is rather more obviously German than Turkish, was one of hundreds of German officers serving in the Ottoman forces. German naval sources spell his name as Gehl and give his rank as 'Torpedist-Captain' – roughly equivalent to a lieutenant-commander RN. As the Dardanelles defences were assigned to the Turkish Army, German naval officers working on them wore Ottoman Army uniforms. Mine specialists belonged to the same branch of the Imperial German Navy (IGN) as torpedo experts.

But in a post-war 'debriefing' interview with Brigadier-General C. J. Perceval of the British Army in 1919, the Turkish Major-General Cefat Pasha, in charge of the Dardanelles defences at the beginning of the war, said: 'I had a special line of eight [sic] mines laid in a line parallel to the Erenkeui Bay on the south side of the channel. I considered these would be less likely to be detected, owing to their being parallel to and not across the channel, and that they might catch a ship keeping to the south ...' The interview is in the records of the Dardanelles Committee of officers from all three British armed services, who investigated every aspect of the campaign in great detail (as distinct from the Dardanelles Commission, which conducted the official inquiry into the defeat in 1917–18). Other Turkish sources give Commander Nazmi the credit for the idea of the eleventh line of mines. General Cefat spoke of eight mines; others mentioned 20 and 24.

The German sources refer to 26, and ascribe the idea to Admiral Guido von Usedom, the German flag officer appointed inspector-general of the defences of the straits by the Turks and given the rank of general in their army for the purpose. The mines had been handed over to Usedom's 'special command' by Admiral Wilhelm Souchon, appointed head of the Ottoman fleet soon after he evaded a British chase and brought the Mediterranean Division of the IGN into Turkish waters on 10 August 1914. His message to Usedom said: 'Fleet [command] recommends mines to be kept in reserve for the time being, and to lay them as a tactical barrier when specific enemy movements can be predicted.' They were delivered to the fort at Chanak, the main bastion on the Asian side of the Narrows. During the heavy Anglo-French naval bombardments of 19 and 25 February the defenders observed that the attacking battleships used Erenkeui Bay, in the broadest part of the strait south-west of the Narrows, to manoeuvre out of the firing line, reverse course and return to their anchorage at Mudros on the island of Lemnos. It seemed safe therefore to predict that in the next attack they would do the same.

Having sailed close to the Asiatic shore the couple of miles from Nagara to the fort, the engines held to 140 revolutions, the crew of the *Nusret* stopped to collect their mines. They weighed anchor again at about five a.m. and crossed over to hug the European coast as far as possible and thus obtain some shelter from the rough weather coming from the north-west over the Gallipoli peninsula. Conditions were less than stormy but had proved unpleasant enough to lead the British to forgo their usual night destroyer-patrol in the area south of the Narrows, a fact noted by the defenders and Commander Nazmi. He seized the opportunity of carrying out his mission, as planned some days before, undetected by the enemy. Dawn was breaking over Erenkeui Bay as the minelayer arrived.

After Hakki had crossed the strait again towards the Asian shore, Nazmi laid his mines in a row that ran from north-east to south-west, in line with the shore of the bay and about one and a half miles out. They were laid at intervals of some 100 metres – considerably less than the length of a battleship – and set to float at a depth of five metres. The sailors let a weighted mine slip into the water every 15 seconds. The sowing lasted less than seven minutes. Smaller ships, such as destroyers, could sail over the mines with impunity, their crews blissfully unaware of their presence in such an area, whereas a battleship with its deeper draught was highly likely to strike a mine while manoeuvring. The *Nusret*, still rolling in the heavy weather, returned to harbour undetected by the Allied besiegers.

The stratagem worked perfectly. On 18 March 1915, the day of the climactic Allied bombardment of the Dardanelles forts, the French battleship *Bouvet*, 12,200 tonnes, coming out of the firing line, turned to leave the strait at 1.45 p.m. She hit a mine, exploded, keeled over and sank in two minutes, with the loss of some 640 men. Fewer than 40 survived.

And that was only the beginning …

'Any sailor who attacks a fort is a fool.'

Vice-Admiral Horatio Viscount Nelson

PART I

THE FATEFUL ALLIANCE

CHAPTER 1

The Turkish Question

The Ottoman Empire that was dying on its feet in 1914 was founded in 1299 and captured Constantinople in 1453, putting an end to the residual eastern Roman or Byzantine Empire. Its power peaked about a century later, when it ruled not only what we now call Turkey but also the Balkans, the Levant, the Arab interior and much of North Africa, including Egypt. Defeated in the great naval battle of Lepanto in 1571 and foiled in its attempt to seize Vienna in 1683, its long decline accelerated, making it possible for expansionist European powers, most notably Britain and France, to acquire direct or indirect control of much of its territory, especially in North Africa, in the nineteenth century. Greece broke away to form an independent state in 1830, to which Crete and western Thrace (Salonica) were later added. Italy came late to the feast, seizing coastal Libya and the Dodecanese islands off the Turkish south-western coast in 1912.

Meanwhile Austria-Hungary, Germany's ally, vied with Russia for influence in the Balkans, a tinderbox of rival nationalisms that flourished in the power vacuum left by the receding Ottomans. Bismarck, architect and Chancellor of the second German Reich, unified in 1870-1, dismissed the region as 'not worth the healthy bones of a single Pomeranian grenadier' – but also forecast that if Europe once again succumbed to war, 'it will come out of some damned silly thing in the Balkans'. Tsar Nicholas I of Russia declared that 'Turkey is a dying man ... He will, he must, die.' It was as if the leading European powers had gathered round a corpse like carrion crows, ready to squabble over the remains of a once-great empire variously referred to for well over a century under such headings as 'the sick man of Europe' or 'the Turkish (or Eastern) Question'.

The rivalry among the powers over Turkey boiled down to Russia's eternal ambition to gain secure access to the Mediterranean from the Black Sea by acquiring control of Constantinople – and the determination of the others to prevent it. As Napoleon had written to his ambassador in St Petersburg in 1808: 'The root of the great question is always there: who will have Constantinople?' In what was merely the latest in a long series of wars between them, Russia invaded Turkey's Danubian provinces (modern Bulgaria and Romania) in 1851 and destroyed the Turkish Black Sea fleet in 1853. This prompted Austria to intervene in the Balkans, while Britain and France supported Turkey and declared war on Russia in 1854. In Britain a disgusted Lord Salisbury, the future Prime Minister, declared that Britain had 'backed the wrong horse'.

The ensuing Crimean War set new standards in military incompetence on both sides, with Russia losing messily by default in 1856. Nevertheless she went to war again in 1877 after the Ottomans had brutally suppressed Slav revolts in the Balkans, imposing harsh territorial terms on the defeated Turks in the Treaty of San Stefano in 1878. But later the same year Russian ambition was once again thwarted at the first Congress of Berlin, where Serbia, Montenegro, Romania and Bulgaria had their autonomy confirmed, Austria gained control of Bosnia-Herzegovina and Britain took over Cyprus. Serbia and Bulgaria effectively became client states of Russia. Under Bismarck Germany had joined the encircling powers in 1875, working to divide non-Turkish Ottoman territory in the Balkans between Russia and Austria in the longer term, with Berlin acting as mediator while generally avoiding closer entanglement in Turkish affairs to avoid alarming Russia.

Yet German involvement in Turkey went back to 1826, when the Sultan of the day sought Prussian help in reforming his army after an internal military revolt – the origin of the German military mission to Constantinople. In the same spirit the British were invited to send a naval mission. In 1883 the German Lieutenant-Colonel Colmar Baron von der Goltz became deputy chief of the Turkish General Staff (and inspector-general of military education); he would play a key role in the Middle Eastern campaign of the First World War and would die in harness in 1916 as a field marshal in the Ottoman Army. In 1913 another future field marshal in that army, General Otto Liman von Sanders, became chief of the German military mission – a year after Rear-Admiral Arthur Limpus was appointed head of the British naval one.

British interest in the Ottoman Empire was closely related to London's central imperial policy: to protect the route to India via the Mediterranean, whose eastern basin the Turks dominated from north, east and south. The British began to take less and less notice of Turkey and its concerns once they had acquired control of Egypt (nominally ruled by a Turkish *khedive* or viceroy), the Suez Canal and Cyprus. After that, what with possessing naval bases and staging posts at Gibraltar and Malta plus their Mediterranean Fleet, the British felt the imperial lifeline was safe, complacency set in and Britain lost active interest in her role as Turkey's traditional patron.

Kaiser Wilhelm II, who ascended the German imperial and Prussian thrones in 1888, was only too ready to fill the resulting gap, especially after he dismissed Bismarck from the chancellorship in 1890. Without the guiding hand of the consummate old statesman and power-broker, Germany managed within a few years to fall out with every major power in Europe except Austria-Hungary, thus demolishing the main element of Bismarck's foreign policy, the shifting network of alliances isolating France to prevent her seeking revenge for her defeat and loss of Alsace-Lorraine in the war of 1870. Undeterred by the brutal and corrupt regime of Sultan Abdul Hamid II, known as 'the Damned', begun in 1876, the autocratic Wilhelm invested heavily in Turkey, most notably by financing the 'Berlin–Baghdad railway' project, inaugurated in 1883. New track slowly wound its way through Ottoman territory (in 1914, just two sections, in today's Syria and Iraq, remained to be built). The overall aim was to complete a line running nearly 1,900 miles across German, Austro-Hungarian or friendly-neutral territory, except for 175 unavoidable miles through Serbia. Talks in 1895 between Britain and Germany on what to do about the crumbling Ottoman Empire led nowhere, thanks to the rapidly diverging interests of the participants. The Kaiser paid a state visit to Constantinople in 1898, during which he encouraged Turkey's aspirations to revive its spiritual leadership of Islam, the caliphate. He can hardly have been unaware that the majority of the world's Muslims lived within the British Empire at the time.

Elsewhere, Britain's old enemy, France, had in 1892 concluded an alliance with Russia – not only Britain's rival in the 'Great Game', the struggle for power in Central Asia, but also Turkey's traditional foe. This marked the end of more than two decades of French isolation in Europe, as fostered by Bismarck ever since the war with Prussia. The accord was reached two years after Germany had, despite Russian pleas, chosen not to renew its 1887 'reinsurance' treaty with St Petersburg, arguably Wilhelm's greatest diplomatic blunder. Under this pact each partner had promised to remain neutral if the other got involved in war with a third party – unless Germany attacked France or Russia attacked Austria. Russia was given a free hand by the Germans to intervene in the Bosporus and the Dardanelles. This secret treaty replaced the 'League of the Three Emperors' (of Germany, Austria and Russia) formed in 1873 and allowed to lapse in 1887, when Austrian and Russian interests in south-eastern Europe diverged. As far as

Berlin was concerned, it had already been superseded in 1879 on the conclusion of the Dual Alliance with Vienna.

Britain stood alone at this time in her concern about the relentless persecution of ethnic minorities by Abdul Hamid II, but the realignment of alliances among the leading powers only encouraged inertia in London: the route to India was safe and the vaguely formulated idea of seizing Constantinople to restrain the Sultan was dropped. London continued for the time being to follow its old policy of avoiding unnecessary entanglements on the continent of Europe, which however would not outlast the nineteenth century by more than a year or two.

By default therefore the Ottoman Empire turned to Germany for protection, especially as Berlin was showing keen interest: and Germany's main ally, Austria-Hungary, Russia's rival in the Balkans, could only applaud the resulting check on Russian ambition. The Germans also poured money into a new port at Haidar Pasha, on the Baghdad railway route and the Asian side of the Bosporus, the channel between the Black Sea and the Marmara. All this now made Germany, rather than Turkey, the perceived main obstacle to the eternal Russian ambition of gaining direct access to the Mediterranean. And Germany's growing dominance in Constantinople in the new century also made it the main threat to the British route to India. But, once the Kaiser and Admiral Tirpitz decided on the rapid expansion of the Imperial High Seas Fleet from 1898, a direct and open challenge to British world maritime supremacy, the main arena of Anglo-German rivalry became the North Sea. The first dramatic consequence of the growing anxiety in London about Germany's headlong naval expansion was the British alliance with Japan in 1902. With the Imperial Japanese Navy, modelled on the British, prepared to help look after British interests in the Far East, the Admiralty could withdraw major naval units to European waters.

Embittered by the loss of Alsace-Lorraine in the war of 1870, France regarded Germany, which had supplanted her as Europe's leading military power, as her main enemy ever since. Now as Britain reacted to the threat posed by the Kaiser's naval challenge, she took another even more important diplomatic step: an understanding with France. The outcome of Wilhelm's rash naval building programme was not only the *Entente Cordiale* in 1904 but also a naval construction programme to outstrip Germany's. France eventually agreed to take the main responsibility for the naval defence of the Mediterranean, enabling the British to reduce their Mediterranean Fleet while they took the naval lead in the Channel, the North Sea and north Atlantic.

Three years after the Entente Britain reached an agreement with Russia, much the lesser threat to British interests when compared with the thrusting new Germany and its ruler's constant demand for an undefined 'place in the sun'. This understanding completed the Triple Entente that the Central Powers would confront in 1914. The latter were members of the Triple Alliance with Italy, but this pact required the Italians to aid their Germanic partners only if they came under attack. Since the Central Powers did the attacking in 1914, the *casus foederis* never arose and traditionally Anglophile Italy began the war as a neutral. All these developments formed the ABC of causation that led to war: Alsace-Lorraine (France v. Germany); Balkan peninsula (Russia v. Austria); capital ships (Britain v. Germany).

The machinations of the European powers as they sought to profit from the decline of the Ottoman Empire were matched by turbulence within it, especially in the period leading up to the war of 1914. The inept and brutal reign of Abdul Hamid II prompted a revolt by a group of relatively youthful intellectuals and military officers who were soon referred to as the 'Young Turks'. They gravitated to the Committee of Union and Progress (CUP), founded by students and young army doctors in 1869 and dedicated to modernising and liberalising the empire before it disintegrated altogether. The reformist constitution announced by the Sultan on his accession in 1876 had been set aside soon afterwards because he took the view that an ignorant population was not ready for it or worthy of it. The newfangled Chamber of Deputies was suspended. Fears of further losses beyond the territorial amputations imposed at the Congress of Berlin, given the endemic unrest in the Balkans and among the Arabs, prompted the CUP in 1908 to threaten revolution unless the constitution was reinstated. This was not the first time the military had intervened in Turkish politics, nor would it by any means be the last. The Sultan complied and the CUP won a huge majority in the ensuing election to the Chamber of Deputies, which reassembled on 17 December.

But the CUP at this stage represented only one of three ideological strands to be found among the politically aware classes in Turkey: the Ottomanist tendency, which wanted to save the empire by modernisation; the Pan-Turkish movement, which wanted to unite all ethnic Turks from central Asia to Anatolia under a single flag; and the Pan-Islamic, which wanted to revive the caliphate and thus re-establish Turkish hegemony over Islam. Rivalry among imperialists, nationalists and Islamists was intense and was by no means discouraged by the end of the Sultan's tyranny. The CUP used its parliamentary advantage to force the Grand Vizier (prime minister), Kemal Pasha, out of office in February 1909, forming a new government. A month later Islamists provoked a rising in Constantinople, supported by soldiers of the army's First Corps, in favour of Islamic rule. The CUP brought in the Third Corps from Salonica to suppress the revolt mercilessly: 60 alleged ringleaders were hanged. Abdul Hamid was deposed and sent into internal exile in Salonica; it is not clear whether he was involved in the failed coup. His younger brother Rashid took his place under the official name of Mehmet V. He was to be the last Sultan – and the first to reign like a constitutional monarch rather than rule like a despot.

So it was not the new Sultan who undermined the new constitutional arrangements but the CUP, which used the abortive revolt as an excuse to suppress opposition parties as it swung towards nationalism, the Turks being outnumbered by non-Turks in parliament. Then a damaging series of wars between the empire and its neighbours began in 1911, when the Italians invaded Tripolitania and Cyrenaica, the coastal regions of modern Libya. Britain undermined Turkey's capacity to resist by declaring Egypt neutral, even though it was officially still Ottoman territory, thus preventing the Turks from sending troops overland from Syria; the superior Italian fleet ruled out a Turkish naval riposte. Not content with their North African conquests, the Italians seized the Dodecanese islands in spring 1912 (Italy withdrew only in 1947, in favour of the Greeks rather than the Turks). The Ottoman government resigned in summer, when Kemal Pasha was reinstalled as Grand Vizier.

Like hyenas scenting moribund flesh, the Balkan states erupted in the hope of gaining territory from the ailing Turks. Tiny Montenegro was the first to declare war on 8 October 1912; ten days later, Serbia, Greece and Bulgaria followed suit. The Turks gained a partial respite on the same day, when a diplomatic settlement was reached with Italy, which was allowed to keep the Libyan territories but agreed to return the Dodecanese – a promise never fulfilled. Sir Edward Grey, the British Foreign Secretary, convened a conference of the leading powers in London in a bid to settle the Balkan wars. Despite the many rivalries among their governments, the diplomats worked constructively and eventually succeeded in producing the 1913 Treaty of London. Turkey signed ceasefire agreements with Bulgaria and Serbia on 3 December 1912, but the Greeks and the Montenegrins continued to fight. At the beginning of 1913 Bulgaria attacked again, aiming to capture Edirne in Thrace, the historic city that had been the Ottoman capital until the fall of Constantinople in 1453.

This prompted the leading figures in the CUP, Enver Pasha, Jemal Pasha and Talaat Bey, to unseat Grand Vizier Kemal Pasha a second time with the false claim that he was planning to give in to the Bulgarians. Talaat Bey had been the head of the Turkish postal service until he led this last putsch by the Young Turks in January 1913 against Kemal Pasha. A deceptively affable giant, he was also much more shrewd than he looked, and ruthless, not least against the Armenians, and was the iron fist of the CUP as Minister of the Interior. He, Enver and Jemal were a minority in the Cabinet, united in their determination to take Turkey to war on the side of their German friends once Enver had won the other two over.

Mahmud Sevket Pasha was appointed Grand Vizier on 23 January. Even so the Bulgarians took Edirne on 26 March. Peace talks led to an armistice and then the London treaty on 30 May. Turkey may thus have arrived at a precarious peace at the cost of yet more territory, including Albania and southern Thrace (the area round Salonica – now Thessaloniki – which went to Greece), but her erstwhile Balkan enemies now fell out and fought each other. Sevket Pasha was assassinated in June 1913, but the CUP remained in the saddle, banishing or executing its political opponents. Bulgaria attacked Serbia and Greece on 29 June; 11 days later Romania attacked Bulgaria. The dashing, not to say reckless, Lieutenant-Colonel Enver saw his opportunity to profit from these quarrels by leading a column to reoccupy Edirne on 22 July. Turkish honour was thus, to a degree, salvaged by Enver who, unfortunately for himself and his country, now developed an exaggerated opinion of his own ability as a military commander. The entire Balkan imbroglio was brought to a close on 10 August by the Treaty of Bucharest. The Ottoman Empire was left with nothing in Africa and a reduced, modest foothold in Europe around Edirne and Constantinople, while retaining the Turkish heartland of Anatolia as well as the Levant and Arabia, Mesopotamia, Syria and Palestine.

As the world's leading naval power, Britain might deploy her squadrons in all manner of places. The Admiralty however had no war staff in the modern sense until just before the outbreak of conflict in 1914, and was committed to a 'Two-Power Standard' (to be as strong as the next two naval powers combined), which meant that contingency plans were rare to non-existent. Until Fisher became First Sea Lord in 1904, the Royal Navy's posture was reactive, prompted mainly by what the actual or potential enemies of the day did. But the main preoccupation of the Admiralty from the eve of the twentieth century onward was inevitably Germany with its rapidly growing battlefleet: Germany plus 50 per cent was the new guideline, and war with Germany was the great contingency for which Fisher made coherent plans. The Royal Navy's long-standing focus on the traditional enemy, France, from ports on the south coast of England was dramatically shifted to Germany at the dawn of the century, when Rosyth in the Firth of Forth was built up as a naval base. Before the end of the first decade the great natural anchorage of Scapa Flow in the Orkney Islands was earmarked in the event of war for the newly expanded and expensively modernised Grand Fleet, while the Cromarty Firth was chosen as an advance base for the fast new battlecruisers that would lead the battleships into action. Eastern and northern Scotland became the Royal Navy's centre of gravity. Destroyers and submarines were based at Harwich on England's east coast and the Channel was to be guarded by more destroyers of the Dover Patrol. This strategic shift came as close as possible to a guarantee that any German attempt at an invasion of England would be thwarted. The admirals – and the general public as war approached – looked to the navy to win a new Trafalgar in the North Sea within weeks of the opening of hostilities.

On the high seas, away from the North Sea arena, the main threat was the IGN's sole 'blue water' formation, the cruiser squadron led by Vice-Admiral Maximilian Graf von Spee and based at Tsingtao, the port of the German enclave of Kiaochow on the north-east Chinese coast. The two heavy and up to four light cruisers were thought in London (and would soon prove) to be capable of operating anywhere in the Pacific, Indian and south Atlantic oceans, which meant that groups of British and allied ships had to be allocated to key areas in all three in order to counter them and protect commerce.

In the Mediterranean the French Navy, supported by the British Mediterranean Fleet, was responsible for meeting any threat from the small but strong Austrian Navy, the German Navy's Mediterranean Division of just two ships (although one of them was the most powerful ship afloat in that ocean), and the considerable Italian fleet, should Italy go to war alongside her German and Austrian allies. Turkey was expected to remain neutral, its decrepit fleet dismissed as of no account in the Mediterranean theatre, even though two of the latest dreadnoughts ('all-big-gun' ships introduced by Britain in 1907 and rendering all earlier battleships obsolete) were nearing completion for the Ottoman Navy in Tyneside shipyards.

Even so, consideration had on several occasions in the nineteenth and early twentieth centuries been given at the Admiralty, the War Office and in the Committee of Imperial Defence to the problem of capturing Constantinople should the need ever arise, though no plan was drawn up. Only the Russians were in a position to do this from the north and east, using the short route via the Bosporus; a western attacker would have to approach from the south-west, passing through the Dardanelles strait into the Sea of Marmara and sailing some 140 miles to reach the Golden Horn on which Constantinople stood.

The precedent to which both sides of the desultory British debates on the practicability of an attack on Constantinople via the Dardanelles paid close attention occurred in 1807, in the context of what was really the first *world* war, against Napoleonic France and its allies. Russia had asked the British for a move against Turkey, to take the pressure off her in the Black Sea area – an appeal she would repeat in 1915. Turkey, influenced by France, had closed the Bosporus and the Dardanelles at either end of the Sea of Marmara to Russian shipping. In October 1806 Admiral Lord Collingwood, commander-in-chief of the Mediterranean Fleet, sent three ships of the line to reconnoitre the defences of the Dardanelles in case the Royal Navy should be required to attack them. In late November Rear-Admiral Sir Thomas Louis entered the Dardanelles, politely exchanged gun salutes with the entrance forts, left two of his three ships of the line and a frigate at anchor off Chanak (now Çannakale) on the Asian side and sailed on to Constantinople in his flagship, HMS *Canopus*, escorted by another frigate. He stayed for a month. Just after Christmas he returned in his flagship, collecting the other two ships of the line on the way out and leaving a frigate behind at the Golden Horn to be at the disposal of the British ambassador, Arbuthnot. Louis brought the Russian ambassador out with him as Turkey had once again broken off relations with St Petersburg. The lone British frigate cut her cables and slipped away the next night with the British envoy aboard as the crisis deepened.

Collingwood meanwhile had received orders from the Admiralty to be ready to go to war against Turkey. Vice-Admiral Sir John Duckworth was to command the squadron detailed for the purpose. General Sir John Moore, second-in-command of British troops then in Sicily, wanted troops earmarked for Alexandria in Egypt to go with the navy to the Dardanelles instead, to make sure of their capture, but his advice was ignored. The order to go ahead reached Collingwood off Cadiz in mid-January and Duckworth sailed in the *Royal George*. Linking up with Louis off the island of Tenedos, Duckworth assembled eight ships of the line with auxiliaries. His objective was to destroy or capture the Turkish fleet and to bombard Constantinople if Turkey refused to surrender the ships. Louis reported that the forts and their guns were in poor condition, while much of the Turkish fleet lay idle in the Golden Horn apart from a squadron based to the north of the Narrows. To forestall traditional Ottoman time-wasting tactics Duckworth, on Arbuthnot's advice, was determined to allow no negotiation with the Turks to last longer than half an hour.

While waiting for some weeks for a favourable wind, Duckworth reported to Collingwood that the Turks, with French assistance, had set up new batteries on the shores of the Dardanelles. 'We are to enter a sea environed with enemies,' he warned in a report, 'without a possible resource but in ourselves; and when we are to return, there cannot remain a doubt but that passage will be rendered as formidable as efforts of the Turkish Empire, directed and assisted by their allies the French, can make it.' Substitute 'Germans' for 'French' in the foregoing and it becomes a perfect description of the position of the Allied fleet off the Dardanelles in February and March 1915. Duckworth promised he would do his best.

On 14 February, just after a dispatch vessel had sailed with Duckworth's letter to his chief, HMS *Ajax*, a third-rate, 74-gun ship of the line, succumbed to an accidental fire and sank with the loss of 250 men. But five days later a favourable, south-west wind took Duckworth's squadron up the straits. Gunfire from the entrance forts proved ineffectual, but the shooting, at shorter range, from the Narrows forts was more effective. The ships gave as good as they got and damage to them was light, with only six British sailors killed and about 50 wounded. On emerging from the Narrows into the Marmara, Rear-Admiral Sir Sydney Smith, commanding the rearguard, took on the Turkish squadron there after it opened fire on Duckworth's line, and all but destroyed it: one 64-gun ship, four frigates and three corvettes were sunk while one corvette was captured. But a brig was able to escape and warn Constantinople that the British were coming. Royal Marines and sailors went ashore and spiked about 30 guns sited at the entrance to the Dardanelles.

Duckworth's squadron sailed on into the Marmara, progressing slowly so that the ships arrived at Princes Island some eight miles from Constantinople at about ten p.m. on 20 February, where he was halted by adverse winds. An exchange of letters between Arbuthnot and the Ottoman authorities led nowhere as the Turks, egged on by Napoleon's agent, General Sebastiani, beefed up the defences by deploying more artillery and such of their ships as were still seaworthy. They set up a battery on the island of Prota between Princes Island and the city; Admiral Louis sent a landing party to destroy it but it was repelled. The Dardanelles defences were also hastily reinforced with new batteries.

After nine days Duckworth drew up his line and offered battle to the five Turkish ships and four frigates facing him. The challenge was ignored; so the British commander withdrew to a point about six miles above the Narrows on 1 March, having waited more than a week for a favourable wind. On the 3rd a frustrated Duckworth led his ships out of the strait before their retreat was completely cut off by the rapidly strengthening defensive artillery. He politely fired a salute of 13 guns as he passed the forts guarding the Narrows, only to be affronted by a bombardment in earnest, which caused considerable damage to his ships and over 160 casualties. The result of the botched foray was a humiliation, reducing British standing in the eyes of their Russian allies, who soon gave up and made peace with Napoleon at Tilsit. On urgent orders from the Admiralty, Collingwood himself essayed a brief attack on the Dardanelles, in concert with Admiral Senyavin's Russian squadron, which attacked the Bosporus at the same time, but both were repelled. Neither admiral had troops at his disposal to land and attack the shore defences from the rear.

Britain and Turkey concluded the Treaty of the Dardanelles in 1809, which *inter alia* declared the Dardanelles and the Bosporus to be open to all merchant shipping. This principle was reinforced by the London Straits Convention of 1841, under which Britain, France, Russia, Austria and Prussia also agreed that Turkey, while at peace, had the right to bar foreign warships from the straits, although the Sultan could admit friendly visits by individual ships coming to 'show the flag'. These provisions were repeated in the Treaty of Paris ending the Crimean War in 1856, and reaffirmed once more at Berlin in 1878. Further, if Turkey remained neutral in a European war, she was required to exclude foreign warships, and to give any belligerent vessel twenty-four hours' notice of expulsion or internment if it was inside the straits when a war broke out. These restrictions were punctiliously observed until August 1914.

The next British admiral after Duckworth and Collingwood to sail to the Dardanelles was Sir Geoffrey Phipps Hornby, commander-in-chief of the Mediterranean Fleet, in 1877, during the Russo-Turkish war of that time in which Britain was neutral. One of his battleship captains was John Arbuthnot Fisher, the future First Sea Lord, who, like his flag officer at the time, concluded that there could be no forcing of the Dardanelles without troops: a combined operation was the only realistic possibility. Hornby did not become involved in hostilities and his ships were not fired upon; he withdrew peacefully. He noted to the Admiralty: 'There seems to be an idea that this fleet can keep the Dardanelles and Bosporus open. Nothing can be more visionary. Not all the fleets in the world can keep them open for unarmoured ships.' One of the dangers he identified was the presence of easily hidden, mobile gun batteries on both sides of the strait, particularly the European, where the rough terrain of the Gallipoli peninsula offered many hills to hide in.

Although Russia won this round, it still did not get its hands on Constantinople. As we have seen, the rival powers saw to that at the Congress of Berlin in 1878. Fisher rose to command of the Mediterranean Fleet at the time of the Boer War (1899–1902) and spent some time based at Lemnos, the island south-west of the mouth of the Dardanelles that assumed so much importance in 1914–15. From there he made a detailed study of the strategic and tactical problems relating to forcing the strait and advancing on Constantinople. He concluded that the only way to do it would be to land troops to secure the Gallipoli peninsula at the same time as the attacking fleet passed into the Marmara. Armoured ships could expect to silence the forts and get through with tolerable losses, but unprotected transports, essential to sustain the fleet, would be wide open to Turkish artillerymen with their mobile German guns (and gunnery 'advisers'): the defences had been strengthened with new German artillery pieces in 1885. He looked at the problem again when he became First Sea Lord, and saw no reason to change his view: such an undertaking would be 'mightily hazardous'.

The Committee of Imperial Defence (CID) was set up by the British government at the end of 1902. It consisted of the Prime Minister, then the Conservative Arthur Balfour, as chairman, the Foreign Secretary, the First Lord of the Admiralty (political chief of the Royal Navy), the Secretary of State for War, a few other ministers as appropriate and naval and military advisers, principally the First Sea Lord and the Chief of the Imperial General Staff or their representatives. Its long-serving Secretary was Lieutenant-Colonel Maurice Hankey (ultimately Lord Hankey), late of the Royal Marine Light Infantry, and its role was clearly defined by its title. It was a sensible response to a deteriorating world situation as anxiety began to grow about the rapid expansion of the German High Seas Fleet, a development which had already led to an unprecedented understanding with Japan in 1902 and would soon lead to *rapprochements* with France and Russia.

One of the main worries of the CID in the opening years of the century was the possibility of war between the Far Eastern rivals Japan and Russia, which might lead the latter to send her Black Sea Fleet through the Dardanelles to reinforce, albeit circuitously, the Pacific Fleet. This would entail a breach of the international conventions mentioned above. In the event, the Russo-Japanese War fought in 1904–5 led to the even more outlandish, and ultimately disastrous, Russian decision to send their Northern Fleet from Archangel right round the Eurasian land-mass to reinforce the Pacific Fleet, both of which were then destroyed by the victorious Japanese.

At its ninety-second meeting in July 1906, 'War with Turkey' dominated the agenda of the CID. Britain and Turkey were at odds about the border between British-controlled Egypt and Ottoman Syria; the Sultan laid claim to the Sinai Desert and the territory bordering the eastern bank of the Suez Canal. Sir Edward Grey, Foreign Secretary, declared that a decision was needed on whether it was possible to force the Dardanelles in defence of Egypt, a question originally raised by General Sir John French. The First Lord of the Admiralty, Lord Tweedmouth, said there was no doubt that the Royal Navy could force the strait alone. But he added that it would be a costly business as the forts had powerful guns and German artillery officers were helping the Turks to man them. Ships would therefore be lost. Seizing islands commanding the mouth of the Dardanelles (Tenedos, Imbros, Lemnos, then all Turkish) might be enough to coerce the Turks. One naval adviser said the question had been considered before, but events at Port Arthur, the Russian enclave in Manchuria, in the war with Japan, had shown that forts had a natural advantage over attacking ships (although the Japanese fleet destroyed the Russians at Tsushima, near the port, the land-based guns repelled the seaborne victors and Japan had to send a large army overland to take it from the rear). The consensus at the CID was that a combined navy–army operation was the only realistic approach; but also that the current border dispute did not justify an attack on the Dardanelles.

At the next CID meeting in November, Admiral Sir John Fisher, the First Sea Lord, said, 'Germany now controls the Dardanelles, and we could no longer hope to bribe the defenders to let us pass.' He was opposed to any attack on the strait, especially one by the navy alone, and hoped it would never happen. The General Staff and the Naval Intelligence Division agreed at a conference on the Dardanelles question in December 1906 that a squadron of older armoured ships might break through to Constantinople but would be battered on the way back; and if the Turks abandoned the city there would be no real profit anyway. The army might be able to land 5,000 troops on Gallipoli for a surprise *coup de main* against the coastal artillery from the rear, but the force would be difficult to extricate and would have to hold on until heavily telegraphed, heavy reinforcements could be landed. That left the possibility of a large-scale combined operation, which could hardly expect to achieve surprise and would therefore have to make a landing opposed by strong defensive forces with modern guns – unless the fleet could somehow cover the landing in such a way as to enable the troops to seize a sufficiently large beachhead from which to launch a landward advance. Naval officers thought their army colleagues were overlooking the huge and swift recent advances in warship technology, including high explosives, rangefinders and massive long-range guns of a new standard of accuracy, but all agreed that large military and naval forces would be needed and heavy casualties were inevitable. War Office and General Staff studies in 1908 and again in 1911 reached the same conclusions.

The CID's ninety-sixth meeting in February 1907 had concluded: 'The Committee consider that the operation of landing an expeditionary force on or near the Gallipoli Peninsula would involve great risk, and should not be undertaken if other means of bringing pressure to bear on Turkey were available.' The subject did not come up again at the CID itself in peacetime, even when Turkish territorial ambitions in the Persian Gulf appeared to threaten British interests in the region. Both the Admiralty and the War Office consistently took it as read that should it be necessary or advisable to attempt to force the Dardanelles in order to coerce the Ottoman government, a full-scale, combined naval and military operation was the only strategy. There could be no question of the Royal Navy attempting the task unaided.

Thanks to its intervention on Turkey's side in the Crimean War, the underlying motive for which was, as ever, to frustrate Russian ambitions in the Black Sea and the Mediterranean, Britain enjoyed lasting prestige and even popularity in Turkey. This endured despite British inroads on Ottoman territory in Egypt, Persia, the Balkans and the eastern Mediterranean plus loud public criticism of Turkish oppression of its minorities (Turkey's cavalier approach to human rights was still a bone of contention a century later). Until almost the end of the nineteenth century Turkey looked to

Britain and its navy for protection from Russian expansionism, but in the last quarter German influence began to gain ground at Britain's expense.

Yet the British naval mission, while hardly hyperactive during this period, was still in place in Constantinople. Rear-Admiral Arthur Henry Limpus led it in his official capacity as naval adviser to the Ottoman government and was personally popular among the Turks. Soon after his appointment by Winston Churchill, First Lord of the Admiralty, in 1912, Limpus displayed energy in trying to revive the Turkish fleet, as part of British efforts to help the Turks recover from their setbacks in the Balkan wars. In this he was encouraged by his political chief, who was virtually alone among British ministers in favouring an alliance with Turkey. Churchill was enthusiastically supportive of the 'Young Turks', especially when they brought down Sultan Abdul Hamid, 'the Damned', who was personally responsible for the persecutions. Churchill met Enver, then briefly military attaché in Berlin, while officially observing German Army manoeuvres in 1909, when the Turk was aged just 27. Enver called on Churchill in London in 1910, the year he became First Lord. In September they met again when Churchill spent five days in Constantinople.

Turkey had already ordered a dreadnought battleship in 1911, to be built on Tyneside and named *Reshadieh*. The ship was launched in September 1913. There was no dock big enough for such a large vessel in Constantinople, so in December 1913, as the ship, 23,000 tonnes and armed with ten 13.5-inch guns, was being fitted out, the Turks concluded another deal with Armstrong's and Vickers, the two shipbuilders whose close co-operation would one day lead to a merger, for shore facilities for her. The two companies were also commissioned to regenerate the neglected ships of the Ottoman fleet but had made little progress when the war broke out. In the same month Turkey successfully made an offer for another battleship, the *Rio de Janeiro*, nearing completion on Tyneside. The ship, 27,500 tonnes with 14 12-inch guns, at the time the world's longest dreadnought, had been commissioned by Brazil, which then found it could not afford the cost. She was renamed *Sultan Osman I*. Both ships were to be ready for delivery in July 1914. The contracts, which ran to a total of £6 million, were funded by nationwide public subscription and special taxes in Turkey and by Ottoman government bonds issued in London, supported by international bank loans. The Turks wanted the ships to shore up their flagging prestige – and quite possibly to recover the Aegean islands they had lost to Greece and Italy in recent years.

But as war with Germany looked imminent it was their friend Churchill who decided to take over both ships as a last-minute, instant reinforcement for the British Grand Fleet in the North Sea. Some 500 Turkish sailors had arrived in a steamer at Newcastle upon Tyne to man the ships and take them home. Under the contracts Britain was actually entitled to commandeer them (with full financial compensation) in a national emergency. Churchill made his decision to do so on 28 July 1914 – the day before the Grand Fleet was sent in a body to Scapa Flow after a naval review at Portland on the south coast of England. This strategic move had a decisive effect on the outcome of the war because it meant that the planned naval blockade of Germany could begin without delay. Regardless of subsequent errors by himself and others, this was Churchill's most important contribution by far to ultimate victory. The Cabinet approved the seizure of the Turkish dreadnoughts on 31 July and British sailors backed by troops took them over on 1 August. The move raised the number of dreadnoughts in the Grand Fleet to 22 (with 13 building), compared with Germany's 13 (10 on the stocks): *Reshadieh* became HMS *Erin* while *Rio de Janeiro,* after only a few days as *Sultan Osman I,* was born again as HMS *Agincourt.* The instant expansion of the Grand Fleet's big-gun strength by 10 per cent understandably caused universal outrage in Turkey, swinging political and public opinion decisively towards Germany at the critical moment.

Unbeknown to the British and most of the rest of the world, the timing could not have been worse.

CHAPTER 2

The German Answer

Germany offered Russia a free run in 1875 to pursue her enduring ambition to dominate the route from the Black Sea to the Mediterranean by achieving control of Constantinople, preferably by occupying it. This was a startling departure from the usually unspoken consensus among the European powers that Russia should never be allowed unfettered access to the Mediterranean. In exchange Bismarck, intent as ever on constraining France, asked the Tsar for a free hand in western Europe. The Russians could not fail to be tempted but, no doubt anticipating trouble with Britain and other powers over such a unilateral settlement of the 'eastern question', turned it down. This prompted an expansionist Second Reich to look eastward to extend its political power and economic interests.

From 1875 the Emperor Wilhelm I and his Chancellor, Bismarck, set out to woo the Ottoman Empire. Germany turned two blind eyes towards the brutal internal repression of Sultan Abdul Hamid which had aroused widespread protests in Britain and western Europe. When British and French banks turned down Turkish requests for loans, Germany would provide. Even though the Congress of Berlin, chaired by Bismarck, effectively dismantled Turkish rule in the Balkans in 1878, the Germans continued with some success to increase their influence in Constantinople. The German military mission was revived and extended. In 1882 Colonel Kochler was appointed deputy chief of staff of the Turkish Army, succeeded on his death in 1883 by von der Goltz; in the same year the railway route from Berlin to Constantinople was opened, with work continuing on the extension to Baghdad. The state visit of Kaiser Wilhelm II, more crudely ambitious for Germany than his father, in 1898, underpinned German domination into the twentieth century.

Enver's reward for his part in the revolution of 1908–9 included a short stint as military attaché in Berlin in 1909, which consolidated his admiration for all things German, especially the army: he became the most enthusiastic supporter of the German connection in the CUP leadership and the government. By then Baron Marschall von Bieberstein, appointed

German ambassador to Constantinople in 1897, had come to personify Germany in Turkish eyes. A bulky, Bismarck-like figure with duelling scars on his face, he exuded confidence and a certain brutal charm. He was succeeded in 1912 by Baron Hans von Wangenheim, another imposing personality in the Prussian mould but rather more polished and subtle. He worked as tirelessly as his predecessor to build up German influence in Turkey. As the threat of general war grew, he bent all his efforts to achieving a formal alliance with the Ottoman Empire. General Liman von Sanders took over, and strongly expanded, the military mission in December 1913, bringing with him 70 officers who effectively took over the Turkish Army within a few months. As war broke out, spreading to Turkey within three months, there were 800 German military advisers, who were soon to be reinforced by naval ones.

In autumn 1912 Turkey, fearing an attack on Constantinople itself by Bulgaria, whose heavy artillery could be heard from the city, had called a meeting of ambassadors of all the participants in the Congress of Berlin of 1878 to ask for an international naval force to protect the Ottoman capital and the lives and property of foreign citizens living there. Nine nations agreed to take part, including Russia. The British sent two cruisers and even the small and elderly Royal Netherlands Navy managed to provide one. The Kaiser, whose country had hosted the Congress, was angry and embarrassed when he awoke to the fact that the Imperial Navy had no presence in the Mediterranean, apart from the modest gunboat it kept at the Golden Horn, like the other powers, to look after its interests and privileges (the humiliating 'capitulations' whereby Turkey conferred virtual legal immunity on resident citizens of the principal powers). The United States was content to be represented merely by the gunboat it normally kept on station. On the advice of Admiral Tirpitz, co-architect with himself of the High Seas Fleet, Wilhelm, always on the lookout for chances to assert Germany's claim to great-power status, created the Mediterranean Division of the Imperial Navy on a whim in November 1912, sending it to fly the Kaiser's imposing black and white naval ensign off Constantinople as the tenth constituent of the protection squadron. It consisted of just two shining new ships, both in the process of completing their sea trials at the time: the battlecruiser *Goeben*, with the light cruiser *Breslau* as her sole escort.

The pair caused a sensation when they arrived at Constantinople on 15 November. The *Goeben* was not only by far the most impressive ship in the squadron and its only dreadnought; it was also the fastest and most powerful capital ship in the entire Mediterranean. The divisional flag officer, Rear-Admiral Kummler, placed himself at the disposal of the French vice-admiral nominally commanding the force, France being the leading naval power in the Mediterranean. The foreign warships were in the event not called upon to take any action as the Turkish front against the Bulgarians managed to hold firm and save Constantinople. The squadron dispersed in due course, but the Mediterranean Division remained in being, free to use the naval bases and harbours of Germany's allies, Austria-Hungary and Italy. The German presence in the inland sea was to be permanent, a new piece on the strategic board which however aroused little concern in the French and British Mediterranean fleets, both of which were much larger: the British alone possessed three battlecruisers in the region, any one of which fired a heavier broadside than the *Goeben*, although each was inferior in armour and speed. Britain also disposed of an array of heavy and light cruisers plus destroyers. The French had two dreadnoughts and 17 other, sometimes elderly, battleships with several squadrons of lesser vessels.

Admiral Kummler was relieved in October 1913 by Rear-Admiral Wilhelm Anton Theodor Souchon, aged 49, son of an artist of Huguenot descent. He hoisted his flag on the *Goeben* in Trieste and immediately set out on a detailed exploration of his area of operations. Showing the flag at friendly, neutral and potential enemy ports not only offered an endless series of floating drinks parties but also opportunities to study local conditions. He met the commanders-in-chief of the Austrian and Italian fleets but was not impressed by their French contemporary, Vice-Admiral Augustin Boué de Lapeyrère, whom he called upon at Messina in Sicily (Souchon's acquaintance with the port would soon prove very useful). He never met Admiral Sir Berkeley Milne, commander-in-chief of the British Mediterranean Fleet, whose policy was to send a strong British contingent to any port visited by the Germans as soon as possible afterwards, to counteract any favourable impression gained by the locals. The Kaiser called this transparent spoiling tactic 'spitting in the soup'.

Rear-Admiral Ernest Troubridge, Milne's second-in-command and flag officer of the First Cruiser Squadron, did not meet Souchon either, but was entertained by the captain and officers of SMS *Breslau* during a visit to Durrazzo in the last week of peace: he left an imposing impression. Uncertain of Italy's semi-detached role in the Triple Alliance, Souchon held talks with the Austrian naval commander-in-chief, Admiral Anton Haus, at his main base of Pola (now Pula in Croatia) and agreed that the Mediterranean Division would serve under the latter's overall command in the event of war.

In May 1914 the *Goeben* continued her unceasing round of showing the Kaiser's flag by calling at Constantinople on the invitation of the Sultan, not for the first time, nor yet the last. While she was in port on 22 May a large fire broke out at a nearby Turkish army barracks. Some 150 sailors volunteered to help (without detracting from their heroism, one may reasonably deduce mixed motives on their part: they were in the midst of coaling ship, the most hated task in the navies of the day). They rushed half-naked and covered in coal dust through the narrow streets to fight the flames; three German sailors died in the blaze and four were injured. Thousands of Turks turned out for the funeral to acknowledge their courage and sacrifice. The gesture was not primarily intended to do so, but undoubtedly conferred invaluable prestige on Germany and its navy at a very useful moment, encouraging the Germanophiles in the divided government.

The CUP coup of January 1913 brought in Mahmud Sevket Pasha as Grand Vizier. His Cabinet had a 'distinct German colouring' in the view of the British ambassador, Sir Louis Mallet. When Sevket was assassinated in June, Prince Said Halim Pasha succeeded him without giving Mallet reason to revise his assessment. The driving forces in both CUP and Cabinet were Enver, Minister of War from early 1914, and Talaat Bey, party leader and Minister of the Interior, originally inclined towards Russia but opportunistically turned pro-German. They formed a ruling triumvirate with Jemal Pasha, who became Minister of Marine in 1913. Halim favoured neutrality, but without passion. Halil, the Chairman of the Chamber of Deputies, and Jemal Pasha, initially pro-French, allowed themselves to be won over to Germany. But there were several other members of the government, such as Javid, the Foreign Minister, who favoured Britain and had supported an offer to London of a formal alliance, declined in 1911. As late as July 1914 the majority in the Turkish Cabinet was friendly disposed towards Britain, Enver and Talaat as usual standing out against such a policy.

Enver was born in 1881 and schooled for an army career. In 1903 he was a staff captain with III Corps in Salonica as well as a committed activist for the CUP. As we saw, his prominent role in the revolution of 1908–9 won him a posting to Berlin as military attaché. A lieutenant-colonel at the time of his counter-attack on the Bulgarians which led to the recovery of Edirne, he was promptly promoted brigadier-general, which brought the title

Pasha. Small, dapper, vain and energetic, he cut a figure rather different from that of Talaat Bey, a hard-working politician of a more traditional mould (and build) with a strong character and a bluff manner that masked considerable intelligence and shrewdness. Just 27 when he led the coup by the CUP in June 1908, Enver was anointed 'Hero of the Revolution' but later unsuccessfully fought the Italians in North Africa, until a humiliating peace was hastily signed with them as general war broke out in the Balkans in 1912. Energetic, ruthless and determined, Enver always cut a dashing and dapper figure and earned the not necessarily affectionate nickname of *Napoleonlik* – little Napoleon. In his study he kept a portrait of the French emperor on one wall and of King Frederick the Great of Prussia on another but the implicit assessment of his own military talent was seriously exaggerated.

Even so, his dash on horseback overnight in summer 1913 to liberate Adrianople (Edirne) in European Turkey (already abandoned by the Bulgars, as it happens) had won him laurels and he became Minister of War in 1914, still only 33. He helped himself to the title of Chief of the General Staff. A convinced Germanophile since his year as military attaché in Berlin not long before the war, he won over the other two members of the CUP's ruling triumvirate, Talaat and Jemal, to the treaty he had secretly been negotiating with Wangenheim. Jemal was finally persuaded when in the last days of peace Churchill seized the two dreadnoughts bought by Turkey.

In the final weeks of peace following the assassination of Archduke Franz Ferdinand, heir to the Austrian imperial throne, and his wife Sophie at Sarajevo, capital of Bosnia, by a Serbian nationalist on 28 June 1914, Wangenheim redoubled his efforts to win over the Turks to a full-blown alliance with Germany. He held out prospects of protection against the old enemy, Russia, and potential territorial gains at its expense on the successful conclusion of a war between it and the Central Powers. He talked of reviving the caliphate and promised a guarantee of Turkish territorial integrity. In the late evening of Monday 27 July the new Grand Vizier, Prince Said Halim, strongly urged on by Enver and supported by Talaat, sent for Wangenheim and formally requested a defensive and offensive alliance against Russia. This was to be kept secret not only from the world at large but even from the rest of the Cabinet. Within 24 hours the German Chancellor, Theobald von Bethmann-Hollweg, telegraphed a treaty text for Wangenheim to show the Turkish conspirators. Earlier that day Austria had declared war on Serbia over the double assassination – and Churchill ordered the seizure of the Turkish dreadnoughts.

The Turks havered and wavered. The particular objection of those in the know was the clause that limited the treaty to the end of the coming war. They thought this would not protect Turkey against Russian post-war revenge. The Turks shared the widespread belief among the future belligerents that the coming war would be 'over by Christmas' or not much later. The clause was therefore amended so as to make the treaty last until the projected end of the tour of duty of General Liman von Sanders as head of the German military mission – 31 December 1918. It would then be renewed for five years unless one party or the other gave six months' notice of termination. Among its provisions were a German guarantee to help Turkey against external threat and Turkish acceptance of a commanding role for Liman von Sanders and his colleagues if the Turkish Army went to war. The alliance was to remain secret until an announcement was made. Enver as War Minister jumped the gun on 31 July by ordering general mobilisation in support of Turkey's declared posture of 'armed neutrality' in the coming conflict. On 2 August he lost patience with his vacillating colleagues, still debating Turkey's stance in wartime, and pressed the Grand Vizier to sign the treaty. Talaat and Halil of the Chamber of Deputies were the only other Cabinet members in the know at the time. Such was the character of the only major diplomatic triumph of Kaiser Wilhelm II in the prelude to the war of 1914. Turkey would suffer for it; but then so would Britain, France, Australia, New Zealand and even Newfoundland.

Wangenheim's main concern, as he impatiently awaited the signing of the treaty (which he was confident was only a matter of time), was how Germany could quickly demonstrate its practical value and significance to the many sceptics in Constantinople. So on 1 August, the day Germany declared war on Russia, he wired Berlin asking for the dispatch of Souchon's Mediterranean Division, a familiar and much-admired sight at the Golden Horn, to Constantinople. The Foreign Office in Berlin replied that the Kaiser did not deem this appropriate; but Grand Admiral Tirpitz, head of the Navy Office, intervened and told Wangenheim on the 3rd, the day Germany declared war on France, that the *Goeben* and the *Breslau* had been ordered to proceed to Constantinople after all. He also suggested that Souchon should be proposed to the Turks as commander-in-chief of their fleet. As Germany violated Belgium's neutrality by sending a vast army through the country to attack northern France, Britain decided to go to war in support of France and Belgium with effect from midnight Greenwich Mean Time on 4 August.

Souchon's orders in the event of war between Germany and France were simple enough: he was to take his two ships and disrupt the anticipated movement of large numbers of colonial troops across the western basin of the Mediterranean from North Africa to metropolitan France. In the dying days of July 1914 the *Goeben* (Captain Richard Ackermann, IGN) was visiting Trieste, then Austrian, while the *Breslau* (Commander Kettner, IGN) was at Durrazzo (now Durres) as part of an international flotilla supporting the government of Albania, newly independent from Turkey after the Balkan wars of 1912. The admiral, uncertain as to who would go to war and when, ordered the two ships to join up at the south-east Italian port of Brindisi on 1 August, so as not to be trapped in the Adriatic. The omens were not good. The Mediterranean Division anchored in the roads outside the harbour and Souchon asked the port authorities for coal – only to be refused. Italy had decided on neutrality, and was not obliged to help the Germans because they had declared war on France rather than the reverse. Souchon ordered his two ships to sail on to Messina, the port at the north-eastern tip of Sicily, just two miles from the Italian mainland. On the way the crews were told after breakfast on 2 August that they were now at war, the articles of war were read out and three cheers raised for the Kaiser.

Once again the Germans anchored offshore in the roads. There too the Italian authorities refused to supply coal, and even food – but later relented. The ships were allowed to load some coal from Italian government and German mercantile bunkers. Since Germany had ordered general mobilisation on 1 August, Souchon now had legal powers to issue orders to any ship flying the German flag. He instructed the East Africa Line ship SS *General* to rendezvous with him at Messina so he could plunder the big liner's bunkers. The passengers were disembarked and sent away with financial compensation while the ship's decks were opened up to gain access to the coal. Anything of potential value to a warship on active service, including naval reservists, was commandeered. The coal was laboriously transferred by barges, lighters and small boats, the *Goeben* acquiring just 173 tonnes and the more accessible *Breslau* 200, bringing her up to almost a full load of 1,200. The larger ship still had only two-thirds of her maximum capacity of about 3,000 tonnes, worrying for Souchon because she was designed for short-range deployment in the North Sea rather than blue-water operations. Her bunker space was small anyway, and now she was one-third short of a full load just as Souchon was preparing to carry out his first war assignment, the bombardment of the Algerian coast. Italian policy looked likely to prevent him getting much more.

None the less at midnight on 2 August the two ships sailed separately northward from Messina, which meant, as decreed by local geography, that they were westward-bound. Souchon ordered them to link up again briefly at a point south of Sardinia, from where the *Goeben* would make for Philippeville (now Skikda) – and her escort for Bône (now Annaba) – on the Algerian coast, each arriving at first light, about 3.30 a.m. GMT. Interestingly, in view of future events much further east, Souchon's orders to his captains included an injunction not to 'waste ammunition by firing at forts'. On the way southward, Souchon received the following message:

Alliance concluded with Turkey. *Goeben, Breslau* proceed at once to Constantinople.

Having come so far, and without consulting Berlin, Souchon decided to complete the mission he had begun, reckoning that the confusion he was bound to cause among the French would be worthwhile. He was more right than he knew.

The subsequent escape of the Mediterranean Division to the Dardanelles, and all the disastrous consequences, are usually blamed exclusively on the British, even by the British themselves. But Souchon's ships crossed the path of the bulk of the French fleet, and were detected by it, not once but at least twice, during their run to and from North Africa; and the French Navy did not have the excuse of the British Mediterranean Fleet that it was not yet at war with Germany when it failed to catch or even challenge Souchon. The first war-task of the French fleet, as the Germans had guessed, was to collect the army's XIX Corps, the 'Army of Africa', from French North Africa and deliver it to Toulon and Marseilles for forwarding by rail to its place in the line in northern France. So urgent was this that Admiral Lapeyrère, the *amiralissime* or commander-in-chief, was ordered to let each troopship sail individually as soon as loaded rather than having it wait to join a convoy. The various divisions of the fleet would cover them by seizing control of the Mediterranean, dealing with the Austrian and Italian fleets if and when necessary, the admiral said before the war broke out. He did not bother to mention the Germans. But on 28 July he startled Paris by questioning his long-agreed orders: now he wanted to form trooping convoys escorted by naval squadrons. The Ministry of Marine overruled him, specifically accepting the risk of individual sailings and pointing out that the French fleet was strong enough to dominate the entire Mediterranean. The message reached Lapeyrère at the main naval base of Toulon on 31 July.

The next day the French government rejected a German ultimatum to stay neutral in a war between Germany and Russia, which meant France was at war. General mobilisation was ordered from midnight on the 1st and Lapeyrère was informed on his flagship, the *Courbet*, at Toulon. The following evening a message from the French naval station of Bizerta in Tunisia reported that the wireless of the *Goeben* had been heard clearly nearby. Assuming correctly, even though the report was a false alarm, that the Germans would try to interfere with French troop movements, the admiral at seven p.m. on the 2nd ordered all troopships to stay in port until naval escorts arrived. As the entire fleet was also still in port, this implied a two-day delay for XIX Corps. Despite the chaos at the Paris Ministry of Marine, following the resignation of the minister after a nervous collapse, the Cabinet cobbled together a message to Lapeyrère, telling him the German ships had been seen at Brindisi on the night of 31 July–1August. He was told unequivocally to 'set sail ... and stop them'. Once again he was ordered to let troopships sail at once, alone if necessary. Once again he stayed in port. Early on the morning of 3 August he was told that the Germans had arrived at Messina on the afternoon of the 2nd. Lapeyrère finally set sail at four a.m.

The fleet was divided into three sections. Vice-Admiral Chocheprat led Group A, consisting of the First Squadron (six of the latest pre-dreadnoughts) and the First Light Division (four heavy cruisers and a dozen destroyers). This amounted to half the fleet and was bound for Philippeville. Lapeyrère himself led Group B in the dreadnought *Courbet*, accompanied by the Second Squadron of five older battleships (Rear-Admiral Le Bris), the Second Light Division and various auxiliaries, all bound for Algiers. The slow Group C, including the elderly Reserve Division of battleships with one extra added and four destroyers, had been sent out of Toulon on the evening of the 2nd and had reached the Balearic Islands, whence it was sent to Oran. All three groups were sailing at an almost leisurely 11–12 knots, Group A to the east, Group B in the centre and C to the west, corresponding to their destinations. All were in close order; amazingly, there was no screen of cruisers or destroyers to scout, despite the known imminence of general war.

On the afternoon of 3 August the French commander-in-chief received an offer of support from Admiral Sir Berkeley Milne, commanding the British Mediterranean Fleet (who embarrassingly outranked the Frenchman under whom he was expected to serve in wartime). He reminded the French that he had 3 battlecruisers, 4 heavy cruisers and 4 light, plus 16 destroyers. Taking his time, that night Lapeyrère thanked Milne, told him he was covering the passage of the Army of Africa and airily asked him to watch the movements of the Italian, Austrian and German fleets. 'You will be informed as soon as I have regained my freedom of movement.' By midnight he knew that Italy had declared herself neutral and that the Germans had left Messina a second time and were being hunted by the British. Just after one a.m. on 4 August he received the text of a message from Paris which had taken an inexcusable five hours to decode and clarify, once again ordering him not to waste time with convoys, to work with the British to provide general cover for the troopships and to 'destroy German cruisers, hostilities with Germany being now declared'. Germany had formally declared war with effect from six p.m. CET on 3 August. Lapeyrère had been ordered three times in 80 hours not to form convoys and twice in under 30 to catch the German ships.

The *Breslau* fired 190 15-cm shells at her target in 19 minutes; the *Goeben*, delayed for an hour by the need to avoid being sighted by two unidentified steamers, opened fire for ten minutes just after five a.m. with her secondary, 15-cm guns; 36 rounds caused a spectacular conflagration ashore. News of the shelling of Bône reached Lapeyrère by five a.m. on 4 August; and that of Philippeville, 60 miles to the west, 80 minutes later. The Germans were reported to be heading west after their bombardments – a feint, as subsequent reports revealed: Souchon was eastward-bound, heading back to Messina, desperately hoping he could find some more coal, especially for the *Goeben*, her bunkers now less than half-full. Lapeyrère ignored the subsequent correction because, like Milne, the French Ministry of Marine and the British Admiralty, he was convinced that Souchon must run west, in a bid to get home to Germany. It was the *idée fixe* of all his opponents. But wherever the Germans might be headed, one or both of them was sure to cross the path of the French Group A. Chocheprat, however, had slowed down because one of his battleships and a destroyer had engine trouble. Later calculations of the courses and timings of the French and the Germans indicated that Chocheprat's left wing, westbound, passed within 40 miles of the *Goeben*, heading east, at about seven a.m. on 4 August. Had the Frenchman been travelling at a normal speed, had he put out a cruiser or destroyer screen in the normal way, he would have sighted Souchon on a morning offering visibility of ten miles. For her part the *Breslau* overheard clear, plain-language signals between two French battleships (of Group A) at about 1.30 a.m. on the 4th. She sighted an unidentified, darkened ship to starboard an hour later.

Neither Chocheprat nor his chief made any effort to find the Germans. Instead the entire French fleet slowed to a crawl to accommodate two limping ships, of no use in their condition, rather than detaching them and pressing on. There was no attempt to link up or co-ordinate with the British, and the fleet was wasting time on a task – shepherding troopships – which it had specifically and repeatedly been forbidden to perform. In fact the French Navy went even further than merely missing a chance to stop the Germans if Milne's second-in-command, Troubridge, is to be believed: Lapeyrère's flagship *Courbet* had actually sighted the *Goeben*'s smoke at a distance of 25–30 miles on the morning of 4 August but the admiral did nothing about it, not even telling the British, because he thought a chase would be futile, despite his orders to try. The French fleet might even have been able to surround the enemy battlecruiser. Lapeyrère disclosed this to Troubridge when they met at Malta on 16 August – by which time, as we shall see, Troubridge was in disgrace.

The two German ships joined up once more south of Sardinia just after nine a.m. and headed eastward for Messina. At 9.15, however, a lookout on the *Breslau* sighted two columns of smoke coming towards them from the west. Kettner alerted the *Goeben* and Souchon, who at first assumed they were from French battleships. But as they drew nearer the Germans could make out two British battlecruisers. This was serious news. The *Goeben* had ten 28-cm (11-inch) guns capable of firing a broadside weighing 6,600 pounds; British battlecruisers each had eight 12-inch guns with a broadside of 6,800 pounds, in combination therefore boasting more than twice the Germans' firepower. But the German big guns were made of better steel, had a higher muzzle velocity, higher elevation (meaning greater range), superior range-finders and more reliable ammunition. British battlecruisers sacrificed some armour to make them faster than battleships whereas German ships of this type had almost as much armour as battleships, together with bigger engines that gave them an advantage of at least two knots over their British contemporaries. Some 20 feet broader in the beam than these early Royal Navy battlecruisers, the *Goeben* (22,640 tonnes) offered a steadier gun platform. The British pair, *Indomitable* (17,250 tonnes) and *Indefatigable* (18,750 tonnes), had a design speed of 25 knots and carried much more coal than a German capital ship. Souchon ordered Kettner to sail away from the scene at top speed towards the north-east: this was no place for a light cruiser.

As the senior of the two British captains, Francis Kennedy, RN, of *Indomitable* commanded the pair and sent a simple wireless signal to Admiral Milne, who was at Malta at the time. Short though it was, it managed to include a mistake:

> Enemy in sight, steering east, consisting of *Goeben* and *Breslau*.

The excitement at the Admiralty when Milne relayed the news at ten a.m. was palpable. Churchill, its political chief, was informed at once. But Kennedy's error, though understandable, was fundamental – the use of the word 'enemy'. His report was timed 9.46 a.m. GMT on 4 August, over 14 hours before Britain would officially go to war against Germany, at midnight. The Germans had been given until then to withdraw from Belgium. Meanwhile Milne's message omitted to include the essential fact in Kennedy's signal that the Germans were steering *east*. Churchill, as he was to do many times during what became known as 'the *Goeben* affair' and then during the ensuing Dardanelles campaign alike, personally wrote the first reply to Milne and Kennedy:

> Very good. Hold her [*Goeben*]. War imminent.

After hasty consultation with the Prime Minister, H. H. Asquith, and the Foreign Secretary, Sir Edward Grey, Churchill added to his message 50 minutes later an order to 'sink the *Goeben*' if the Germans attacked French transports. But the full Cabinet cancelled this and the Admiralty rescinded the order just after two p.m. There was to be no act of war before midnight. This was merely the first of many slaphappy or merely sloppy signals from the Admiralty to Milne, his deputy Troubridge and individual ships, as will be shown. The ultimately disastrous abuse of the new invention of wireless at sea, a blessing but also a burden, by the Admiralty and Churchill in particular contrasts sharply with the way the Germans treated Souchon.

Routine administrative and informative signals were sent to his flagship and every other German naval detachment afloat or ashore. The admiral was in touch by wireless with the highly important naval *Etappe* (staging post), ably run by Commander Hans Humann in Constantinople, with some of the colliers the Imperial Navy had positioned in carefully chosen, out-of-the-way spots in the Mediterranean in case of need as well as other merchant ships such as the *General*, and of course with the Navy Office in Berlin. But he was sent only one brief order in the vital opening days of war and then left to get on with his work. He used his own discretion in deciding to carry out his predetermined first war-task, disrupting the French, regardless of the new instruction to go to Constantinople at once. By the moment he received it, very little extra time would be needed to obtain a rich dividend from confounding French movements: he saw no need to clear this with Berlin, even though there was a risk (not much of one as it turned out) that he might get involved in an action with French ships, which could have compromised his mission to Constantinople.

Souchon wondered whether to dip his colours in salute, as peacetime courtesy decreed, to the two approaching British ships, which he assumed would be commanded by an admiral likely to be senior to him. He decided not to, in case the gesture was misread as hoisting a battle flag. The *Goeben* was cleared for action – guns manned and loaded, ready ammunition in place, rangefinders hard at work – but kept her guns aligned fore and aft. The British, who must have known the *Goeben* had an admiral aboard whereas they did not, also refrained from saluting. The eastbound Germans and the westbound British approached each other at a combined speed of well over 40 knots, passing each other, the *Goeben* to the south, at a distance of 9,000 metres (10,000 yards or five nautical miles), well within the range of the guns of both sides. The British big guns tracked the Germans but held their fire as the two battlecruisers turned in a wide arc to swing behind the *Goeben*, beginning what must stand as the most dramatic race in naval history.

The British had no means of knowing that the *Goeben* was badly afflicted with boiler trouble. Had the ship been given more time to 'shake down' when first commissioned this might have been dealt with, but as it was some 4,500 boiler tubes had to be replaced at Pola just before the battle-cruiser was readied for war service. Even that did not solve the problem, which meant that the *Goeben* was probably some two knots short of her design speed of 27 knots.

The two British battlecruisers also had their problems. Neither had a full complement for war service. Both needed maintenance; one had been forced to set sail from Malta in the middle of refitting. All this reduced their design speed of 25 knots by a similar margin. The Germans therefore crept inexorably ahead as the three big ships sent up towering columns of black smoke over the Mediterranean.

But the price paid by the Germans for opening a gap was very high. Below deck every available man, including the off-duty watch, officers, even telegraphists, was roped in to help with trimming coal, feeding the insatiable furnaces and clearing hot ash as the *Goeben* piled on steam.

Two hours in that hell below was all a man could stand [Telegraphist Georg Kopp recalled]. Smarting and irritating, the fine coaldust in the bunkers penetrated the nose and clogged the throat. Lungs laboured heavily as the men struggled at their work. A crust of coaldust would form in the throat and cause a racking cough. Coffee and lemonade were constantly and greedily gulped down. But the relief did not last ...

In silence, but pluckily and undismayed, the stokers stuck to their work – half naked ... they served the fires ... The sweat ran in streams down their gleaming torsos. The searing heat streamed from the furnaces, burning the skin and singeing the hair. And still the work went on in the torrid stokeholds.

It was here that the issue was being fought out.

The effort involved would have challenged a contemporary coal-miner. It was not just a case of shovelling coal out of a midships bunker into the furnaces close by; as this was being done, others were shovelling fuel along the sides of the hull from more distant bunkers towards midships, fighting to keep their balance on the shifting coals and gulping down dust in the filthy air. One Seaman Westphal died of asphyxiation on the run to Messina; before the *Goeben* reached her goal, Captain Ackermann would work another three men to death.

Breslau reached Messina at four a.m. on 5 August, *Goeben* almost three hours later. The larger ship was escorted for the last 90 minutes of her run by five Italian destroyers, three ahead and two astern, as a courtesy. Ackermann was able to stop briefly to bury Seaman Westphal at sea. The battlecruiser was down to her last few hundred tonnes of coal, but the *General* and four other German merchant ships were waiting in the roads and the exhausted sailors were put to work again on the dispiriting task of taking coal aboard. Sicily in August was not cool, but the crew of the *Goeben* performed the herculean labour of loading 1,600 tonnes in little more than

12 hours. They were plied with drinks and music from the ship's band and those who collapsed from heat and exhaustion were allowed a few hours off in the comfortable bunks of the liner *General*, followed by a bath. Souchon reluctantly stood the men down when his flagship had loaded some two-thirds of her coal capacity, about 2,100 tonnes. The light cruiser acquired 495 tonnes for a total of 920. The Germans even managed to buy the cargo of a British collier that happened to be in port.

With the Italians officially neutral, Souchon and his men had every reason to feel rather lonely in a sea dominated by France and Britain. The German admiral therefore appealed to Admiral Haus, the Austrian naval chief, to send supporting ships to escort him from Messina. As Austria was not yet at war with the British or French, Haus declined, and Berlin warned Souchon that Austria was unlikely to help anyway, urging him to press on eastwards. The Italian authorities told him he would not be allowed to coal in their harbours again. And an overnight signal from Berlin to Souchon received early on 6 August told him that 'Entry to Constantinople [is] not yet possible at present for political reasons'. The Turkish Cabinet was as divided as ever about the alliance with Germany; once again Enver acted behind the backs of the sceptics by ensuring that the German ships would at least be allowed into the Dardanelles when they got there. But Souchon must have wondered whether he was about to put his head in a noose when Turkish attitudes were so equivocal. Even so he suppressed his doubts and signalled:

I shall break through to the east.

Meanwhile Admiral Milne had done very little. He had sent the two battlecruisers westward to block the Strait of Gibraltar because he believed the Germans were bound to try to run for home, especially after their bombardment of the Algerian coast. He ordered the light cruiser *Dublin*, visiting Bizerta (see below), to join up with the battlecruisers. Once the Germans were in Messina they ostensibly still had two options (Turkey did not yet figure at all in British or French naval calculations): to run for home or to join the Austrians in the Adriatic. If westward-bound from Messina, a ship must leave northwards and then turn west; if heading east she must run southward first and turn eastward round the 'toe' of Italy.

On 30 July 1914, Milne had received the following message, personally drafted by Churchill and so important in the light of subsequent events that it needs to be cited in some detail:

Should war break out and England and France engage in it, it now seems probable that Italy will remain neutral … The attitude of Italy is, however, uncertain, and it is especially important that your squadron should not be seriously engaged with Austrian ships before we know what Italy will do. *Your first task should be to aid the French in the transportation of their African Army by covering, and, if possible, bringing to action individual fast German ships, particularly* Goeben *who [sic] may interfere with that transportation.* You will be notified by telegraph when you may consult with the French admiral. *Do not at this stage be brought to action against superior forces,* except in combination with the French, as part of a general battle … We shall hope later to reinforce the Mediterranean, *and you must husband your forces at the outset* [author's emphases].

The significance of this verbose message, quoted at length but still not in full, will become clear; suffice it to say here that wireless was in its infancy in 1914, which meant that signals, transmitted in cipher and Morse code, had to be relayed, often contained garbles which necessitated repeats, and might take half a day or a lot longer to get through, whereupon they had to be deciphered. Churchill's text looks more like a draft of a parliamentary speech than an operational message to an admiral about to go to war. The above text is copied verbatim from Admiralty signal records in the British National Archives. This is part of how it was reproduced in Churchill's history of the war of 1914–18, *The World Crisis*:

It now seems probable should war break out and England and France engage in it, that Italy will remain neutral … Except in combination with the French as part of a general battle, do not at this stage be brought to action against superior forces … You must husband your forces at the outset and we shall hope later to reinforce the Mediterranean.

Churchill thus tidied up the punctuation, reconstructing the three sentences quoted here (he also changed '*Goeben* who' to '*Goeben* which'!). He commented: 'So far as the English language may serve as a vehicle of thought, the words employed appear to express the intentions we [Churchill and Fisher, the First Sea Lord] had formed.' There can be no denying that the revised version changes the emphasis in the original text, which is badly drafted and therefore open to more than one interpretation. To take one example, was Milne not supposed to engage German ships unless they were 'individual' *and* 'fast' *and* interfering with the French transports? Was he not to cover them if the German ships (there were after all only two) were sailing together? Nor is there any definition of 'superior forces', which turned out to be a tragic omission.

Milne, not unreasonably, read the message as meaning that his absolute priority was to protect the French transports, a task which rightfully belonged to the much bigger French fleet. He relayed the gist of the message to Troubridge, in his sailing orders issued at Malta on 2 August, ending with the words: 'I am to avoid being brought to action against superior force. *You are to be guided by this should war be declared* [author's emphasis].' On the same day the Admiralty told Milne:

> *Goeben* must be shadowed by two battlecruisers. Approach to Adriatic must be watched by cruisers and destroyers. Remain near Malta yourself.

That evening Troubridge took his squadron of four heavy cruisers, the light cruiser *Gloucester* and eight destroyers to watch the mouth of the Adriatic. The two battlecruisers were temporarily placed under his command as well. Milne, told he could link up with the French fleet as war was imminent, asked if he could now open his secret war orders, which contained the Anglo-French cipher to be used in wartime – even though his standing orders, issued in May 1913, specifically called for this in the circumstances. The affirmative reply took more than 12 hours to reach him, so there was a total of 24 hours' delay before Milne on the afternoon of 3 August offered his support to Lapeyrère. Reply came there none. Milne now sent the light cruiser *Dublin* to Bizerta – the wrong direction – to look for Lapeyrère and to hand over a letter he had written repeating his offer of help; it was never delivered.

Sir Archibald Berkeley Milne inherited his title from his baronet father, an admiral of the fleet. From the age of 27 he entered upon a series of postings to royal yachts, culminating in his appointment as flag officer commanding all of them, in the rank of rear-admiral, in 1903. He was 48. Though both a dandy and a ladies' man, and a close friend of Princess Alexandra, frequently wronged wife of the Prince of Wales who became King Edward VII in 1901, Milne never married. Lord Fisher, the former and future First Sea Lord of humble origins, detested him. The lower deck called him Arky-Barky, but Fisher, in retirement in 1912 when Milne was given the plum Mediterranean command, protested strongly to Churchill as First Lord: 'I consider you have betrayed the navy,' he wrote, and much more. He called

Milne many names, the shortest of which was Sir B. Mean; after the *Goeben* scandal Fisher called him Sir Berkeley Goeben. His main base was Malta, and in 1914 he flew his flag on the battlecruiser HMS *Inflexible*.

Milne's second-in-command and flag officer of the First Cruiser Squadron was of an entirely different stamp. Affectionately known to the lower deck as the 'Silver King' for his mane of white hair, Ernest Charles Thomas Troubridge was descended from one of Nelson's close associates and a distinguished naval and military family. Strongly built, with a ruddy face and a bluff, jovial manner, he got on well with both his juniors and his seniors. Like Milne and so many other senior naval officers, he came from an upper-class background, but unlike Milne he was no courtier. In 1888, at the age of 26, he won a Royal Humane Society award for diving into the sea at night to save a sailor who had fallen overboard from a torpedo-boat. A captain by 1901, he was an official observer during the Russo-Japanese War of 1904–5, producing important reports that influenced future tactics in the Royal Navy. The gifted seaman and leader of men was also good at staffwork, becoming Naval Secretary to Churchill's predecessor as First Lord and rising as a rear-admiral in 1912 to naval chief of staff, the first man to hold this new post. Fisher was one of his greatest admirers, though this would change …

In 1914 Troubridge commanded a squadron of four heavy cruisers from one of their number, HMS *Defence*. Significantly, the Imperial German Navy, the Royal Navy's upstart rival whose fleet, ship for ship, was the best in the world in many respects, deployed only two of this type on front-line service in 1914, in Graf Spee's squadron: they were the last built by the Germans (in 1904). Displacing about 14,000 tonnes, the heaviest armament of the British 'armoured cruisers' was the 9.2-inch gun and their maximum armour six inches thick while their top speed was barely 23 knots. A heavy cruiser was no match for a capital ship, which it could not even outrun, slower and less nimble than a light cruiser, and of no value in a fleet action, as the Battle of Jutland in 1916 would prove: *Defence* was sunk there. None was laid down in Britain after 1905.

The Germans entered Messina from the north. Milne had been ordered not to enter Italian waters for fear of upsetting neutral sentiment; as the strait is only two miles wide at its narrowest, there could be no question of a chase down the channel. British warships, including the *Dublin* (Captain John Kelly, RN), stayed the requisite three miles offshore as the Germans took on supplies in full view. Milne ordered Troubridge to detach the light cruiser *Gloucester* (Captain Howard Kelly, RN, brother of John) to watch the southern exit of the strait.

Sicilians and Italians lined the shore on both sides as a powerful sense of impending drama spread. While the small vessels fed the large grey ones with coal, enterprising local traders from Messina sailed out to them, offering food and drink. Other boats were crowded with sightseers; musicians came out to serenade the sweating German sailors; local newspapers pulled out all the stops in their headlines: 'Into the jaws of death', one paper proclaimed; 'Towards death and glory – the bold venture of *Goeben* and *Breslau*', shouted another. There would not be another scene like it until 1939, when the German 'pocket battleship' *Admiral Graf Spee* prepared to leave Montevideo on the River Plate after taking refuge there following a fight with three British cruisers. Thousands of locals watched avidly and the scene was broadcast live round the world by radio. There are other parallels with this later drama, as will become clear. After a five-hour respite for the crews, the two German ships quietly began to raise steam for full speed. Some 36 hours after their second visit to Messina inside a week, the *Goeben* and the *Breslau* weighed anchor and moved off.

At 5.10 p.m. on 6 August there was an urgent message from HMS *Gloucester* on her lonely patrol at the southern exit of the Strait of Messina: the *Goeben* had just come out, 'steering east'. Ten minutes later the *Breslau* appeared. Both ships were careful to hug the coast, within the three-mile Italian territorial limit, as they rounded the Italian foot and headed northeast towards the Adriatic.

Howard Kelly's light cruiser was three knots slower than the *Breslau* (28 knots), and her heaviest guns were a pair of six-inchers, one fore, one aft. She also had ten four-inch guns and two torpedo tubes. By keeping contact with the Germans in dangerous conditions the *Gloucester* was able to discover, at considerable risk, where Souchon was actually going, and only gave up the pursuit on a direct order from Milne, when it was clear that the Germans had outpaced the rest of the British fleet and would get away. The conduct of the ship was a beacon of courage and competence in a sorry saga of ineptitude and hesitation, salvaging some honour for an embarrassed Royal Navy.

When Kelly's report reached him, Milne was about one-third of the way along the north coast of Sicily, heading east. Mindful of the order not to enter Italian waters, he saw no alternative but to turn about and take the long route round the great island, which meant he could never hope to catch the Germans. That this did not interest him overmuch is shown by the fact that he took his ships at a far from urgent speed back to Malta – to collect coal which the capacious British battlecruisers did not need. By the time an Admiralty message not to worry about territorial waters reached him it was too late to be relevant. *Dublin* and two destroyers had left Malta at two p.m. to join Troubridge; Milne diverted them to seek the Germans and make a torpedo attack on them. John Kelly worked out that he would not catch up until mid-morning the next day; but at least he put his foot down, on the practical principle that you never know what may turn up – perhaps one of Souchon's ships might break down.

His brother in the *Gloucester* kept up the pursuit despite a close pass at him by the *Breslau*, though neither side opened fire, at a range of less than 4,000 yards. At 9.46 p.m. on the 6th the British light cruiser sent another electrifying message:

Urgent. *Goeben* altering course to southward.

The Germans were not entering the Adriatic after all: the north-easterly course had been a feint. John Kelly now calculated that he might be able to cross the enemy's path just after midnight – his reward for getting a move on. Unfortunately evasive manoeuvres by the Germans prevented him from making an attack, despite a flow of information from his brother. He gave up just before three a.m.

Admiral Troubridge, on learning the Germans were apparently headed for the Adriatic, decided to make an attack, hoping to intercept them between 2.30 and 3 a.m. GMT, with luck in the confined waters north of Corfu, where he might hope to offset the *Goeben*'s advantages in armament, armour and speed. On hearing of Souchon's change of course away from him he still hoped to cross the Germans' path around three a.m. or later, though further south. Unable to sleep for tension on the way southward, Troubridge had doubts, which were encouraged by Captain Fawcet Wray of the *Defence*, his flag captain and a gunnery specialist. He argued that the *Goeben* was a force superior to the four heavy cruisers because she could pick them off at her leisure from outside the range of their own guns and move a good deal faster too. At 2.55 a.m. on 7 August Troubridge changed his mind, called off the hunt and sheered off to sheltered waters. It made no difference that he could have spread his cruisers out and sent in his fast destroyers to make torpedo attacks, thus offering *Goeben* a bewildering plethora of targets.

All he needed to do was to clip the Germans' wings, to inflict enough damage for the British battlecruisers to catch up and finish them off: the enemy, once slowed down, had no refuge or source of extra ammunition.

One knows instinctively that a John or Howard Kelly would have 'had a go' in the not unreasonable hope that something would turn up. Troubridge however put discretion before valour, and paid a high price for it. A court of inquiry determined that he should be tried by court martial for negligence or default in his failure 'to pursue ... an enemy then flying'. He was acquitted, despite Milne's best efforts to stab him in the back with his evidence, but never got another seagoing command and became a pariah in the navy. So at least did Milne, who was never charged over his part in the débâcle forever known as 'the *Goeben* affair'. So did Wray.

John Kelly having missed the Germans and Troubridge having declined to take them on, there was now nothing between the Mediterranean Division and its goal, the Dardanelles, except for the open sea. The *Gloucester*, after an inconclusive exchange of shots with the *Breslau*, reluctantly abandoned the chase south of the Peloponnese. This was fortunate as Souchon had planned to spring a trap on the irritating contact-keeper by hiding behind a headland in the *Goeben* while using his other ship as a lure. Howard Kelly was rightly acclaimed for his bold and sustained pursuit. He had divined Souchon's intentions and reported his manoeuvres: it was more than a great pity that Milne's blunders and Troubridge's defection had ensured his crew's best efforts in keeping up speed and sending quick and clear signals were all in vain. The performance of the brothers Kelly, who both became admirals, showed up the contrast between the high quality of many individual ships' captains and the indifferent performance of so many admirals of the time.

The unquestionably competent Souchon carried on, pausing to take up coal from two German colliers deployed for his benefit at Dhenousa among the Greek Aegean islands. The rendezvous duly took place on Sunday 9 August; the admiral found time to order a church service. After 12 more hours of sweated labour the *Goeben* had built her coal stocks up to just half a full load. On Monday 10 August at 4.45 a.m. Souchon ordered his ships to weigh anchor and steer north.

Urged on by Berlin and Commander Humann in Constantinople, the German ships arrived at a point five miles off the entrance to the Dardanelles. The flagship signalled by wireless, lamp and flag to the entrance forts: 'Send me a pilot immediately.' A Turkish torpedo-boat came out flying the flag-signal 'Follow me'. Within minutes Admiral Souchon's command passed Cape Helles and entered the Dardanelles, its mission apparently accomplished. Unbeknown to his new hosts, however, Souchon had been given another order which would change the course of world history – but would take ten weeks rather than ten days to execute.

PART II

THE ALLIED RESPONSE

CHAPTER 3

Blockade

Admiral Sir Berkeley Milne, having learned from several signals on the night of 5–6 August that the German ships had returned to Messina after their raid on the Algerian coast, was as convinced as ever that they were bound eventually to head westward for home. He therefore decided to block their presumed route, which as we have seen meant heading very briefly north out of Messina before sailing west along the lengthy northern coast of Sicily. He had taken his ships to Bizerta, in French Tunisia, to enable some of them to take on coal; by 6.30 a.m. on the 6th he reached the north-western tip of Sicily for a slow sweep eastward. Lacking any further intelligence of the enemy, he resolved to guard the northern exit from the Strait of Messina. He sent the light cruisers *Weymouth* and *Chatham* ahead of the two battlecruisers in company, his flagship *Inflexible* and the *Indefatigable* (Captain Kennedy of the *Indomitable* was still coaling in Bizerta, having wasted 12 hours looking for a suitable French official to authorise access to a loaded collier already in port).

By failing to divide his forces so as to block the strait with firepower superior to the Germans' at each end, summoning reinforcements from Troubridge at the mouth of the Adriatic if necessary, Milne made his first major error. Hindsight enables us to see that it was also his biggest tactical mistake, with strategic consequences out of all proportion; but it should have been obvious to him at the time that if he was strong enough to block both ends at no added risk to himself or his fleet, he should have done so. While it might not have seemed remotely likely to him that Souchon would seek to link up with the Austrians, thus locking himself up in the Adriatic, Milne could not have known what orders the German admiral had received and should have catered for the possibility. Had he done so, he would coincidentally have frustrated the Germans' real purpose, of which he was entirely ignorant through no fault of his own, by a happy accident.

Urgency was not uppermost in Milne's mind after Souchon's second departure from Messina: he took his two battlecruisers to Malta to stock up on coal, although their bunkers contained enough to get them to the eastern end of the Mediterranean *and back*, even at high speed. Souchon would doubtless have given his eye-teeth for such copious coal capacity. This was Milne's second major blunder. He took 17 hours at an average speed below 15 knots to reach Valletta, where *Indomitable* and her three destroyers rejoined his flag from Bizerta. On his way west at about ten a.m. on the 6th, Milne, ironically, received the following redundant message:

> If *Goeben* goes south from Messina, you should follow through the Straits, irrespective of territorial waters.

As Captain John Kelly in the *Dublin* had left Malta with two destroyers at two p.m. on the 6th to join Troubridge, Milne diverted him to chase and attack the Germans with torpedoes. Both Kelly brothers coaxed more than their design speed out of their respective light cruisers. It has proved impossible to establish exactly how close John Kelly came to the *Goeben* that night before breaking off the chase, even as his brother Howard maintained contact with the Germans from astern. The *Dublin* sighted smoke – but it could just as well have been the *Gloucester*'s. Now the Royal Navy's only chance to catch the *Goeben* lay with Rear-Admiral Troubridge in the Adriatic. But, as we saw, he sheered off his interceptive course – at about the moment the *Dublin* gave up the hunt, 2.55 a.m. GMT on the morning of 7 August. Shortly after dawn *Gloucester* was ordered by Milne to fall back to avoid capture. Howard Kelly reported later:

> … as it was essential to know if the enemy were making for Egypt or for the Aegean Sea, it was considered permissible to continue shadowing.

The *Gloucester* therefore showed a rare initiative by carrying on against orders, and even engaged in an inconclusive exchange of fire with the *Breslau*. Just before that was broken off, Kelly received the order from Milne to abandon the pursuit due south of Cape Matapan, the southern extremity of Greece. This time he obeyed. At least one commander in the sorry saga of the Royal Navy and the *Goeben* had shown initiative and a Nelsonian fighting spirit. Souchon, although he did not know it yet, now had a clear run to Turkish waters.

Milne however had not quite given up the idea of going after him: the three battlecruisers and the light cruiser *Weymouth* set out from Malta in the first hour of 8 August, albeit at a stately 14 knots. At about noon the hapless admiral, in common with all other British naval commands and ships at sea, received a short message: 'Commence hostilities at once against Austria.' Three hours later came another: 'Negative my telegram hostilities against Austria.' A signals clerk had blundered; Austria was not yet at war with the Entente (though it would be, soon enough). Milne's entirely correct reaction to this false alarm was to alter course northward to link up with Troubridge, so as to prevent the Austrian fleet from coming out of the Adriatic and getting between his eastbound ships and their base at Malta. The ever-cautious admiral also lost more time awaiting an answer to his querulous (but in the circumstances entirely justifiable) signal asking for confirmation of the cancellation. It took half an hour to arrive. Another half-hour after that there was a further message from the Admiralty: 'With reference to the cancellation of telegram notifying war on Austria, situation is critical.' Milne had thus received three gratuitous answers to the unasked question as to whether he had to reckon with the Austrian fleet: Yes; No; and finally, Maybe! None of them should have been sent. All this embarrassing confusion took more than seven hours to resolve. Milne finally got round to resuming the 'chase' of the Germans at lunchtime on 9 August, and then only on the direct order of the Admiralty: 'Not at war with Austria. Continue chase of *Goeben* which passed Cape Matapan early on 7th steering north-east.'

But by now the trail was stone cold. The pusillanimous decisions of Milne and Troubridge had been compounded by extraordinary ineptitude at the Admiralty, for which Churchill, with his penchant for prolix signals and interference in matters of operational detail, must bear the lion's share of responsibility. The British Mediterranean Fleet was now 59 hours behind the German Mediterranean Division. Even so, for a while Milne positioned his battlecruisers between the Peloponnese and Crete to block a westward move by Souchon, still Milne's *idée fixe* despite the mounting evidence to the contrary.

On the morning of the 10th, however, he led his three battlecruisers and two light cruisers on a sweep of the Aegean Sea with its myriad islands and hiding places, finding nothing. At 9.30 a.m. German wireless traffic was intercepted, indicating that the *Goeben* could not be far away; but radio direction-finding did not yet exist. Milne's search continued for more than 24 hours until he received a message from London, relayed via Malta, saying that the German ships had reached the Dardanelles, as had been reported by a local British vice-consul 15 hours earlier, and adding:

> You should establish a blockade of Dardanelles for the present, but be on the lookout for mines.

Once again the master-quibbler Milne sought confirmation, and once more he was justified, as the Admiralty reply shows:

> No blockade intended … carefully watch the entrance in case enemy cruisers come out.

The same slapdash drafting of signals prevailed at the Admiralty, unfazed by the premature declaration of war against Austria. Blockade is an act of war; Turkey had, however duplicitously, declared herself neutral and London had no reason yet to believe otherwise. Milne was quite right to wonder aloud whether he was really meant to open hostilities against the Ottoman Empire. Twenty-four hours after the Germans entered the Dardanelles, HMS *Weymouth* (Captain W. D. Church, RN) had approached the entrance, on the afternoon of 11 August. Two Turkish torpedo-boats came out and signalled by flag: 'Heave to.' When Church disingenuously allowed his ship to 'drift' towards the entrance, two blank warning shots were fired and the guns of the entrance forts swung towards the light cruiser. He then asked for a pilot and was refused. Church took up a position on the three-mile limit. On the morning of the 12th a torpedo-boat brought a Turkish Army lieutenant, who boarded the British watchkeeper with a message: the two German ships were in Turkish waters and had been purchased by the Ottoman government. The *Goeben* was now the *Sultan Yavuz Selim* and the *Breslau* had become the *Midilli*, he explained in halting English. Church asked if he might sail up the straits as far as Chanak, the town overlooking the Narrows from the Asian shore, and was flatly refused. The stable door was firmly closed in the face of the Royal Navy – after the horses had bolted safely inside.

For the time being the Germans dropped anchor off Chanak. Souchon was still well over 100 miles from his objective of Constantinople; Enver was still unsure of his Cabinet colleagues' resolve, although he felt with some justification that things were moving his way. The German admiral on 12 August received a message, dated the 10th, from the Admiralty in Berlin, urging him to go on to Constantinople as soon as possible 'in order to press Turkey to declare for us on basis of concluded treaty'. It was followed by another signal containing orders to be carried out if he was not allowed to stay in Constantinople. There were, it seemed, two possibilities:

(1) With tacit consent or without serious opposition from Turkey, break-through [into] Black Sea to attack Russia, or
(2) Attempt breakthrough [to] Adriatic Sea. Report as soon as ready to sail out, so that Austria [can] make move [on] Otranto …

Otranto is at the mouth of the Adriatic, where the French fleet assembled a blockading force soon after Austria joined in the war against the Entente on 12 August. Souchon, assuming a heavy British presence outside the Dardanelles, could only have regarded such a breakout as suicidal and dismissed it out of hand. Instead he told Berlin: 'I intend to move forward against the Black Sea as soon as possible.' Taking on the Russian Black Sea Fleet, even though it was not inconsiderable, must have seemed the better bet. Besides, his real mission was to exploit the alliance with Turkey against Russia, Germany's main enemy, by provoking a new war between the two ancient rivals.

In accord with the Turkish lieutenant's statement to Captain Church of the *Weymouth*, Souchon told his two ships' crews that 'Turkish government [is] declaring, with knowledge of German government, that *Goeben* and *Breslau* have been sold to Turkey. For political reasons it is necessary not to counter these rumours. *Ships of course remain German*' [author's emphasis]. This was a neat ruse, agreed with Enver, which annoyed the British: Turkey had decided to 'buy' the two German ships, purportedly to replace the two dreadnoughts commandeered by the Royal Navy. Preparing his detailed report to Berlin about the run east, Souchon made an interesting but understandable miscalculation. He attributed HMS *Gloucester*'s lack of support while shadowing his ships to the success of his own telegraphists in jamming her wireless. Obviously he could not understand how he had been able to elude the attentions of the rest of the British Mediterranean Fleet so easily after having been so energetically chased by two of its battlecruisers. Captain Howard Kelly was fully aware of the jamming, signalling at one point, 'I am deliberately being interfered with' (the future admiral was addicted to the feeble *double entendre*: when his ship returned to Malta after her long chase, Captain Wray signalled from the flagship of the Cruiser Squadron: 'Congratulate you on your splendid feat.' Kelly replied, 'Yes, they are very large'). The efficiency of his wireless operators was just one of the attributes of a well-run ship.

Meanwhile the Germans' most pressing practical problem was the serious dilapidation of the *Goeben*'s boiler tubes, exacerbated by the exertions of the run east, during which four of the battlecruiser's crew had been worked to death. Captain Ackermann reported that no fewer than 8,000 tubes were blown and 50 boilermakers would have to be brought from Germany with replacements to repair them. But at least by 13 August the ship's bunkers were full with 3,000 tonnes of coal for the first time in weeks. Souchon and his flag captain realised that if the battlecruiser had to sail, she could not expect to exceed 18 knots as the unavoidable running repairs were made on three or four boilers at a time. Until that process was complete, the ship would forfeit one-third of her design speed.

Souchon left this headache behind, sailing to Constantinople in a dispatch boat for talks with Enver. The German commander was alarmed by what he had seen of the defences of the Dardanelles as he entered them and almost immediately signalled Berlin with a shopping list. He suggested sending two admirals, ten seaman-officers plus technical experts as reinforcements for his division and for the Turkish defence as soon as possible. More communications equipment, guns, ammunition, torpedoes and mines were badly needed. His sense of urgency about the defences make it clear that he anticipated the need to prepare for a British attack on them sooner rather than later from the moment he entered Turkish waters. Enver explained that so long as the attitudes of as yet neutral Bulgaria and Romania were in doubt, many of his Cabinet colleagues remained hesitant about activating the still-secret alliance with Germany. Souchon, having agreed with Enver that he should take over the command of the Ottoman fleet, next met Jemal, the Navy Minister, and demanded that the British officers and technicians of Admiral Limpus's naval mission be removed from all Turkish warships and naval installations. Reluctantly Jemal agreed.

Souchon also called on Ambassador Wangenheim to discuss the political situation in Constantinople. The admiral was impatient to carry out his mission against Russia while the diplomat urged understanding of Turkish hesitation so long as the position of their Balkan neighbours remained unclear. The Bulgarians and Romanians were clearly waiting to see how the Central Powers progressed against the Triple Entente in the campaigns to the north and west. The two German officials agreed fully in principle on the objective of exploiting their hard-won advantage, gained from the alliance and boosted by the arrival of the navy: the only issue between them was the timing.

The Admiralty in Berlin signalled to Souchon on 14 August: 'Concur proposal undertake operation [in] Black Sea [with] agreement *or against the will* of Turkey' [author's emphasis]. But the admiral was also urged to co-operate with Wangenheim, and to wait until Turkish mobilisation was further advanced. Souchon's military opposite number, General Otto Liman von Sanders, was no less impatient as he struggled to galvanise the Ottoman Army. Its condition initially left nearly as much to be desired as that of the Turkish fleet, which had been allowed to rot for more than 20 years. The British naval mission had made little progress beyond securing the abortive orders for two dreadnoughts, and Souchon was determined that its German replacement would get to grips with the derelict condition of most of the fleet. He returned to his flagship on the 15th.

On 16 August – the same day as an alarmed Russia offered a disdainful and increasingly confident Enver a defensive military alliance – the British mission members were expelled from the Turkish fleet while the *Goeben* and *Breslau* sailed for Constantinople. On the way the names *Sultan Yavuz Selim* and *Midilli* were painted on their respective sterns, the Turkish flag was hoisted (though the German command pennants remained in place) and the crews exchanged their floppy, beribboned, dark-blue sailors' caps for red fezes. Anchored at the southern end of the Bosporus, off the Golden Horn, the gleaming German ships were cheered by Turkish crowds lining the shore as Jemal Pasha formally appointed Souchon commander-in-chief of the Ottoman fleet on the deck of the *Goeben/Yavuz* in a ceremony complete with brass band. Souchon took the salute when such Turkish warships as were sufficiently presentable (and mobile) passed in review. He was then conveyed ashore for an audience with the Sultan at the vast and ornate Dolmabahçe Palace on the shore of the Bosporus. His fleet sailed back to the Sea of Marmara and dropped anchor in Tuzla Bay: the two German ships, two old Turkish battleships and eight destroyers. Souchon soon rejoined them and reflected on the magnitude of his task; but he had at least been able to fulfil the first part of his orders, to proceed to Constantinople. It had taken less than a fortnight. The admiral now bent his formidable energy and organising ability to the task of fulfilling the second part, the bearding of Russia.

On 18 August Admiral Limpus of the unwanted British naval mission visited Enver with a friendly message from Churchill, who as noted had met the War Minister several times. He apologised for the 'unavoidable' sequestration of the two dreadnoughts, promised full compensation and offered to release them to Turkey after the war. Limpus advised Enver to send the German sailors and military advisers home, warning of disaster for Turkey if they were not and recommending a continuation of the stated policy of neutrality. Enver rejected this advice, even though there was still stiff resistance in the Cabinet to the German connection and to active participation in the war. German naval officers and ratings poured into Constantinople by train, munitions and other supplies came by rail and by barge down the Danube and along the Black Sea coast into the Bosporus; all protests from the Allies were ignored, even when some German sailors openly travelled in uniform, in flagrant breach of international law.

His Britannic Majesty's Mediterranean Fleet was now assembled in considerable strength outside the Dardanelles: the three battlecruisers, four light cruisers and smaller vessels. In the early hours of 13 August, Admiral Milne was told, correctly this time, that Britain had been at war with Austria since the previous day. He was ordered to sail back to Malta with the bulk of his ships, to lay down his command and return to Britain, where inquiries were already under way into the acutely embarrassing failure to stop the Germans reaching the Dardanelles. Outside the gates the battlecruisers *Indefatigable* and *Indomitable* and the gallant light cruiser *Gloucester*, a force large enough to outgun the vanished Germans should they come out, remained on guard, temporarily under the flag of Rear-Admiral Troubridge, pending a decision by London on what to do next.

Milne was replaced in the command of the Mediterranean Fleet, with singular lack of imagination, by Vice-Admiral Sir Sackville Carden, the lacklustre erstwhile admiral-superintendent at Malta, who relieved Troubridge off the Dardanelles. Carden was replaced in the deskbound command at Malta by Rear-Admiral Limpus, the former head of the British naval mission and thus the man on the British side with by far the most detailed knowledge of Turkish naval dispositions and facilities. But the Foreign Office, on the advice of Sir Louis Mallet, ambassador to Turkey, developed the remarkable view that appointing Limpus as commander of the force at the Dardanelles would offend the Turks. Of course Mallet had as yet no knowledge of the Turco-German alliance and still hoped Turkey would remain neutral.

There was little activity off the Dardanelles during September 1914 as various units of the British Mediterranean Fleet, and later also of the French Navy, kept watch. But on the 26th a Turkish torpedo-boat emerged into the Aegean, like a rabbit taking a peek from its warren at the waiting foxes. A party of British sailors and marines boarded the little warship from a destroyer – and found a few Germans among the crew. The British therefore did not hesitate to order the ship to put about and go back into the strait. The German General Weber Pasha, 'adviser' to the Turkish General Staff on the defence of the entrance forts, did not hesitate either. On his own authority, without even informing his Turkish allies in advance, he took the momentous decision to close the Dardanelles. Extra mines were soon laid under the tutelage of the German Vice-Admiral Usedom (sent to stiffen the defences at Souchon's request) in the approaches to the Narrows, the lighthouses were extinguished and the strategic waterway, to which free access had been guaranteed by several international treaties, was blocked. Scores of Russian grain-ships queued in vain in an unprecedented maritime traffic-jam to get out, but eventually had to return home. Nearly all Russian exports and imports were cut off, terminating the possibility of trading grain for munitions from Britain and France and thus grievously undermining both Allied strategy and the Russian war effort.

The British were soon forced to rely on food imported from North America. This recourse opened up their transatlantic shipping to the eventually catastrophic depredations of the German U-boat campaign, which came closest of all factors to knocking the United Kingdom out of the war. The closure of the Dardanelles amounted to an inverted blockade: the Allied naval forces waiting outside were not conducting such a procedure against officially neutral Turkey but were notionally watching for the enemy German ships to come out. They were legally entitled to stop and search a warship in case it was carrying enemy German sailors, just as they would have been entitled to stop a merchant ship carrying supplies meant for the Germans, in order to prevent their delivery. But when the Turks accepted Weber's action, it was as if they also accepted that they would soon be under siege and might as well raise the drawbridge in their own time before the inevitable attack came.

The dread consequences of the Turco-German treaty and the arrival of the Mediterranean Division eight days later were not so obvious at the time. The closure was an act of war by, or on behalf of, a supposedly neutral power, but the British and French, their attention naturally focused on the burgeoning impasse on the Western Front, showed little immediate inclination to do anything about it. There was as little activity in the Aegean for the whole of October as there had been for most of September and indeed since Souchon's arrival. It was a different story in the Sea of Marmara, the Black Sea and the Bosporus strait which links them.

The impatient Souchon had been pressing the Turks for permission to exercise in the Black Sea since early September; this was reluctantly granted in mid-month, initially for two ships at a time, excluding the 'purchased' German pair for the time being. At this point, on 16 September, Admiral Limpus took his rejected men out of Constantinople and sailed away to Malta. Enver and his political supporters told Souchon there were to be no naval 'demonstrations' off the coasts of Bulgaria and Romania for fear of causing unnecessary alarm. Once General Weber had closed the Dardanelles on the 26th, events in the Turkish fleet gathered pace. On 3 October Souchon sent the *Goeben* and *Breslau* into the Black Sea for the first time, to exercise with two Turkish battleships. On the 8th *Breslau* was sent there again to scout for the Russian Black Sea Fleet, which however the Russians had prudently confined to port in their main base of Sevastopol, to avoid provoking the Turks. On the 12th Souchon risked sending his entire serviceable fleet into the Black Sea on manoeuvres, receiving a metaphorical slap on the wrist from a complaisant Enver.

German and Turkish naval staff were hard at work on operational plans and orders. A German 'soft loan' at this juncture helped to underpin a nascent pro-war majority in both the CUP leadership and the Cabinet: the Turks were now confident enough to demand, from all the warring powers, an end to the demeaning 'capitulations' conferring extra-territorial status on privileged foreigners. The Entente powers were no less keen than the Central powers to comply.

Although the anti-war faction was slowly dwindling, Enver felt from about the middle of October that in the absence of a smashing new triumph on the part of the Germans and their allies and/or a decisive step by Turkey, the rising tide of support for war would peak and begin to ebb. On 22 October he drew up a plan for Turkish intervention in the war and put it up to the German General Staff for comment: it included a move to seize the initiative in the Black Sea complete with military moves against Russia, against Britain in Egypt and in the Balkans, depending on developments there. The General Staff approved and politely looked forward to early delivery. Two days later Enver personally presented Souchon with his orders to enter the Black Sea in strength, attack the Russian coast and seize maritime supremacy, whenever he was ready. Individual orders went to Turkish naval officers to follow the German admiral's instructions.

On 26 October Souchon signalled to Berlin that he was 'entering Black Sea with fleet under guise of fleet exercise, with intent to attack …'. The next day a Turkish fleet entered the Black Sea from the Bosporus intent on war for the first time in 36 years. The ships, including *Yavuz* and *Midilli*, both sporting the red and white Ottoman flag, formed groups to bombard four Russian naval bases – Sevastopol, Odessa, Feodosia and Novorossiysk – and to lay mines along the Russian Black Sea coast. Souchon ended his fleet order with the pseudo-Nelsonian envoi, also hoisted in flag form on the *Goeben/Yavuz* as she turned away for Sevastopol: 'Do your utmost: the future of Turkey is at stake.' Never was truer word spoken.

The fleet command allowed the whole of 28 October for preparation, rehearsal, final training and detailed orders to the crews, and for the task groups assigned to each target to get into position for the concerted series of attacks at dawn on Thursday 29 October. The pair of torpedo-boats assigned to shell Odessa, displacing a mere 160 tonnes each, jumped the gun in the most literal sense by opening fire early. Panicky wireless messages in plain language were quickly broadcast from Odessa, alerting all Russian naval stations in the Black Sea: 'War has begun … war has begun …'

Soon afterwards a Turkish gunboat appeared off Novorossiysk on the north-east coast of the Black Sea, east of the Crimean peninsula, under a white flag. A cutter brought a Turkish officer ashore with a warning: the port's oil tanks and corn silos, and ships in harbour, would come under shellfire in four hours' time. This gesture was made in order to enable the authorities to evacuate civilians. At 10.50 a.m. the modern, four-funnelled light cruiser *Midilli* duly appeared and fired no fewer than 308 rounds of ten-centimetre ammunition at Novorossiysk in salvo after salvo. The oil tanks blazed fiercely, sending streams of burning fuel downhill into the town and forcing people to flee for their lives; 14 ships were sunk or damaged. A vast pall of smoke hung over the harbour like a funeral pyre. A Turkish cruiser appeared off Feodosia and also delivered a warning, well before opening fire on the town.

Alerted by the wireless warnings from Odessa, the forts of Sevastopol opened a fierce shellfire as soon as the long grey shape of the *Goeben* with her five gun turrets, each showing two long 28-centimetre guns, appeared in the light haze about four miles offshore as the sun came up at about 6.30. She was accompanied by two small Turkish escorts. The whole city shook to the tremors from the defensive barrage. Considering that the coastal artillery had not fired a shot in anger in 60 years, the Russian gunners performed well, even though much of their ammunition fell short. Some of it did not: the attacking trio were seen to move backwards and forwards in an attempt to put them off their aim. Two ten-inch shells passed through the *Goeben*'s after-funnel, her wireless antennae were damaged, a search-light destroyed and a boiler-room was also hit. One of the flagship's treacherous boilers failed. Only 47 rounds of 28-centimetre shells were fired, along with a dozen shots from the battlecruiser's secondary 15-centimetre armament – a light barrage that could only have been a tribute to the spirit of the defenders (and quite possibly evidence of a shortage of German 28-centimetre shells). Little damage was done to the city, and unaccountably no Turkish or German shell came near the bulk of the Black Sea Fleet moored in harbour.

On the way back to the Bosporus, the flagship came across a Russian steamer which had been converted into a minelayer – the *Prut*. Captain Ackermann signalled her to stop, lower her lifeboats and abandon ship. He then ordered her sunk by gunfire, sending her with her 700 mines to the bottom. Some of the crew, including the captain, were taken prisoner, the rest allowed to row to safety. A Russian Orthodox naval chaplain refused to leave the doomed ship, standing at the stern by the Russian flag, beard flowing in the breeze, with a holy book in one hand and crossing himself with the other: he went down with the blazing wreck. Shortly afterwards three small but modern and fast Russian destroyers tried a torpedo attack, which took more than 130 rounds of 15-centimetre shell to drive off. A Russian collier was also seized. Mines were laid by the attackers in several parts of the northern Black Sea, including the Kerch Channel leading to the Sea of Azov (by the *Midilli*) and off Sevastopol. The mines would soon claim victims. The Turkish warships also sank a Russian gunboat and three steamships.

Inevitably, as a result of all this unprovoked aggression, Russia declared war on Turkey. The other members of the Triple Entente, Britain and France, followed suit. Rear-Admiral Wilhelm Souchon of the Imperial German Navy was now fully entitled to say: 'Mission accomplished.'

CHAPTER 4

Councils of War

The first three months of war in Europe had already thrown up a series of spectacular events from which only one clear conclusion could be drawn: the war could not 'be over by Christmas' and might well last very much longer. The Germans, having decided to knock out France, Russia's ally, so that they could deal with Russia herself, the main enemy, at their leisure, violated Belgium's internationally guaranteed neutrality in strength on 3 August in order to outflank the French Army, thus ensuring that Britain would enter the war on France's side, in defence of Belgium. This heavily weighted right hook was intended to swing round the French armies positioned close to the German border and take Paris – the Schlieffen Plan. The Germans also brought up formidable siege artillery, including their new heavy howitzers, against the Belgian fortress complex centred on Liège, which fell on 17 August, opening the way for the main attack on France.

The British Expeditionary Force (BEF), initially of just four divisions, was safely transported across the Channel to take up its place, as agreed in pre-war staff talks, on the French left – just in time to be attacked by the German First Army at Mons in Belgium. The Allied left wing conducted a fighting retreat that lasted for two weeks until French reinforcements arrived from further east and the German advance was halted at the Battle of the Marne in the early days of September. The Germans fell back on the River Aisne, broadly the line they were to hold, with only minor adjustments, for the next four years.

The Belgian Army was dug in at the western end of its exiguous national territory and the BEF, augmented to six divisions, moved up alongside on its right. The Germans, trying to rescue the Schlieffen Plan that had been botched by their own generals and halted at the Marne, threw fresh troops into the right of their line and launched a fierce new outflanking attempt, which became the First Battle of Ypres, on 30 October. After enormous losses they fell back on 11 November, frustrated by the machine-guns and unmatched musketry of the flower of the British regular army, which also suffered heavy casualties. The German strategy of a breakthrough on their right was permanently frustrated, but the Germans did capture the main Belgian ports, including Antwerp and Zeebrugge – a headache for the Royal Navy when German light naval forces, including U-boats, began to operate from them.

In mid-August Winston Churchill, who wanted, and sometimes seemed to manage, to be 'everywhere at once' (he had, for instance, gone far outside his naval brief to persuade Kitchener in the first hours of the war not to return to his command in Egypt and then persuaded Prime Minister Asquith to make him Secretary of State for War), had used spare naval manpower to form a Royal Naval Division (RND), initially of 8,000 men who had volunteered for service at sea. When the Germans laid siege to Antwerp on 26 September, once again deploying their giant howitzers, the First Lord of the Admiralty volunteered to lead the fight for the great port on the Scheldt when it appeared about to fall. This offer, regarded as 'mad' by his political and naval contemporaries, was not taken up, but he did throw in the half-trained RND to support the hard-fought defence of the city (BEF units arrived too late to save it). He also made a brief visit to the front there. Some 1,500 RND men were interned in neutral Holland while nearly 1,000 surrendered. Antwerp fell on 10 October. Perhaps the strongest impression Churchill carried away from the lost battle was the awesome power of the German heavy siege-guns. They certainly worked in Flanders …

On Germany's eastern front, only a few divisions had been left to hold off the Russians in East Prussia pending the fall of France. A smashing Russian victory at Gumbinnen was a false dawn; the Russians were out-generalled by the newly appointed team of Hindenburg (army commander) and Ludendorff (chief of staff), suffering a shattering defeat in East Prussia at Tannenberg and another at the Masurian Lakes. But the Russians fared better on their Austrian front, where the Habsburg armies lost over two million men in a series of inconclusive or bungled battles, despite German reinforcements. By Christmas the war of movement for which the great European powers had prepared was effectively over; but there was stalemate on all fronts as the belligerents, trying to cope with terrible losses, began to train up new armies and dug in for the long haul. The trench line on the Western Front soon stretched from the Channel to the foothills of the Alps and the border of neutral Switzerland. Further to the south-east, the Austrians confronted the Serbians and Russians in the Carpathians and the Balkans; and to the north-east, the Germans faced the Russians in East Prussia and Poland.

At sea in the first three months the Royal Navy and the Imperial Navy confronted each other warily, an approach that led to several skirmishes and incidents but not the great knock-out blow of a second Trafalgar that the admirals on both sides were half-expecting and purportedly wanted (there were private misgivings in both camps). The Kaiser ordered the High Seas Fleet to remain on the defensive for the time being. On the British side, with the whole country looking to its navy for salvation and triumph, Churchill and his more discerning admirals came close to despair as one piece of bad news followed another. Only hindsight would show just how decisive was the Royal Navy's first strategic move, which happened before war broke out: the order to the Grand Fleet, handily mobilised in full for a royal review, to sail direct to Scapa Flow, its designated main base against Germany, on 29 July without standing down the reservists. The guardian of the nation, manned by 60,000 sailors, formed a grey steel line over 18 miles long as it steamed 800 miles up the east coast of the United Kingdom, taking two days to arrive. The Grand Fleet was the ultimate guarantor of the traditional British naval strategy against a continental European enemy: blockade, now silently directed against Germany, albeit from an unprecedented distance for fear of mines and the unproven but feared submarines. The Grand Fleet in Scottish waters barred the northerly route from Germany to the broad Atlantic; the southerly route via the Channel was blocked by the destroyers of the Harwich Force and the Dover Patrol, supported by submarines and ultimately by the 15 pre-dreadnoughts of the Channel Fleet, stationed along England's south coast.

On 5 August two Harwich destroyers sank the German minelayer *Königin Luise* (a converted passenger ship) 50 miles off the Suffolk coast. Unfortunately she had already laid her 180 mines, two of which sank the cruiser HMS *Amphion* the next day with the loss of 151 men. The Royal Navy soon rounded up several German merchantmen in the Atlantic as the Tenth Cruiser Squadron became the Northern Patrol, covering the area between Scotland and Norway round the Shetland Islands (in November the cruisers were replaced by 18 auxiliary cruisers taken up from the Merchant Navy and armed with old guns). On 9 August the light cruiser *Birmingham* caught the *U15* repairing her engines on the surface in the North Sea, rammed and sank it with the loss of all hands – the first victory of a surface ship against a submarine and a rare event for many a long month.

Despite the pre-war concentration of resources on the Grand Fleet in the North Sea, the Royal Navy still possessed a profusion of ships round the globe, starting with the Mediterranean Fleet, modern enough for its role except for Troubridge's white-elephant heavy cruisers. And despite the purge of outdated ships and the rapid construction of new ones during Admiral Fisher's original term as First Sea Lord (1904–10), there were far too many inadequate vessels, such as most of Admiral Cradock's South American Squadron, so comprehensively beaten by Graf Spee's cruisers at the Battle of Coronel on 1 November 1914. Many old cruisers in particular remained in service, trying to cover the commitments of a Royal Navy globally overstretched, despite the unprecedented strategic understandings with Japan and France. Naval technology had been advancing so rapidly for decades and over the turn of the century that warships had an extraordinarily brief front-line life of just a few years: steam power, steel armour, turbines, wireless, bigger and bigger breech-loading guns, firedirection, rangefinders, torpedoes, mines, seaplanes and submarines …

The worst possible demonstration of the vulnerability of older ships came on 22 September 1914, when the primitive, paraffin-powered German submarine *U9* (Lieutenant-Commander Otto Weddigen, IGN, the world's first submarine 'ace') sank the 14-year-old cruisers *Aboukir, Hogue* and *Cressy,* 12,000 tonnes each, in 95 minutes off the northern Dutch coast. More than 1,450 sailors drowned; fewer than 900 survived. This terrible feat remains unequalled in the short but immensely destructive history of submarine warfare: three large warships sunk by a single boat in an hour and a half. Only four days earlier Churchill, warned of the weakness of this 'live-bait squadron' by staff officers during a visit to the Grand Fleet, had ordered First Sea Lord Battenberg to call a halt to such patrols. Even so, on 15 October Weddigen delivered a bleak postscript by sinking the even older cruiser *Hawke* off north-east Scotland with the loss of 525 sailors; just 21 survived. But two days later four German destroyers on a mine-laying mission were sunk by a light cruiser and her four British destroyers, off the Dutch-Frisian island of Texel.

Off the south Norwegian coast on 20 October the *U17* became the first submarine to sink a merchant ship, the British SS *Glitra*: halted by a shot across her bows, she was boarded and scuttled by the Germans. They let the crew get into their lifeboats and even gave them a tow towards land in a display of chivalry worthy of the legendary *Emden*, detached by Graf Spee earlier to cause havoc in the Indian Ocean (see below). Such courtesy would not last long. The early U-boat successes, and mounting fear of mines, prompted Jellicoe, Commander-in-Chief of the Grand Fleet, temporarily to evacuate his poorly protected main base at Scapa Flow and move his ships first to Loch Ewe on the west coast of Scotland and then to Lough Swilly on the north coast of Ireland. The Grand Fleet was in effect homeless as it succumbed to the new affliction of 'periscopitis', or sighting submarines (and sometimes firing heavily at them) where there was none. Beyond the gun and the ancient naval tactic of ramming there was as yet nothing available to surface warships with which to sink or disable a submarine, and the gun was effective only if the submarine was on the surface. Then on 27 October the modern battleship *Audacious* hit a German mine 25 miles out to sea from the lough. Despite the best efforts of the passing British liner *Olympic*, then the largest in the world, to tow her to safety, she sank eight hours later; all but one of the crew were rescued from the first dreadnought ever to succumb to enemy action. The loss was covered up until *Olympic* passengers gave their photographs to an American newspaper two weeks later. On the last day of October the *U27* sank the seaplane-carrier HMS *Hermes* just eight miles north-west of Calais, a bold stroke indeed in the strongly guarded 'English' Channel.

On 13 August, Graf Spee, bound for the Pacific after abandoning his doomed base at Tsingtao, north-west China (under threat from the Japanese fleet), had detached from his squadron the light cruiser *Emden* (Captain Karl von Müller, IGN) to attack commerce in the eastern Indian Ocean. Entering it on 8 September after a long evasion through the East Indies, the *Emden* in barely two months sank or captured 22 ships, shelled Madras, raided Penang sinking two small warships – and generated a stream of favourable propaganda for the German cause. The enemy, even Churchill himself, publicly acknowledged Müller's skill and chivalry towards his civilian and merchant-seamen victims. The failure of more than 70 ships of the Royal Navy and its Japanese, Russian and French naval allies to catch him caused prolonged embarrassment to the Allies. In the end it was an Australian light cruiser, HMAS *Sydney*, that shelled the graceful *Emden* to pieces with her heavier guns and forced the blazing wreck aground in the Turks and Caicos Islands on 9 November. It was the first battle in the history of the new Royal Australian Navy.

Another German light cruiser, SMS *Königsberg*, caused chaos on the western side of the Indian Ocean, sinking several merchant ships and a British cruiser before taking refuge in the Rufiji River in east Africa. A third, the *Karlsruhe*, and a fourth, the *Dresden*, briefly cut a swathe through British merchant shipping in the Atlantic before the former mysteriously blew up and the latter rejoined Spee for the battle off Coronel. A handful of auxiliary cruisers (converted liners with strengthened decks and fitted with guns), such as the *Kormoran* in the Pacific and the *Prinz Eitel Friedrich* in the Atlantic, caused discomfiture to the world's mightiest navy in the opening weeks and months of the war at sea.

One brief burst of light in the early gloom came on 28 August, when an overwhelmingly superior British group of destroyers and light cruisers from the Harwich Force, backed by Beatty's battlecruisers, sank three German light cruisers and a fleet destroyer, damaging others, without loss and only limited damage, in the Battle of the Heligoland Bight; the German battlecruisers set out too late to intervene. But faulty signalling (always Beatty's Achilles' heel) and unintelligent use of intelligence marred this morale-boosting but insignificant victory. British submarines too managed, albeit to a lesser degree than their German rivals, to hurt the enemy, notably when three of them stole into the Baltic to operate from Russian bases.

The other enormous advantage gained by the Royal Navy, second only to the well-timed move to Scapa, arrived at the Admiralty on 13 October – in the shape of the entire main signal book of the Imperial German Navy. This most closely guarded secret of the war at sea came courtesy of Britain's Russian allies, who had found it clasped in the arms of a dead German warrant officer, floating in the Baltic after the Russian Navy had trapped the light cruiser *Magdeburg* in the Gulf of Finland and driven her aground on 26 August before shelling her. The Russians offered it to the British, who gratefully sent a cruiser to collect it on 10 October. The book was the foundation of an invaluable intelligence operation conducted from Room 40 in the Admiralty's Old Building for the duration of the war, foreshadowing the better-known assault on German codes and ciphers at Bletchley Park in the Second World War. But such a coup could hardly be made public.

By the end of October 1914, therefore, the Royal Navy apparently had only a few small successes to show against a depressingly long list of setbacks: the escape of the *Goeben*, the three 'Cressys' and other losses to the apparently uncatchable U-boats, the fall of Antwerp, the *Emden* and other detached German cruisers, the *Audacious*, the *Hermes* ... The fleet's greatest success of this period was and is seldom mentioned: the entirely safe transportation of the BEF across the Channel along with its supplies and reinforcements. This continued throughout the war; not one soldier was lost to enemy action on the cross-Channel route, even when U-boats and light craft were operating from the Belgian ports. At the beginning of 'First Ypres' a British naval flotilla under Rear-Admiral Hood made a valuable contribution by shelling German targets from offshore with the heavy guns of two cruisers, three monitors (floating gun batteries) and four destroyers. Tethered balloons with observers aboard were used to spot the fall of shot.

While Churchill was frustrated and depressed by the lack of major action at sea and of good news from the navy, the nation was disappointed and the press increasingly critical of the fleet and its political chief. He was accused of interference in operational detail and of not listening to the experts at the Admiralty. Battenberg almost resigned over Churchill's intervention at Antwerp; the First Lord meanwhile in the last days of October was touting the idea of replacing the excessively Germanic First Sea Lord with the 74-year-old Lord Fisher. King George V did not like or trust Fisher and did not want the mercurial but vastly experienced old sailor to make a comeback at the expense of his royal cousin; Churchill himself was apparently prepared to resign over the issue until Asquith, the Prime Minister, persuaded all parties to accept the change at the head of the Royal Navy on 29 October – just three days before what was in psychological terms the worst naval disaster of them all: the destruction by Graf Spee of Cradock's squadron.

Unusual vigour was shown by the Admiralty in investigating the *Goeben* fiasco. Preliminary enquiries began within a week of Souchon's escape. It has to be remembered that there was no clue to his further intentions at this stage. As far as the Royal Navy was concerned, the Germans in the end had made for the only refuge available to them; an attempt to get home would have been suicidal, and Austria was not yet at war with Britain and France, so was unlikely to intervene to help Souchon (this assessment, as we saw, was entirely correct). The only apparent result was initially seen as positive for the Entente: with the Italians neutral and the Germans locked away in the Sea of Marmara, the only naval enemy left in the Mediterranean was the Austrian fleet in the Adriatic, a real but surely containable threat. It included 2 dreadnoughts (with 2 more on the stocks), 6 pre-dreadnought and 8 more antiquated battleships, 4 modern light cruisers, 6 old armoured cruisers, 21 mostly recent destroyers and a small but high-quality submarine arm of a dozen boats, soon to be reinforced.

None the less, Milne's lacklustre, not to say inept, performance and Troubridge's failure to engage the Germans were matters of profound shame in the Royal Navy. The general feeling in the not altogether silent service was that the two German ships could, and should, have been caught and sunk. 'To think that it is to the Navy to provide the first and only instance of failure. God, it makes me sick', Vice-Admiral Sir David Beatty, then commanding the battlecruiser force in the Grand Fleet, wrote to his wife on the *Goeben* affair. Fisher, all his warnings about Milne vindicated, was apoplectic but far from speechless. 'Sir Berkeley Goeben' had been due to take over the Nore command on the Thames estuary (a demotion) but the outbreak of war supervened; when he finally laid down his Mediterranean post he never got another. Having handed over to Carden on 17 August 1914, he sailed to Plymouth in the *Inflexible*. He defended his actions and decisions in a series of letters to the Admiralty. So did Troubridge, also by the end of August. An important difference between the former commander-in-chief and his erstwhile second-in-command concerned the two battlecruisers, *Indomitable* and *Indefatigable*, temporarily assigned by Milne to Troubridge on the very eve of war. In effect, the latter said he changed his mind about attacking the *Goeben* when he belatedly realised they would not be available to him after they had been detached on 3 August; Milne said he had never promised to return them. Milne's defence at the court of inquiry, convened to determine whether there should be a trial by court martial, was jesuitical and self-serving, while Troubridge's was emotional and disorganised.

Prince Louis Battenberg, still First Sea Lord at this time (he was hounded out of office two months later), read the two admirals' exculpations and concluded that while Milne had acted more or less correctly with one or two exceptions, Troubridge was definitely and seriously at fault: 'He failed to carry out his clear duty … to attack the enemy … Not one of [Troubridge's] excuses can be accepted for one moment … The escape of the *Goeben* must ever remain a shameful episode …' And, Battenberg concluded, the flag officer responsible should never command at sea again. Troubridge, like Milne, never did; he had been elected scapegoat, not only for Milne but also for the appalling inefficiencies at the Admiralty itself. While Milne could hardly be condemned without reference to the Admiralty's major contributions to the fiasco, Troubridge apparently could. His main defence was that the *Goeben*, with her long-range, 28-centimetre guns and high speed, was a force superior to his four lumbering armoured cruisers in the prevailing conditions, and he, like Milne, had been under orders not to engage a superior force.

Curiously, the not inconsiderable factor of the German capital ship's superior armour was never mentioned, whether at the inquiry or at Troubridge's ensuing court martial: even if his cruisers had been able to get within their own firing range before being knocked out, the shells from their contemporary type of 9.2-inch guns might well have have bounced off *Goeben*'s main armour, made from Krupp's finest steel plates. But Troubridge could have deployed his light cruisers and fast destroyers in simultaneous torpedo attacks from several directions at once, while his heavy cruisers, suitably positioned, would have added to a plethora of targets which the Germans could not possibly have disabled, or even engaged, simultaneously. Even in 1939 capital ships proved incapable of coping with more than two targets at once. When Commodore Harwood's three cruisers took on the German pocket battleship *Admiral Graf Spee* in the south Atlantic that year, she could engage only two of them at a time, enabling the weaker British ships to 'wing' her and drive her into Montevideo (she scuttled on emerging from harbour rather than face the enemy again). All this is to miss the point: Troubridge's real offence was to put discretion before valour, to let his head rule his heart, to adopt the gallant course at first and then change his mind: he failed to try. All he needed to do was to 'wing' the *Goeben* so that the battlecruisers could come up and finish her off.

Accordingly the court of inquiry on 22 September, chaired by Admiral Sir Hedworth Meux, commander-in-chief at Portsmouth, supported by Admiral Sir George Callaghan, immediate past commander-in-chief of the Grand Fleet, concluded that Troubridge did indeed have a case to answer. The Admiralty therefore wrote to the rear-admiral saying he would be tried under the Naval Discipline Act, on a charge that he did 'from negligence … forbear to pursue the chase of His Imperial German Majesty's ship *Goeben*, being an enemy then flying'. Had the word 'cowardice' been substituted for 'negligence' here, Troubridge would have faced the death penalty. The trial of an admiral for avoiding battle in wartime was an extreme rarity; even so, while it was not held in secret (except when national security was deemed to be involved), no journalist applied to attend. It began at Portland on 5 November 1914, aboard HMS *Bulwark*, the 15,000-tonne pre-dreadnought battleship which flew the flag of the commander-in-chief, Plymouth, Admiral Sir George Egerton. He presided, assisted by a vice-admiral, three rear-admirals, four captains and the deputy Judge Advocate of the Fleet. The prosecutor was Rear-Admiral Sydney Fremantle, who had the moral courage to resist the pressure from within a vengeful Admiralty to charge Troubridge with the hanging offence of cowardice. Mr Leslie Scott, KC, MP, a prominent advocate, was 'the Accused's Friend', the technical term for the defender at a court martial, and managed to make a strong case for his client.

Unfortunately for Troubridge, his trial began just one week after Souchon had taken his command under the Ottoman flag into the Black Sea to shell the four Russian naval ports. The 5th of November was the day on which, in consequence, Britain and France formally declared war on Turkey, three days after Russia and Serbia; on 9 November, the final day of the court proceedings, the Sultan of Turkey declared a jihad, or holy war, against the Entente. The dreadful consequences of Souchon's preventable escape into the Dardanelles were at last appallingly clear for all to see three months after the event, and Troubridge now faced condemnation by hindsight.

Yet he was acquitted. The court accepted, however reluctantly, that in the absence of the battlecruisers Troubridge was entitled in the particular circumstances to regard the *Goeben* as a superior force which he had been ordered not to engage, and that he had been right to give priority to the watch on the Adriatic, as also ordered. The members of the Board of Admiralty were invited, in reverse order of seniority, to minute their comments on the verdict. Nearly all were hostile; the most penetrating came from the Third Sea Lord, Rear-Admiral Frederick Tudor: 'That the ... Cruiser Squadron stood a chance of being severely punished ... can be accepted, but that they [*sic*] could have been destroyed, or nearly destroyed, before the *Goeben* had expended all her 11-inch ammunition appears to me to be out of the question.'

There was one tragic, if indirect, consequence of the *Goeben* affair half a world away. Rear-Admiral Sir Christopher Cradock, a man already possessing a record of exceptional courage, took on the formidable heavy and light cruisers of Admiral Graf Spee off the coast of Chile at the Battle of Coronel on 1 November 1914 with a scratch squadron, as we saw. Spee's heavy cruisers, the only modern ships of their type in the German Navy, were superior in speed, protection and number of guns to British armoured cruisers. Expressly determined to avoid the ignominy heaped on Troubridge's head by the *Goeben* affair ('I will take care I do not suffer the fate of poor Troubridge', he wrote to a brother-officer shortly beforehand), Cradock could have avoided action without disgrace – an 1897 battleship that should have been with him had fallen 300 miles behind – but he deliberately took on an obviously much stronger force. Two British heavy cruisers (similar to Troubridge's) were sunk with the loss of all hands, including Cradock; one auxiliary cruiser and one light cruiser escaped. Cradock, in preserving his honour and avoiding Troubridge's fate, incurred something rather worse; unfortunately so did more than 1,600 men of the Royal Navy, lost with him. At the Admiralty Cradock was criticised for not falling back on his sole battleship, HMS *Canopus*, which at least had four 12-inch guns (Spee reported after the battle that he would not have expected to overcome the British had she been on hand; as it was, his victory had cost him half his ammunition). It was the worst British naval defeat in more than a century, since the American victory at Lake Champlain in the War of 1812. Lord Fisher wrote to his most celebrated protégé, Admiral Beatty: 'Steer mid-way between Troubridge and Cradock and all will be well. Cradock preferred ...'

When war broke out in August 1914, the Committee of Imperial Defence, whose pre-war ruminations on what to do in the event of war with Turkey were considered in detail in Chapter One, became the War Council. It was now a war Cabinet in all but name (the term was not used before 1939) and had the same overall membership as the CID: the Prime Minister in the chair; the Secretaries of State for Foreign Affairs, War and India; the Chancellor of the Exchequer and the First Lord of the Admiralty, supported by the former premier, Arthur Balfour, and advised by the First Sea Lord and the Chief of the Imperial General Staff. A few other key officers such as the Director of Naval Intelligence attended when needed. As with the CID, the secretary was Maurice Hankey, whose personal note of the proceedings is the main source of what took place at the War Council's meetings.

The official reaction in London to events at the Dardanelles and beyond, apart from a short bombardment of the entrance forts by Carden's squadron on 3 November 1914, was remarkably lethargic. It is inconceivable that the humiliating escape of the German ships into Turkish waters and the potential implications thereof were not discussed, at least informally: Churchill and Kitchener met at the end of August, for example, to consider what action to take in the event of war with Turkey. They debated the idea of an attack on the Dardanelles by the Royal Navy in conjunction with a landing by the Greek Army on Gallipoli as a combined threat to Constantinople. The Prime Minister of neutral Greece, Eleutherios Venizelos, was well disposed towards the Entente; the King of Greece, Constantine I, however, related by marriage to the Kaiser's House of Hohenzollern, was not. This was an interesting variation on the generally accepted belief on the Allied side that an attack on the Dardanelles should take the form of a combined operation, on land as well as water, something to which Churchill at this time subscribed as unquestioningly as the admirals and generals did.

But the minutes of the War Council contain no mention of Turkey before 25 November 1914. At that time there was concern about defending Egypt and the Suez Canal against a possible Turkish attack from Syria. The First Lord, Churchill, argued that the best way of defending Egypt was to attack the Gallipoli peninsula: 'This, if successful, would give us control of the Dardanelles, and we could dictate terms at Constantinople.' It was, however, a 'very difficult operation requiring a large force', he said. Fisher, the First Sea Lord, suggested persuading the Greek Army to attack Gallipoli. Churchill said that at this juncture one battlecruiser and one light cruiser were stationed off the Dardanelles, with three British and three French submarines; France had been asked to send three battleships. Although the French had the leading naval role in the Mediterranean, they were content to leave the command in the Aegean Sea at its eastern end to a British admiral, while retaining responsibility for guarding the Adriatic against any Austrian naval initiatives.

Churchill recognised as clearly as anyone at the meeting that the 'ideal method' of defending Egypt was a combined operation against the Dardanelles and the Gallipoli peninsula which overlooked the straits. Not for the first time, still less the last, Kitchener, as Secretary of State for War, said that there were no British or imperial troops available; they were all needed on the Western Front. This view was naturally supported by Sir John French, commanding the BEF, and the French Army, which wanted all the help it could get. There was also a shortage of shells, which were being expended at an alarming rate in France and Flanders. The admirals, most of the politicians on the War Council – the Chancellor, Lloyd George, to the fore, and not least Hankey, its secretary, who may well have thought of it first – were in favour of Churchill's idea, which amounted to outflanking the Central Powers: such a move could knock Turkey out of the war and persuade Italy and the Balkan neutrals to join the Entente. In the end, Kitchener's flat insistence that no troops could be spared for a major initiative in the Near East was decisive. In matters of grand strategy his word was law. There the matter rested as, after five months of war in Europe, 1914 drew to a close.

The Royal Navy managed to deliver a sensational piece of good news from the other end of the world in December. It came from the south Atlantic. Acting with unusual dispatch and determined to avenge Admiral Cradock, Fisher detached Vice-Admiral Sir Doveton Sturdee from his duties as Chief of Naval Staff and ordered him to take a squadron led by two battlecruisers, *Invincible* (flag) and *Inflexible*, with three heavy and two light cruisers, to find and destroy Graf Spee's squadron. A third battlecruiser, HMS *Princess Royal*, armed with six of the latest 13.5-inch guns and supported by an armoured cruiser, provided distant cover by guarding the central Atlantic in case Spee tried to run home (as indeed he planned to do after one last stroke against Britain).

Sturdee arrived off the Falkland Islands, a British dependency in the south Atlantic, on 7 December 1914. HMS *Canopus*, which had avoided Coronel because her chief engineer, Commander William Denbow, RN, terrified of a battle, had faked engine trouble (he was certified by three doctors and sent home on a cargo ship even before battle was joined), was already there. Captain Heathcoat Grant, RN, had beached her so she could serve as a coastal battery, part of the defences arranged by Grant in case Spee came calling. Just before dawn on the 8th, lookouts sighted two German ships, *Gneisenau* (heavy cruiser) and *Nürnberg* (light), off Port Stanley; they had been detached to make the port unusable for the British and further to damage their morale. Spee never acknowledged repeated warnings from Berlin, relayed by the German transmitter at Valparaiso, Chile, that a British heavy squadron was after him. The message may never have reached him. His two detached ships soon sighted the unmistakable tripod masts of the battlecruisers in harbour and reported them to Spee. The British ships were busy coaling, to such effect that warning visual signals from *Canopus* were not seen amid the coal dust (she had no telephone connection with Sturdee). The old battleship however opened accurate fire on the Germans, who retired southward on their admiral.

This gave Sturdee a couple of hours to finish coaling and raise steam for full speed. Two heavy cruisers and the two battlecruisers, with the battered light cruiser *Glasgow*, survivor of Coronel, as scout, moved out in line ahead into remarkably calm south Atlantic waters to meet Spee as he headed northward, also in line ahead, consisting of *Scharnhorst* (heavy cruiser and flagship), *Gneisenau* and three light cruisers. The battlecruisers opened fire at nine miles, one more than the German heavy cruisers' biggest, 21-centimetre guns could manage. But the British shooting was abysmal; the Germans were far more accurate as Spee dispersed his light cruisers and turned to face the battlecruisers. But there was only one way the action could end, even though it was the first director-controlled (i.e. centrally synchronised) gunnery engagement in British naval history. The 12-inch guns began to strike home as the range closed, and after expending more than 1,100 12-inch shells the British saw Spee's graceful pair of heavy cruisers sink (the shattered *Gneisenau* scuttled herself only when her last gun was immobilised) with the loss of some 2,200 men, including Spee and his two lieutenant-sons. Only one of his three light cruisers, the *Dresden*, got away from the scene (to be caught and sunk only in March 1915). Sir Christopher Cradock and his men were well and truly avenged. In Britain Churchill and the Admiralty were grimly satisfied even as they acknowledged the gallantry and proficiency of Graf Spee and his ships and crews. The press and the public were delighted: this, at last, was what they had longed for and expected from the Royal Navy.

CHAPTER 5

'We have no troops'

The dread news of Coronel had reached London on 4 November. The day before, Admiral Carden, commanding what was now styled the East Mediterranean Squadron, led a bombardment of the forts guarding the entrance to the Dardanelles. At that time his command consisted of the battlecruisers *Indomitable* and *Indefatigable*, two old French battleships (*Suffren* and *Vérité*), the Kelly brothers' light cruisers, *Dublin* and *Gloucester*, a few destroyers and six submarines (three British, three French). Churchill ordered the bombardment as an early response to Souchon's attacks on the Russian Black Sea ports. As the First Lord wrote to the First Sea Lord on 30 October, 'Admiral Slade should be asked to state his opinion on the possibility and advisability of a bombardment of the sea-face forts of the Dardanelles. It is a good thing to give a prompt blow.' Vice-Admiral Sir Edmond Slade was a former Director of Naval Intelligence who advised the Admiralty on oil supplies and shipping during the war. He wrote to Churchill, 'The forts are difficult to locate from the sea at anything like the range at which they will have to be engaged ... It may be possible to make a demonstration to draw the fire of [the] guns and make them disclose themselves ... A little target practice from 15 to 12 thousand yards might be useful.'

Churchill's consequent order to Carden of 1 November is worth quoting extensively because it is a small but perfect example of how the First Lord verbosely interfered in matters of detail. Even allowing for the admiral's lack of initiative or talent, Churchill abused the tortuous, two-edged invention of wireless to state the obvious:

> Without risking the Allied ships a demonstration is to be made by bombardment on the earliest suitable day by your armoured ships and the two French battleships against the forts at the entrance of the Dardanelles at a range of 24,000–12,000 yards.
>
> The ships should keep underway. Approaching as soon after daylight as possible.

A retirement should be made before the fire from the forts becomes effective. The ships' guns should outrange the older guns mounted in the forts.

Latest information about guns herewith.

First Sea Lord concurs.

'Bombard entrance forts at long range as demonstration only. Do not risk your ships' would probably have sufficed. Be that as it may, Carden divided his squadron in two: the British heavy ships concentrated on the fort at Sedd el Bahr, next to Cape Helles at the southern extremity of the Gallipoli peninsula, while the French pair fired at Kum Kale, the fort on the opposite, mainland or Asian, shore. The four heavy ships approached in line ahead at dawn. The British opened fire from the safe distance of 13,000 yards (six and a half nautical miles); the guns of the French pre-dreadnoughts had less range, forcing them to move close enough to shore to come within the reach of some of the Kum Kale guns. The defenders' shooting was erratic at first, but soon became sufficiently accurate to drive the French back amid high columns of water thrown up by the exploding near-misses. The engagement lasted about ten minutes before Carden withdrew; there were no casualties and no noticeable damage was sustained on the Allied side, which expended a modest total of 76 heavy shells. The brevity of the engagement was attributed in Constantinople to the spirited shooting of the defenders, apparently driving off the Allies who were too downcast or simply afraid to return.

The short bombardment provoked much debate and even anger at the Admiralty in London, despite the fact that three German battlecruisers had caused alarm on the east coast of England on the same day, when they briefly shelled Great Yarmouth as they covered a mine-laying operation off the Suffolk coast. Jellicoe, commanding the Grand Fleet, called Carden's foray an 'unforgivable error'. Other admirals used words like 'lunacy' and 'irresponsible' to describe it, because they believed, at the time and later, that the manoeuvre had alerted the Turks and Germans to the need to strengthen the defences of the strait. David Lloyd George, the Chancellor of the Exchequer, also complained that the only result was to alert the Turks.

There are two good reasons for dismissing this as an over-reaction: we know from the previous chapter how Souchon was appalled by the state of the defences as soon as he saw them, nearly three months earlier, and immediately urged Berlin to send experts and supplies to remedy the deficiencies as a matter of urgency, to which the German General Staff (which also controlled the Imperial Navy) responded at once. Obviously he anticipated an attack, or at least regarded it as essential to be ready for one, something he would not have failed to mention to his Turkish allies. More pertinently, it cannot be seriously suggested that the defenders would have been surprised by a major attack on the straits once Turkey became involved in hostilities with the Entente. Why else was a strong Allied squadron sitting off the entrance to the Dardanelles if not to attack? The only real question, surely, was when. But while the Germans had already shown the necessary sense of urgency, the short bombardment did have the effect of dispelling traditional Ottoman inertia for long enough to prompt an acceleration in defensive preparations on the part of the Turkish Army, which was officially responsible for the fortifications. The defences of the Bosporus, the passage between the Black Sea and the Marmara, were being reinforced at the same time against the no less obvious possibility of an attack by the Russian Black Sea Fleet. Britain's ultimatum on 31 October had demanded that the Turks send the German crews of the *Goeben* and *Breslau*, along with all their compatriots in Turkish service, back home. It was of course refused.

The brief shelling of 3 November had one other consequence of considerably greater importance. A couple of lucky shots from the British battlecruisers scored direct hits on an ammunition dump at Sedd el Bahr. Some 300 artillery shells blew up, creating a column of smoke 500 feet high, causing 150 Turkish casualties, destroying the fort and blasting all its guns off their mountings. The ground on which it stood remains flattened to this day. This huge explosion, the like of which never happened again at the Dardanelles despite a great deal of heavy shelling later on, engendered a belief in the Royal Navy that the latest naval guns were indeed capable of destroying defensive strongpoints and their armament, in defiance of the received wisdom about ships versus forts. It was one of the reasons behind the eventual decision to try to overwhelm the straits by warships alone, unsupported by a major military landing on the Gallipoli peninsula. Another reason was Churchill's own observations of the effect of the German heavy shells on the Belgian forts.

The wrong lesson was learned from both exemplars: the sieges in Flanders were won by howitzers that lobbed their shells into the air in a high, curving trajectory, which meant they struck home like aerial bombs, from a great height. The trajectory of the big naval guns of the day was as near flat as possible except at extreme range: the armour-piercing shells had surprisingly little effect unless they scored a very rare direct hit, and were quite capable of burying themselves deep in the earth without exploding. The latest guns' long range, ten miles or more, meant that capital ships could open fire with impunity, beyond the reach of the artillery in the entrance forts, but also implied that if shelling was to be effective, pinpoint accuracy was needed, which meant that the fall of shot had to be closely observed, something that local conditions seldom allowed, as we shall see. Even 30 years later, shattering naval bombardments by Allied navies in the Pacific and off Normandy had remarkably little effect on coastal defences except when rare direct hits were scored.

The Turks admittedly were prompted by this first bombardment to speed up the programme, already begun, to strengthen the defences: the fixed gun-batteries were linked by field telephones, extra searchlights were set up, German rangefinders, the world's best, were introduced and buoys placed out to sea to assist the gun crews in ranging their fire. Most important of all, more mobile batteries of field guns, light and medium howitzers were deployed, not only to support the cannon emplaced in the forts but also to protect the all-important lines of mines, whose number in the Narrows area was gradually increased after November from five to ten. No new large-calibre artillery could be obtained for the forts, but some of the *Goeben*'s secondary 15-centimetre guns were unshipped and set up on land and new artillery pieces were shipped down the Danube and the western Black Sea coast to the Bosporus from Czech factories, then within the Austrian Empire. In the end, however, the defenders had all the time in the world to prepare for the next attack and did not exert themselves unduly: it was to be more than three months before the Anglo-French fleet tried again.

Towards the end of November 1914 the Admiralty was considering handing over the blockade of the Dardanelles to the French Navy, which by pre-war agreement was responsible for the Mediterranean naval theatre overall. The French fleet was using British Malta as its base for operations in the eastern basin, where its main task was to guard the mouth of the Adriatic against the Austrian fleet. As in the North Sea, the blockade was a distant one, a precaution against submarine attack. The British naval presence off the Dardanelles had for the time being been reduced to a force just sufficient to deal unaided with the unlikely event of a breakout by the German ships: one battlecruiser (*Indefatigable*), one light cruiser (*Dublin*), six destroyers and three submarines. But also recently arrived to join

Carden's flag was a French heavy squadron commanded by Rear-Admiral Émile Guépratte, consisting of the *Gaulois* (flag) and three other pre-dreadnoughts, plus six destroyers and three submarines. Rear-Admiral John de Robeck was Carden's deputy, and Commodore Roger Keyes (previously based at Harwich in command of submarine forces) was chief of staff; both were competent officers.

The destruction of Graf Spee's squadron on 8 December brought not only a boost to naval and national morale but also a useful strategic dividend. Only very few, isolated German light cruisers and auxiliary cruisers were left at large (but not for long), which meant there was no longer any need to keep groups of heavy ships scattered across the broad oceans to protect merchant shipping against an attack by an enemy squadron. No such formation now existed outside German home waters. The Germans would run a dangerous handful of disguised merchant cruisers, much better armed and more dangerous than mere auxiliary cruisers, with some success for most of the rest of the war, but each one operated alone, with effects that were hardly noticeable once the U-boat campaign got into its stride. Meanwhile dozens of Allied cruisers and other vessels could be redeployed to such areas as the Mediterranean. Vice-Admiral R. H. Peirse, for example, left his Bombay base and the East Indies station and moved his flag to Suez, to reinforce the naval protection of Egypt with patrols off the Syrian coast. The Russian light cruiser *Askold*, temporarily attached to his flag, explored as far north as Alexandretta (Iskanderun) and was followed by the British light cruiser, the misleadingly gentle-sounding HMS *Doris*.

The latter's commander, Captain F. Larken, RN, appears to have come from the same mould as the brothers Kelly, his light-cruiser colleagues. As the official naval historian, Sir Julian Corbett, noted, 'Captain Larken at once went north and proceeded to interpret the Admiralty instructions in a liberal manner.' He conducted a series of pinprick raids along the coast, bombarding coastal defences, cutting telegraph wires and blowing up railway tracks and equipment, particularly at Alexandretta, where many Turkish troops were based. Information from *Doris* prompted the thought at the Admiralty of making Alexandretta, at the northern end of the Syrian coast, a target for a substantial military and naval intervention against the Turks. It was an easier target than the Dardanelles and would involve not only less risk but also fewer resources. A landing there could inflict permanent damage to the strategic Baghdad and Hejaz railways and bolster Britain's positions in Mesopotamia (modern Iraq) and Egypt. It could be attacked instead of the Dardanelles, or if an assault on the straits were frustrated.

Another example of the contrast between the mostly uninspired admirals and the gumption of individual British commanders was provided by Lieutenant Norman Holbrook in the primitive submarine *B11* on 13 December 1914. Carden's Captain (D), C. P. R. Coode, RN, commanding the six destroyers and also the three submarines with the squadron (*B9*, *B10* and *B11*), chose Holbrook for a mission he had had in mind for some time. Holbrook's boat was built in 1905 (ancient in submarine terms), was 135 feet long, displaced just 280 tonnes (315 submerged) and was armed with only two torpedo tubes. Her maximum underwater speed was eight knots and she had a crew of 16. Holbrook was ordered to enter the Dardanelles to look for a target to sink. The boat was specially fitted with mine 'bumpers' – metal fenders at the bow which were intended to push aside the anchoring cables of mines like curtains, without setting off the explosive charges. As yet there were still only five completed lines of mines across the strait and Holbrook passed under them unscathed, making slow headway against the eternal current.

Just short of Chanak at the Narrows he sighted an old 10,000-tonne battleship, which he proceeded to hit fair and square with a single torpedo fired from 800 yards. A large explosion ensued and the unfortunate ship, the *Messudieh,* turned over and sank in ten minutes. She had been commissioned in 1874, though rebuilt in 1902, and had a main armament of two 9.2-inch guns. She had been moved to her exposed position by the Germans, against Turkish protests, as a floating battery to defend the Narrows. Only 10 officers and 27 men were killed; a dramatic rescue operation involving the cutting of holes in the upended hull rescued more than 600 of her crew.

Holbrook dived and turned to escape, only to discover that the glass of the boat's compass was fogged. He steered blind and bumped along the bottom, using the periscope fleetingly to try and locate his position. After nine hours submerged, the *B11* returned to base with only minor damage. Holbrook won the first VC of the submarine service for his unprecedented stroke, and every other crew member received a high decoration. A month later the French submarine *Saphir* tried to repeat the exploit, but ran aground and was lost.

The British war leadership in general and Churchill in particular were casting about at the end of 1914 for a way of using their huge naval margin in secondary ships, without weakening the Grand Fleet in the North Sea, for a blow against the Central Powers and their allies, who enjoyed the advantage of internal lines of communication all the way across Europe. The traditional British tactic, whether on the individual battlefield or in a war against a continental enemy, was the flank attack, a classic example being the campaign in the Iberian peninsula against Napoleonic France.

Theoretically there were five possibilities for exploiting Britain's over-whelming maritime advantage:

- A move against Germany in the north by British warships and Russian troops, focused on the Baltic (but the Russians were heavily engaged elsewhere against the Germans, Austrians and Turks).
- A drive up the Adriatic against the Austrians and their fleet (impossible without Italian support and dangerous because of submarines).
- A landing at Salonica to take the pressure off isolated Serbia (out of the question without Greek participation, which was unavailable so long as Bulgaria's intentions remained unknown).
- A northward thrust by the BEF in Belgium, supported by naval guns, to expel the Germans from the captured ports, including Zeebrugge and Ostend.
- A combined operation against the Turks at the Dardanelles aimed at Constantinople (or something less ambitious against Alexandretta).

Kitchener, Sir John French, commanding the BEF, and his staff insisted that all freshly raised and trained British troops must be sent to the Western Front – even as they admitted that there was no foreseeable chance of a strategic decision there. If there were to be such a development it would have to come on the Eastern Front, where there was enormous room for manoeuvre and huge reserves of manpower – but a shortage of munitions, thanks to the closure of the Dardanelles. French favoured the Belgian coast option, Fisher and Churchill the Baltic, while France believed a knockout blow against the Germans on the Marne was still possible, given the necessary reinforcements.

We saw how the War Council finally got around to considering what to do about Turkey at its first wartime meeting on 25 November 1914, when an attack on Gallipoli and the Dardanelles was considered. The minds of Britain's war leaders were drawn back to the question at the turn of the year. On 30 December the Russian commander-in-chief, Grand Duke

Nicholas, told Sir George Buchanan, the British ambassador to Petrograd (formerly and now St Petersburg), that his armies were under pressure from the Turks in the Caucasus. He asked for help, in the form of a diversionary 'demonstration' against Turkey. Buchanan informed Grey, the Foreign Secretary, of this request on New Year's Day in a telegram that arrived on 2 January 1915. Grey forwarded it to Kitchener, who showed it to Churchill on a visit to the First Lord's office. Prior to this development, Churchill's opinion had been in favour of Fisher's idea of an intervention in the Baltic, seizing the German Frisian island of Borkum as a base for naval operations. Clearly now the Russians were in no position to mount a large invasion of north Germany.

Faced with Churchill's proposal to respond to the Grand Duke's call for help with a combined operation at the Dardanelles, including a landing at Gallipoli, Kitchener suggested a demonstration at the Dardanelles by the navy alone, deploying what was to become his mantra in the coming weeks: 'We have no troops to land anywhere.' Churchill therefore eventually decided on a purely naval operation. Kitchener sent a telegram to the Grand Duke via the Foreign Office, committing Britain to a demonstration at the Dardanelles. It was not shown to Churchill, or even to the Prime Minister apparently, as noted in a curious paragraph in the first report of the Dardanelles Commission, published early in 1917: 'Mr Asquith thinks that he did not see this telegram before it was sent, but it must not be by any means inferred on that account that he would not have approved of its dispatch if he had seen it'! The available evidence suggests that Kitchener had only a demonstration in mind, and not the all-out naval attempt to force the strait which Churchill was to make of it: he still had no troops to offer. Kitchener's aim was merely to deter or distract the Turks from sending more troops to the Caucasus against the Russians.

The idea was discussed by the Admiralty War Group of senior admirals on 3 January amid general pessimism, shared at this stage by Churchill himself, who was still thinking about the Baltic. The old admirals reluctantly endorsed a naval demonstration. Fisher favoured all or nothing: a full-blown Dardanelles strategy – provided the Russians and the Balkan armies (Serbs, Greeks, Bulgarians, Romanians) joined in with enough troops to overwhelm Gallipoli and march on Constantinople: 'But as the great Napoleon said, "CELERITY" – without it – "FAILURE"'!' Fisher's memoranda, notes, minutes and letters were full of exclamations, capital letters and underlinings, often in green ink. Maurice Hankey, secretary to the War Council, had suggested in more measured tones a similar cam-

General Lord Kitchener of Khartoum in 1900.

The Rt. Hon. Winston Churchill, MP, First Lord of the Admiralty, in 1915.

Admiral of the Fleet Lord Fisher of Kilverstone.

Lieutenant Norman Holbrook, RN, and the crew of submarine *B11* after sinking the battleship *Messudieh* inside the Dardanelles, December 1914.

Admiral Alfred von Tirpitz, architect of the Imperial German Navy.

Hans Freiherr von Wangenheim, German Ambassador to the Ottoman Empire, in 1914.

Rear-Admiral Wilhelm Souchon, commanding the Mediterranean Division of the Imperial German Navy, in 1914.

General Otto Liman von Sanders in Turkish service, defender of Gallipoli 1914-15.

The Allied fleet sailing for the Dardanelles

SS *River Clyde* grounded at 'V' beach after playing 'Trojan horse' for the Cape Helles landing.

French soldiers from the Colonial Regiment inspect a smashed searchlight.

The Kaiser and Enver Pasha converse on the deck of the *Goeben*.

The commanders and chiefs of staff on HMS *Triad*: (L to R) Commodore Roger Keyes; Vice-Admiral John de Robeck; General Sir Ian Hamilton; Major-General W.P. Braithwaite.

The man who answered the Turkish
Question, Mustafa Kemal Atatürk.

The undoing of the Allied fleet. The
Turkish minelayer *Nusret* — the modern
copy at Çannakale.

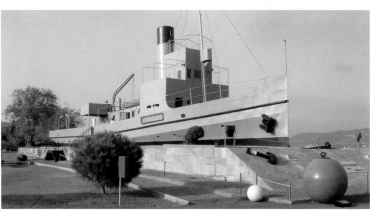

Atatürk's verdict on the Dardanelles and Gallipoli campaigns.

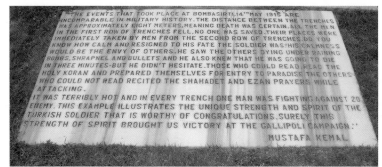

"THE EVENTS THAT TOOK PLACE AT BOMBASIRTI.14TH MAY 1915 ARE
INCOMPARABLE IN MILITARY HISTORY. THE DISTANCE BETWEEN THE TRENCHES
WAS APPROXIMATELY EIGHT METERS, MEANING DEATH WAS CERTAIN. ALL THE MEN
IN THE FIRST ROW OF TRENCHES FELL, NO ONE WAS SAVED. THEIR PLACES WERE
IMMEDIATELY TAKEN BY MEN FROM THE SECOND ROW OF TRENCHES. DO YOU
KNOW HOW CALM AND RESIGNED TO HIS FATE THE SOLDIER WAS? HIS CALMNESS
WOULD BE THE ENVY OF OTHERS. HE SAW THE OTHERS DYING UNDER RAINING
BOMBS, SHRAPNEL AND BULLETS AND HE ALSO KNEW THAT HE WAS GOING TO DIE
IN THREE MINUTES-BUT HE DIDN'T HESITATE. THOSE WHO COULD READ, READ THE
HOLY KORAN AND PREPARED THEMSELVES FOR ENTRY TO PARADISE, THE OTHERS
WHO COULD NOT READ RECITED THE SHAHADET AND EZAN PRAYERS WHILE
ATTACKING.
IT WAS TERRIBLY HOT, AND IN EVERY TRENCH ONE MAN WAS FIGHTING AGAINST 20
ENEMY. THIS EXAMPLE ILLUSTRATES THE UNIQUE STRENGTH AND SPIRIT OF THE
TURKISH SOLDIER THAT IS WORTHY OF CONGRATULATIONS. SURELY THIS
STRENGTH OF SPIRIT BROUGHT US VICTORY AT THE GALLIPOLI CAMPAIGN."

MUSTAFA KEMAL

paign in a memorandum to Asquith, the Prime Minister, as recently as 28 December; Fisher used this to underpin his own plan for a combined operation. Lloyd George was also in favour, writing a paper of his own in support. Balfour and Grey too agreed.

So on 3 January Churchill sent a telegram to Admiral Carden, asking whether forcing the Dardanelles by naval gunfire was practicable: 'The importance of the results would justify severe loss.' Two days later Carden replied that it could be done, though slowly and with a suitable number of ships. On the 6th Churchill asked the admiral how he would do it and what he needed. Five days later Carden telegraphed his considered reply:

… Possibility of operations.
(a) Total reduction of defences at the entrance.
(b) Clear defences inside of straits up to and including Kephez Point battery no. 8.
(c) Reduction of defences at the Narrows, Chanak.
(d) Clear passage through minefield, advancing through Narrows, and final advance to Marmora.
…
Whilst (a) and (b) are being carried out a battleship force would be employed in demonstration and bombardment of Bulair lines and coast [at the north-eastern neck of the Gallipoli peninsula] and reduction of battery at [near the south-western end].

Force required 12 [pre-dreadnought] battleships … three battlecruisers … three light cruisers, one flotilla leader [light cruiser], 16 destroyers … six submarines, four seaplanes … 12 minesweepers …

And a dozen support ships, including a hospital ship and supply vessels. And piles of shells. Carden's long telegram went on to describe in detail the programme of action, step by step, starting with silencing the entrance forts and sending the battleships, preceded by minesweepers, up the straits, bombardments over the peninsula from the Aegean followed by shorter-range direct shelling, with the seaplanes observing the fall of shot: 'Might do it all in a month about. Expenditure of ammunition would be large.' Carden made no mention of a combined operation or of troops to support the fleet.

On 4 January, just five days after the Grand Duke's plea for help, the Russians turned the tables on the Turks in Armenia, defeating them in several actions. Nicholas neglected to tell his British allies of this favourable turn of events, and they went on believing that their Dardanelles intervention, whatever form it took, was for the immediate relief of Russia, as well as for her and the Entente's long-term benefit. There were 129 merchant steamships, Allied and neutral, totalling 350,000 gross register tons, locked up in the Black Sea. Freeing Russia's main trade route would salvage her economy, solve her munitions shortage, guarantee Anglo-French grain supplies, impress the wavering Balkan states and the Arabs under Turkish rule, and quite possibly Italy too. All this was an understandably dazzling prospect.

Churchill took Carden's exhaustive shopping list to the meeting of the War Council on 13 January 1915. A low-key discussion was almost electrified, and certainly enlivened, when he produced it. Sir John French was still arguing for the Zeebrugge attack, on which a final decision was postponed until mid-February, when two new Territorial Army divisions would be ready for the Western Front. Meanwhile General Joffre, the French commander-in-chief, had pulled 100,000 troops out of the line immediately to the right of the BEF to form part of his mobile reserve, which meant that the temporarily exposed British Army could not risk an advance on the Belgian ports.

The First Lord explained that a dozen slow old battleships, of little use against the High Seas Fleet but usually carrying four 12-inch guns, could be used as floating batteries to destroy most of the Dardanelles fortifications. Fisher not only agreed at this stage that old battleships could be spared but threw in the latest pre-dreadnoughts, the *Agamemnon* and *Lord Nelson* – and on the eve of the Council meeting he suggested to Churchill that the new *Queen Elizabeth*, with eight 15-inch guns, the world's most powerful battleship of the day, could go too. The First Sea Lord's enthusiasm for a massive bombardment obviously knew no bounds: he was going to go 'the whole hog – *totus porcus*', as he said later, when the final decision on the nature of the attack was taken, against his advice, at the end of the month; but he soon developed misgivings when it became clear to him that Churchill was pursuing a *totus porcus* of his own: a naval breakthrough followed by an attack on Constantinople, *after* Kitchener had repeated that no troops were available. This would entail considerable, possibly serious, losses; while some old ships could be spared, their trained crews, needed as reserves for the Grand Fleet, could not; and in the event of a defeat of the Grand Fleet the Channel Fleet's pre-dreadnoughts would be the only reserves left against a German invasion. Total domination of the North Sea and Channel was Fisher's absolute strategic priority. A bombardment from a great distance was one thing; a short-range duel with Krupp cannon amid the mines in the Narrows was something else altogether.

Carden wanted three battlecruisers to tackle the most modern of the defences (and the *Goeben* if the chance offered), the First Lord said. There were already two battlecruisers in the Mediterranean; and the *Queen Eliza-beth* could join them to complete her gunnery trials against real targets. Churchill did what would now be called a hard sell on the stupendous gun-power of the new maritime colossus, displacing 28,000 tonnes. Even the normally impassive Kitchener was impressed. He thought a massive naval demonstration worth trying (he had no troops to offer, after all) and added, naïvely or disingenuously: 'We could leave off the bombardment if it did not prove effective.' On this basis, the War Council imprecisely decided on a navy-only attack on the Dardanelles: 'that the Admiralty should ... prepare for a naval expedition in February to bombard and take the Gallipoli peninsula with Constantinople as its objective'. Fisher did not speak at the meeting. Churchill told the French government and Grand Duke Nicholas of the plan on 19 January, inviting their active co-operation at the Dardanelles and the Bosporus respectively: the Russians pleaded maritime weakness in the Black Sea (where Souchon was giving them a lot of trouble) but the French promised naval reinforcements. On the same day Churchill wrote to Fisher with a detailed analysis of the comparative strengths of the Grand and High Seas fleets to underpin his argument that the Royal Navy could well spare some of its older ships for the Mediterranean.

The Admiralty war staff accordingly started to plan an attack with a target date of 15 February. Fisher's doubts grew. Churchill claimed he was unaware of them until the old admiral sent a dissenting memorandum to Asquith on 25 January; but Fisher had told Jellicoe, the Grand Fleet com-mander, on the 19th that he was thinking of resigning because he disagreed with the navy-only plan; Jellicoe urged him to stay on. Two days later the First Sea Lord told him that he 'abominate[d]' the idea unless it became a combined operation, preferably with 200,000 troops.

Fisher sent a copy of his prime-ministerial memorandum to Churchill, saying he had three main objections: the Baltic option was better; the Grand Fleet would be indirectly weakened; and only a combined operation could secure the Dardanelles. On the 27th Fisher told Asquith that he did not want to come to the War Council meeting on the following day because he disagreed with his political chief. The Prime Minister therefore called Fisher and Churchill to his office before the meeting began on the morning of 28 January. Having listened to both his leading naval advisers, Asquith said that as far as he was concerned, Zeebrugge was off and the Dardan-elles was on. He did not say it would be done by the navy alone.

The War Council met three times on the 28th, their deliberations marked by high drama. The first session began at 11.30 at Number 10, Downing Street. Churchill said he had heard from both the Russians and the French that they were in favour of a British naval attack on the Dardanelles starting in the middle of February. Fisher objected that he had understood from the Prime Minister before the meeting that the matter would not be raised on this day. He then got up to leave. Kitchener all but jumped to his feet and cut him off before he could reach the door, engaging Fisher in an animated conversation in a window bay: 'I am never going back to that table,' the admiral said. The field marshal with uncharacteristically visible emotion pointed out that he, Fisher, was the only opponent of the plan, and it was his duty to remain: Kitchener actually begged him to stay. Fisher returned to his seat.

Kitchener now waxed enthusiastic about the naval plan, which he thought could be worth the same as a major victory on land if successful. Once again he said the attack could always be broken off if it did not make progress. After lunch Churchill invited Fisher to his office and persuaded him to supervise the preparations. As usual, albeit against his better judgement, he threw himself into the task: *totus porcus*, he promised. He was utterly loyal to Churchill, not least because the First Lord had recalled him from retirement for one of the most important posts in the conduct of the war. But his reservations remained, as subsequent events would show, even if he kept them to himself for now. He had only recently initiated a vast naval building programme for some 600 ships; and he took comfort in the fact that the War Council agreed with Kitchener that the operation, by ships that could be spared, could be broken off at any time if it faltered. Nobody of importance seems to have questioned this extraordinary piece of wishful thinking at the time. If the Royal Navy called off a major operation for 'lack of progress' there was only one way the enemy would quite reasonably interpret it: as a victory for the defence. The damage to British prestige would be incalculable.

The War Council met again at four p.m. on 28 January. Fisher was not present. The main topic was the isolation of Serbia and the possibility of helping that beleaguered ally via Salonica. The day's third session began at 6.30 p.m. Fisher was present this time, along with Admiral Henry Oliver, the Admiralty's Chief of War Staff. Churchill announced that the Admiralty was going ahead with preparations for a naval attack on the Dardanelles, as agreed by the War Council on 13 January. Oliver said the first shot would be fired in about two weeks, say 3 February. The main base for the enterprise would be the spacious harbour of Mudros on the island of Lemnos, well placed off the mouth of the Dardanelles but not too close. The Admiralty was exploiting the limbo status of the island in international law. It had been taken from the Turks by the Greeks during the Balkan wars, along with other Aegean islands. As it had not been ceded to, but was only occupied by, the Greeks, it was in law Turkish and therefore enemy territory, which the British could take over (Greek consent was readily granted: their garrison withdrew). Some 45 minesweepers, 24 French, 21 British (actually requisitioned trawlers complete with their civilian fish-ermen-crews), along with 16 destroyers, were gathering at Mudros. Rear-Admiral Rosslyn Wemyss was appointed Senior Naval Officer in command of the base, which had almost no facilities either for maintaining ships or for troops.

The Council formally approved the attack, for political more than military reasons. The politicians felt that, given the stalemate on the Western Front, something had to be done somewhere, and there had been no major initiative against the Turks, despite the promise to the Russians. The Balkan states had no Allied success to admire as a reason for joining the Entente, and Bulgaria was clearly leaning towards the Central Powers, which would mean no help for the Allies from the friendly Greeks. Romania was losing interest in the Entente cause, and Serbia was in danger from the Austrians. Despite the fact that all the admirals, the politicians and even 'no-troops' Kitchener believed that a combined operation was the only realistic strategy, the War Council was by all accounts carried away by the rhetoric, the persuasive skill, the enthusiasm and energy of Winston Churchill.

Ironically, indeed sadly in the light of what happened, Churchill told parliament and the Dardanelles Commission long after the event that if he had known in February 1915 that an army of 100,000 was available (as Kitchener at the time still insisted was not the case), he would not have ordered a navy-only attack. As will be shown, troops were indeed available but Kitchener refused to allocate them to the Dardanelles. At the time of the War Council's decision Churchill was clearly dazzled by the prospect of bursting into the Sea of Marmara in a naval cavalry charge and pointing the huge guns of the fleet at Constantinople to force a Turkish surrender. He recalled the success of the big German guns in Belgium, apparently not appreciating the significance of the short range, high angle of fire and associated high trajectory of the big howitzers. Churchill played down or ignored the at best lukewarm enthusiasm of his naval advisers and presented his view as that of the Admiralty as a whole. Fisher never spoke of his doubts to the War Council as such (though nobody there could have been unaware of his misgivings after the contretemps with Kitchener), believing that the role of advisers was analogous to that of Victorian children, to be seen but not heard, to speak only when asked. He had given his advice to his chief elsewhere and if it was discounted or ignored, that was that: he had done his duty. No advice was sought from army artillery experts, nor was the General Staff consulted about the plans. The navy's leading gunnery expert, Admiral Sir Percy Scott, was sceptical. His inconvenient opinion was discounted.

British naval guns of the time had a maximum elevation of 15 degrees (the *Queen Elizabeth* however had 20; German capital ships, including *Goeben,* had 30 degrees, which considerably increased the maximum reach of their lighter guns, making howitzer-like falling shot a possibility at extreme distance). At anything much less than extreme range, British naval shells had an almost flat trajectory, although falling shot could be achieved to some degree at shorter ranges by reducing the explosive charge behind the shell; but the necessary calculation of the quantity of propellant required was neither simple nor reliable. The politicians knew nothing of these things. Churchill was a rarity on the War Council in that he had been an army officer in Africa as a young man (which however did not make him an expert on naval matters); even so he privately dismissed his ministerial colleagues as 'ignorant'. The sage advice against letting ships attack forts given by Lord Nelson, the greatest hero of the Royal Navy, and supported by almost every admiral in 1915, was ignored by Churchill. Nelson knew what he was talking about, because he had tackled the forts at Copenhagen in April 1801 and had a very hard time of it, even though he emerged victorious (but then Nelson's success as a commander was often based on ignoring precepts and even direct orders).

Nelson's battle was however fought within the relatively short range of the naval cannon of the day (perhaps 4,000 yards), which meant that the gunners could at least see what they were shooting at. This would not be the case at the Dardanelles, where fire would be opened from many miles away, and the precise positions of the defending guns would only be revealed when they opened fire themselves. These would also have the advantage of a stable firing platform whereas the ships, even if not constantly on the move to evade incoming shells, would be clearly visible and had to contend with the often turbulent surface of the sea. British naval gunnery was generally poor, as demonstrated by Sturdee's squadron, not least because admirals were often disinclined before the war to expend expensive ammunition on exercise and did not like their gleaming ships to be sullied by gun smoke. Nobody on the British side took the threats from the mobile howitzer batteries or even the mines sufficiently seriously, though both were known to exist in ever-growing numbers and in spite of the spectacular successes of mines against the battleships of both sides in the Russo-Japanese War just ten years earlier. Submarines were recognised as a threat, a little prematurely since there were as yet no U-boats in the area. None of the foregoing can be dismissed as hindsight: all of it was known at the time the operations were being planned. Even Duckworth had complained about mobile batteries a century earlier.

Only one old admiral, Sir Henry Jackson, ventured to ask what the fleet would do when it got to Constantinople. How could its voracious need for supplies be met when enemy artillery on the Gallipoli peninsula was free to fire on the unarmoured merchant ships that would have to deliver them? Under such circumstances the fleet would be forced to retire in a week or two. The War Council seemed airily to assume that the Turks would simply surrender under the threat of the broadsides aimed at the Golden Horn. Jackson's even more venerable colleague, Admiral Sir Arthur Wilson, VC, thought a bombardment of Constantinople would unite Turkey rather than disable it.

To summarise: everybody on the War Council, at the Admiralty and the War Office, including Churchill and Kitchener, believed before the event that a combined operation was the right strategy for taking the Dardanelles, itself the right and only practicable strategy for outflanking the Central Powers. When Kitchener insisted that no British or imperial troops were available, and neither the Russians, the Greeks nor the Balkan states would provide any, Churchill pressed and won the case for a purely naval attack, with the positive support of only one or two fairly senior naval officers, by 28 January 1915, and planning for it went ahead. The First Lord, having been denied army help, also decided not to use his under-strength Royal Naval Division, still recovering from its futile deployment at Antwerp, in support of his operation, but on 6 February he did detach two Royal Marine battalions, 2,000 men, from the RND to Lemnos for brief tactical landings, such as to complete the destruction of guns and forts begun by the fleet (they arrived only on 23 February).

Yet in the opening days of February 1915 the strategic situation in the Middle East, and to some degree on the Western Front, changed sufficiently to lead even Lord Kitchener into thinking the previously unthinkable: perhaps troops were available after all, and in unexpected numbers. In the Middle East, a feeble Turkish attempt to attack Suez from Syria under the German General Kress von Kressenstein was decisively beaten off, and the Turks moved troops from Syria and Palestine to the Caucasus; only three divisions were left to protect Constantinople. With the pressure off Egypt, the Australia and New Zealand Army Corps (ANZAC), which had landed there in mid-December 1914, was underemployed. Although still in training, the two divisions, some 39,000 men in all, were the flower of their countries' youth.

At the War Council meeting on 9 February the plight of Serbia was discussed once again. Kitchener announced that the British 29th Division, consisting of seasoned regular soldiers who had been serving in various parts of the Empire, could be sent to Salonica. The offer was not taken up, but it revealed for the first time that the best division available in Britain was not now going to Egypt as planned, nor to France, the obvious alternative, and was effectively at a loose end. Kitchener also assured the Royal Navy that if it became necessary to land troops at Gallipoli, 'assistance would be forthcoming'. The French, too, had a division of colonial troops available.

A week later, the War Council met again at Number 10, Downing Street. Among its conclusions were confirmation of the role of the two RND marine battalions, a decision to send the 29th as soon as possible to Lemnos, officially made available by the Greeks on 9 February, and an order to the Admiralty to build transports and lighters for 50,000 troops. Churchill reiterated his argument for the Dardanelles plan as the only means available to strike a blow at the enemy, given the stalemate on the Western and Eastern fronts against Germany. Now that the 29th was going, the rest of the RND, another ten battalions, could go too, along with the ANZAC divisions, which included 30,000 infantry. The Greeks had definitively refused to invade Gallipoli for fear of hostilities with Bulgaria and Romania. The Russians were not going to help either: indeed they had recoiled in horror at the prospect of the Greek Army occupying their eternal objective, Constantinople, their gateway to the Mediterranean. Their attitude was roundly condemned by the leading strategist and historian Sir Basil Liddell Hart, who wrote: 'Russia would not help even in helping to clear her own windpipe. She preferred to choke rather than disgorge a morsel of her ambition.'

The First Lord's stated aim now was to have 50,000 troops within striking distance of Gallipoli – but as a follow-up to the planned naval attack, not in combination with it. Churchill admitted that the fleet could guarantee the passage only of armoured ships up the straits, once they had broken through. If merchant ships were to follow, troops would have to go ashore to clear the peninsula. In a memorandum on 15 February, Admiral Jackson wrote: 'The naval bombardment is not recommended as a sound operation unless a strong military force is ready to assist it, or at least to follow it up immediately the forts are silenced.' Kitchener however was beginning to waver about the 29th Division in view of recent Russian setbacks. No final decision was therefore taken on its deployment. Meanwhile Carden had received his orders on the 13th to go ahead with the purely naval assault.

The bombardment of the Dardanelles forts was postponed from 15 February to the 19th because of bad weather.

PART III

FAILURE AND AFTER

CHAPTER 6

The Battle of the Dardanelles

For those who believed in portents, 19 February 1915, the day finally chosen for opening the assault on the Dardanelles, was the 108th anniversary of Admiral Duckworth's advance (unopposed) into the strait. One week earlier Admiral Carden had received the news that the new super-dreadnought HMS *Queen Elizabeth* had stripped the blades of one of her turbines while trying out her guns off Gibraltar, and lost half her maximum speed of 25 knots. She would need a week to get to the Dardanelles.

Admiral Wilhelm Souchon, commander-in-chief of the Ottoman fleet, had been forced by political considerations to stay in the Sea of Marmara for ten weeks before he took the law into his own hands, burst into the Black Sea and provoked Russia into declaring war on Turkey by shelling her ports under the Turkish ensign. After that he was anything but idle. The Grand Vizier, Prince Said Halim, who had not been told in advance, tried to disown the raid of 29 October 1914 and suggested apologising to the Russians with an offer of compensation. He ordered Enver to recall the fleet, which he did. His message was immediately followed by another from Commander Humann of the German naval bureau in Constantinople, saying that Enver had told him to tell Souchon to ignore the recall. The admiral allowed the handful of Russian merchant ships still stuck in the straits to go home and ordered the lighthouses on Turkey's Black Sea coast to be extinguished before he returned to Constantinople on 31 October, his main task achieved.

Souchon was not impressed by the performance of his Turkish sailors, despite their exuberance after the raid. He initiated new programmes of training and repair because he not only anticipated having to help defend the Dardanelles but was also determined to take on the Russian Black Sea Fleet in what became a protracted private war.

The Russians had five old battleships and supporting vessels (including nine new 33-knot destroyers) in the Black Sea, led by the competent

Vice-Admiral Eberhard. Three super-dreadnoughts were under construction in Black Sea yards, two of them due to enter service in autumn 1915. They would have ten 12-inch guns, 12 inches of armour and a speed of 24 knots. The *Goeben/Yavuz* could outrun them, boiler tubes permitting, but she was the only modern capital ship under Souchon's flag: a single mine, torpedo or lucky shell could deprive him of the only ace in his hand. Souchon was determined to do as much damage as he could before the odds against him worsened.

The Russians for their part lost no time in striking back at sea. They shelled the northern coast of Anatolia in the opening days of November, sinking three unescorted troopships with heavy Turkish losses. At the same time, the *Breslau/Midilli* sailed to the eastern end of the Black Sea to shell Poti on the Georgian coast. On 17 November the bulk of the Black Sea Fleet bombarded Trebizond (Trabzon), prompting Souchon to set out in pursuit. He sighted two Russian cruisers in patchy fog off Balaclava on the Crimean coast but as he turned towards them his ships came under heavy fire from battleships at 5,000 yards. The two sides exchanged quite accurate broadsides as they sailed in parallel lines; one 12-inch shell from the flagship *Ievstafi* hit the side of the *Yavuz*, blowing a whole armoured casemate containing a 15-centimetre gun into the sea and setting off an explosion of its ready ammunition. Only rapid flooding below deck prevented a disaster. It was nearly the lucky shot that was all the Russians needed to cripple Turkey's new-found sea power. After ten minutes Souchon ordered a withdrawal. On the way back to the Bosporus, the Turkish fleet paused and sank two Russian schooners. Their disembarked crews were taken prisoner and revealed to a satisfied Souchon and his staff the extent of the panic unleashed by the 29 October raid. Other prisoners taken in various actions towards the end of the year by the *Midilli* told how the *Yavuz* had become the subject of wild stories: she was a devil-ship, she had a doppelgänger (presumably the *Midilli* when they were sighted from a distance sailing together), and Russian crews were under orders to remain on the spot for 24 hours should they witness the sinking of the German battlecruiser – in case she returned to the surface!

At Christmas 1914 the two German ships with Turkish escorts were sailing along the north Anatolian coast on their way back to the Bosporus. Field Marshal Colmar Baron von der Goltz, one of the German commanders of the Ottoman armies, was a guest aboard the *Yavuz* when she struck a mine on her starboard side, causing her to list alarmingly. The list was soon corrected – by another mine under her port side, as another 600 tonnes of water poured in. The Russians had tethered the mines in a record 600 feet of water off the mouth of the Bosporus. The field marshal's tunic was scorched by escaping steam. The flagship limped home under her own power. As Constantinople had no dock capable of handling such a large vessel, Souchon ordered temporary repairs with wooden beams and sent for materials and equipment for coffer dams to be built round the two holes, each of which was about as large as a double-decker bus. The whole affair was almost a disaster: the battlecruiser was not repaired until late March and was unable to intervene in the Allied bombardments of the Dardanelles, although she raised steam during the final naval attack in case her 28-centimetre guns were required for a last-ditch stand. All she could do meanwhile was to unship some of her 11 remaining 15-centimetre guns and lesser cannon for coastal defence and send her machine-gun teams to contest hostile landings.

On other seas, all five available German battlecruisers under Rear-Admiral Franz von Hipper shelled Whitby in North Yorkshire and Hartlepool, Co. Durham, on 16 December 1914 for half an hour, causing more than 700 casualties. Although Room 40 had been able to give advance warning of the sortie, a counter-move by Beatty's battlecruisers was foiled by the usual poor signalling as well as bad visibility. This failure was on balance a good thing, because Hipper was trailing his coat, trying to lure Beatty on to the bulk of Admiral Ingenohl's High Seas Fleet, which had come out in the hope of picking off a vital part of the Grand Fleet, just as Tirpitz had envisaged.

A foretaste of the future in maritime warfare was provided by three British seaplane-carriers on Christmas Day, when they launched aircraft to bomb the Zeppelin sheds near Cuxhaven on the German North Sea coast. No damage was done to them; some bombs were ineffectually dropped near by. The one casualty on the German side was a battlecruiser, which ran aground and was badly damaged when she over-hastily removed herself from the scene. In a counter-attack, two Zeppelins and German seaplanes tried but failed to hit the raiding force in the first air attack ever made on warships at sea. A British destroyer hit one Zeppelin with no noticeable effect: it drifted away safely.

The menacing potential of submarines was demonstrated once again in the Adriatic on 21 December, when the Austrian *U12* scored a hit on the new French fleet flagship, the dreadnought *Jean Bart*: damage was not serious but the crew were upset by the fact that the torpedo had destroyed the on-board wine store. The ship proceeded under her own power to Malta for repairs. On New Year's Day 1915, the 1898 battleship HMS *Formidable* was sunk by the German *U24* in rough weather in the western Channel, a stark reminder of the threat from enemy boats newly based at Zeebrugge. Only some 200 men out of a crew of 780 were saved. The Germans were also busy assembling small, fast torpedo-boats to operate off the Flanders coast from Belgian ports.

Before a reorganisation of the Grand Fleet was completed in February, the first action in history involving dreadnoughts on both sides took place in the North Sea, on 24 January. Room 40 had discovered a few days earlier that two German battlecruisers were already at sea and other preparations for a sortie appeared to be taking place on the German North Sea coast. The Harwich Force, supported by Beatty, made sweeps but found nothing. On the night of 19–20 January two Zeppelins dropped bombs on King's Lynn, Yarmouth and Sheringham in Norfolk, killing 4 civilians and injuring 17 in the first ever aerial bombardment of non-military targets on land. On the 23rd German fast vessels consisting of a destroyer flotilla and four light cruisers, supported by Hipper's battlecruiser force, gathered for a sweep of their own in the direction of the Dogger Bank. Forewarned by Room 40, Beatty's five battlecruisers on hand and escorting light cruisers, as well as Commodore Tyrwhitt's destroyers from Harwich, set out for the Dogger Bank while Jellicoe's battleships came out from Scapa Flow in distant support 150 miles to the north. All this was according to a new plan to trap major units of the High Seas Fleet when they next came out to bombard the English coast, a mirror image of German tactics.

Just after dawn on the 24th, a British and a German light cruiser sighted each other and opened fire. The German force turned for home with Beatty in pursuit of Hipper's three battlecruisers and the slower hybrid, not-quite-dreadnought SMS *Blücher*. Beatty's flagship HMS *Lion* opened fire at about 22,000 yards. A confused action followed, in which once again poor signalling led to individual British battlecruisers concentrating on the wrong targets so that the unfortunate *Blücher* was unnecessarily pulverised while Hipper's three other ships managed to escape. But there was very substantial damage to his flagship, the *Seydlitz*, whose stern was almost blown off by internal explosions. On the British side, Beatty's flagship was severely damaged by 17 hits and reduced to 12, later 8, knots, falling out of the line. The *Blücher* was a burning wreck by the time she struck her colours. British ships were moving in to rescue her crew when she suddenly turned over and sank; 250 German sailors were saved, but nearly 1,000 were lost in the battle. The *Lion* was taken in tow by the *Indomitable* and the other British ships present formed a screen round the two battlecruisers against submarine attack as the pair crept into the safety of the Firth of Forth. It was later established that the British had scored 73 hits with 958 shells (all but 3 on the *Blücher*) while the Germans scored 25 (17 on the *Lion*) from 1,276 fired in what became known as the Battle of the Dogger Bank, a missed opportunity for the British.

It was however a useful victory for the Royal Navy, if not much of one given that five battlecruisers with the advantage in guns and speed had been in play against three and a half. But Hipper's squadron had lost a ship, suffered considerable damage to all three others and had fled the scene, lucky to escape: for the time being, pending extensive repairs, the Germans had no battlecruiser ready for sea (they only ever built seven, including the *Goeben*).

On 30 January *U20* sank two British ships off Le Havre by torpedoes fired from underwater without warning – the first time such a tactic had been used against merchantmen. Within a week Germany declared the waters round Britain to be a war zone in which any vessel, including neutrals, could be sunk without notice. This fateful step was, according to an official announcement, to take effect on 18 February but was postponed to the 22nd.

The naval battle for the Dardanelles opened at last on 19 February 1915. The seaplane-carrier *Ark Royal* had arrived two days before, her aircraft earmarked for reconnaissance and observation. Only one of the first four attempts to reconnoitre the entrance forts succeeded in adverse winds. Admiral Carden returned from Malta on the 18th to take command in the battlecruiser *Inflexible* (flag), still bearing the scorch-marks of her broadsides against Graf Spee's squadron at the Falklands. At his disposal were 12 heavy ships, which he organised into three divisions: the first included his strongest ships – the flagship as well as the *Agamemnon*, a recent pre-dreadnought, and the super-dreadnought *Queen Elizabeth*, ready for action after repairs to her turbines. All three had arrived on the eve of the attack. The Second Division consisted of five older British battleships, commanded by Admiral de Robeck in HMS *Vengeance*; and the Third, of four French pre-dreadnoughts led by Admiral Guépratte on the *Suffren* (flag). Carden also had 4 light cruisers, 16 destroyers, 5 submarines and 21 minesweeping trawlers, all British; the French provided, or were about to provide, 14 minesweepers, 6 destroyers, 2 submarines and a seaplane-carrier.

Carden's plan was straightforward and deliberate, in seven phases, starting with the reduction of the entrance forts on either side of the strait. Then the minesweepers with escort were to sweep up to the Narrows, where more forts would come under heavy bombardment in their turn. Next the main minefields at the Narrows would be cleared, enabling the battleships to move on and bombard the inner forts immediately beyond. The bulk of the fleet would enter the Sea of Marmara, where the final phase, including general clearing operations against the Turkish fleet, would be carried out.

The first-phase attack on the outermost forts would be in three stages: bombardment at long range (including indirect fire across the Gallipoli peninsula) by the heaviest guns, then at medium range with secondary armament, and finally at 4,000 yards or less with all guns that could be brought to bear. A battleship from the Second Division, *Albion*, with a light cruiser and seven minesweepers, was briefly detached and sent up the Aegean coast of the peninsula to clear an area off Gaba Tepe so that the *Queen Elizabeth* could bombard the Narrows forts 'over the top' from there in phase three. Other ships were assigned various forts as targets in phase one: *Inflexible* for example took on the main fort at Sedd el Bahr on the European side while the *Suffren* attacked its opposite number on the Asian side, Kum Kale. From their various positions individual ships were expected to observe each other's fall of shot.

At 9.51 on the morning of 19 February HMS *Cornwallis* of the Second Division, a 1901 battleship with a main armament of four 12-inch guns, fired the first shot, at Orkanie, a secondary fort on the Asian shore, from a position where she could not be hit by the Kum Kale guns. The French flagship started shooting at Kum Kale itself at 10.32. It was a curiously desultory, not to say hesitant, bombardment. Carden, apparently inhibited by a shortage of ammunition (as also experienced at this time by the British Army on the Western Front), ordered all bombarding ships to drop anchor so as to maximise the precision of their shooting. *Cornwallis* had a broken capstan and could not comply, so was replaced for a while by the *Vengeance*. The flagship *Inflexible* initially opened fire on the fort at Cape Helles, adjacent to Sedd el Bahr, at 11.50 a.m. – just two rounds at 15,000 yards, which fell short. She moved 2,000 yards closer and started again at 12.20. The battleship *Triumph* of the Second Division fired 14 shells from her ten-inch guns at the same target between ten and 12.15, or one about every ten minutes. Each one missed. At one p.m. the *Inflexible* switched targets from Cape Helles to Sedd el Bahr. A seaplane went up that afternoon and reported that all the guns at Sedd el Bahr, Kum Kale and Orkanie were intact.

Even so, Carden was sufficiently satisfied with the apparent accuracy of the first-stage shooting to order stage two to begin at two p.m. – bombardment of the entrance forts at closer range, the ships to keep on the move this time in case they were fired upon by the defence. The forts however remained silent. Kum Kale appeared to be in ruins, especially after the French flagship stepped up her rate of fire at 4.10 p.m. Half an hour later Carden ordered de Robeck to sail in the *Vengeance* to examine the condition of the forts. The old battleship made for the entrance at her best speed – and was taken aback when the subsidiary forts at Orkanie and Helles, which had been silent all day, suddenly emitted a hail of shot. De Robeck did not turn tail but headed towards Helles, firing salvoes from his forward-facing armament, to the admiration of the French, whose ships came up in support; they even fired shots over the top of *Vengeance* at the forts on the European side while maintaining their bombardment of Orkanie, which stoutly kept up its lively barrage. *Agamemnon* and *Inflexible*, the fleet flagship, also came up in support. At the end of a slow day the expenditure of ammunition by both sides reached a crescendo in the last half-hour, before Carden issued the general recall in the fading light at 5.20 p.m. De Robeck appealed for permission to initiate stage three, especially as no ship had been hit, but Carden refused, not wishing to sustain casualties at the end of the first day, when the ships at sea made much clearer targets than the defences; he was now also more concerned about his ammunition supply. 'Cease firing' was signalled at 5.30. Only Orkanie was still shooting back as the fleet retired unscathed.

There was much food for thought on Carden's part: he was beginning to realise that even heavy naval guns could not make much of an impression on static defences such as earthworks, and also that direct hits were too rare, yet essential if the guns of the defence were to be knocked out. Indirect 'over-the-top' fire was ineffective without close spotting, which was not available. The best shooting came from anchored ships, but this was clearly risky at anything but long range. Both Carden and the Admiralty were however cautiously optimistic on reviewing the course of the first day of bombardment, their only reservation being the conclusion that battering down the defences was going to take even longer than the cautious admiral had predicted. He believed however that another hour of full daylight would have seen the complete destruction of the entrance forts.

In London, meanwhile, consideration was being given to sending more troops to support the navy at the Dardanelles (as distinct from mounting a combined operation). Two more battalions of Royal Marines were ordered to Lemnos to reinforce the two already there. Churchill, changing his mind, decided to send the only other troops at his disposal, the convalescent and still not fully trained RN Division of ten battalions, as well, on 27 February; his aim now was to have 50,000 troops available within striking distance of the Dardanelles, to be ready to exploit and consolidate a breakthrough by the navy. The First Lord openly acknowledged that if the fleet broke in, only armoured ships could go up the straits. If thin-skinned supply ships were to follow, troops would have to be landed to eliminate shore-based enemy artillery and snipers. At the War Council meeting of 16 February it was provisionally decided to send the 29th Division of experienced British troops to the Aegean rather than France: but only in case of emergency, and not yet. Kitchener still had reservations and would not commit himself because the Russians were once again in difficulties, especially facing the Germans, which meant the latter might soon be free to switch many divisions from east to west. The first of Kitchener's 'new armies' would not be ready for France until April.

With the threat of a Turkish invasion of Egypt removed, however, the 39,000 men of ANZAC were also available; without them there would still be more than 40,000 men left to garrison Egypt, largely from the Indian Army. The Admiralty was instructed to speed up the assembly of transports and lighters to carry and land 50,000 troops. This could not be done in less than three weeks. ANZAC plus RND plus RM made about 50,000; but there were no seasoned troops among this number. Yet the French seemed prepared to send a division of 15,000 men; with the 29th and possibly 10,000 or more from Russia, perhaps even a corps, around 100,000 troops would be available.

The ill-defined Dardanelles plan was now in danger of falling between two stools. The original concept was a purely naval diversion at the straits to distract the Turks as a means of relieving some of the pressure on the Russians in the Caucasus – a purely *tactical* 'demonstration'. As time went by and Souchon made the most of his arrival in the Sea of Marmara, the stalemate on the Allied fronts west of Russia prompted Churchill and others to regard a serious attack on the Central Powers at their weakest point – Turkey – as a highly attractive, indeed the only, possibility of outflanking the enemy, a *strategic* shift in the conduct of the war, exploiting Britain's overwhelming but underemployed naval strength to force the straits and threaten Constantinople.

As noted above, everybody in the Allied war leadership, including Churchill, accepted the received wisdom, dating back more than a century, that a combined operation was the only realistic approach to forcing the Dardanelles and that it would be difficult – but that a success could be decisive for the course of the war because it would be an enormous help to the cause of the Entente in general and Russia in particular. Kitchener's understandable if frustrating refusal to commit his last reserve of battle-hardened soldiers that might yet be needed on the main front in France prompted Churchill and others to cast about for troops elsewhere – the Greek Army, then the navy's own marines plus the RN Division, the two ANZAC divisions, a French division …

But why? Kitchener believed that 150,000 men would be needed to capture and hold the Gallipoli peninsula, which was not only the main threat to a fleet advancing up the strait but was also the overland route to Constantinople from the Mediterranean. The generals simply did not believe the navy could do it alone. A scratch, mostly unblooded, force of 50,000 was neither fish nor fowl: much larger than was needed for pinprick raids to spike shore-based guns for the navy (which could be done by the four marine battalions plus bluejackets), and too small for a landing in strength as part of a combined operation. Nevertheless Kitchener issued orders on 20 February to Lieutenant-General Sir J. G. Maxwell, the commander-in-chief in Egypt, to prepare ANZAC, under the British Major-General Sir William Birdwood, for service at the Dardanelles. Kitchener told Maxwell to contact Carden and find out if he needed troops before 9 March, when the transports for ANZAC would be ready at Alexandria. If so, Maxwell was to send an advance party in locally available transports at once. The Admiralty had already mustered six troopships at Alexandria which would be ready to leave on 27 February. In south-west England the Admiralty had also organised transports for the 29th, which were ready on 22 February; Kitchener however had told the Admiralty the day before that the division would not be leaving.

Admiral Carden intended to continue his bombardment of the entrance forts the next day, 20 February. But, as so often at the Dardanelles in winter, the weather turned hostile. A gale was blowing, and stormy conditions prevailed until the afternoon of the 22nd. Carden had hopes of completing the destruction of the outer forts the next day, but the weather turned foul again. Meanwhile he had told General Maxwell that he wanted 10,000 troops to be landed at the south-western end of the Gallipoli peninsula, at a point where it was just five miles wide, as soon as the outer forts had been silenced. They could occupy the local high point at Achi Baba, from which accurate spotting of the fall of shot should be possible (although a visit to the unachieved objective of the later British landings shows that it was not high enough anyway). This proposal alarmed the War Office; and Maxwell on his own initiative dispatched just one infantry brigade of Australians to Lemnos on 23 February. On the same day he sent Birdwood to confer on the spot with Carden and assess the military possibilities and requirements.

The War Council debated the Dardanelles again on 24 February. Churchill reported on the frustrating weather conditions. Kitchener opined that if the fleet did break through, Turkish troops on the peninsula would probably retire towards Constantinople to avoid being cut off and starved. The 29th Division figured prominently in the discussion. The 'easterners' made the point that one division, however good, was hardly likely to make a noticeable difference on the Western Front, whereas it could play a decisive role at the Dardanelles as a first-class leavening for otherwise raw troops. Everyone recognised that if it were to be sent east, the decision would signify a strategic shift, nothing less than the opening of a new front. If it did go, the last shred of credibility attached to Kitchener's airy theory, that the attack on the Dardanelles could simply be abandoned if progress were not made, would disappear. A commitment of 100,000 men (including the promised French and Russian divisions), with a crack British division in the van, could not be cancelled after a landing without severe loss of prestige. The concept of a combined operation appeared to be gaining ground as if by stealth. But the Admiralty did not go that far, regarding the troops as strictly supplementary to the fleet, to be used for limited local operations against strongpoints and the like. Kitchener was prone to oracular pronouncements, and he chose this stage of the debate to announce that the Allies could not afford to fail at the Dardanelles, a 180-degree change of course on his part. The loss of prestige would be catastrophic. The Secretary of State for War followed his own argument to its conclusion: if the navy did not succeed alone, then the army would have to see the job through.

The next day, 25 February, Carden was at last in a position to resume the bombardment of the entrance forts, completing the third stage of phase one of his plan, although the wind was too strong for seaplanes to be able to go up to spot the fall of shot. The Royal Marines were ordered to be ready to make local landings against gun positions. Four battleships operating in pairs, one British, one French, were ordered to try for direct hits on the forts at Orkanie and Helles at quite close range, down to 3,000 yards, with their secondary armament. Behind them three British battleships, including the *Queen Elizabeth*, and one French, would fire heavy shells at all four forts to deter the defenders from manning their guns. The *Queen Elizabeth* was soon engaged in a lively exchange at 10,000 yards with the Helles guns, which were firing coolly and accurately. The supporting *Agamemnon* was hit seven times in ten minutes, taking moderate damage and three fatalities. Both ships returned to the fray and by noon appeared to have knocked out the two 24-centimetre guns of the battery. Their crews were seen fleeing. The Helles fort was also putting up a spirited defence, straddling the *Gaulois*, which blasted the fort in return to such effect that it too was apparently silenced. The main forts at Sedd el Bahr and Kum Kale took many hits and fired few shots in return. The effect, if any, on their guns could not be discerned.

Even so, by three p.m. Admiral Carden felt confident enough to start the next phase – minesweeping inside the strait. The trawlers, escorted by destroyers and covered by three battleships, moved up an hour later. All four target forts were silent. HMS *Albion* approached the Asian and *Triumph* the European shore until 2,000 yards off, opening a brisk fire with their secondary guns. *Vengeance* stood by in reserve. Only Orkanie shot back, and was immediately shelled by *Agamemnon* and *Irresistible* as well as *Albion*. Helles and Kum Kale got off one shot each; Sedd el Bahr appeared to have been silenced altogether. A handful of hidden, mobile guns fired a few ineffectual rounds. At four p.m. the minesweepers started work in pairs, each pair towing a cable between them to dislodge tethered mines, which would then be set off by rifle fire if necessary. It was very slow work for the trawlers as their underpowered engines struggled against the current. Three battleships remained on station behind them as the rest of the heavy ships retired. Carden and Guépratte reported in optimistic terms to their respective governments that evening.

The distance from the entrance of the Dardanelles to Kephez Point, a small promontory on the Asian side, is about ten nautical miles. Here the strait is at its narrowest, some 2,800 yards (2,500 metres) wide, except for the Narrows themselves at Chanak, about 1,200 yards wide and nearly three miles further in. *Albion* and *Triumph* were ordered to sail as far as Kephez, flanking another old battleship, HMS *Majestic* (1895), just arrived from England on the 25th and exhibiting an unusual temporary feature: each of her two 12-inch-gun turrets sported a howitzer on top for engaging inland targets. The trio were preceded by the trawlers, which began sweeping overnight to about four miles inside the strait. They had found nothing by eight a.m., when the battleships began their advance, their purpose to bombard the forts on each shore and destroy gun-batteries, a bridge, an observation post and suspected land-based torpedo tubes south of Kephez. Among the main targets were Fort Dardanos on the Asian side and a new Fort Messudieh (armed with the eponymous torpedoed ship's recovered guns) on the European, roughly opposite each other on a line about one mile short of Kephez, and each supported by subsidiary batteries covering the minefields, some fixed, some mobile.

On their way in, the battleships sought to complete the destruction of the main entrance forts, Sedd el Bahr and Kum Kale, from 'behind' or inside the strait. After that, *Albion* and *Majestic* began shelling Dardanos from six miles away. Only the occasional shot was fired in reply. Dardanos itself did not respond. At three p.m., as the range from shore to sea shortened, the defenders sharply increased their rate of fire, mostly from concealed and/or mobile batteries which neither lookouts on the ships nor even scouting seaplanes were able to pinpoint. Dozens of these guns, as well as mortars, had been added to the defences in the preceding three months. They were able to concentrate their fire in such a way as to force incoming ships to keep moving in order to evade potentially serious damage from plunging shot. The *Majestic* took a direct hit below the waterline before de Robeck on the *Vengeance* ordered the cease-fire. The damage was not serious.

Carden's second-in-command had been checking the shores nearer the entrance for mobile batteries and found one abandoned on a beach near Kum Kale. De Robeck decided to land demolition parties to destroy the guns spotted on both shores. Half a dozen battleships and cruisers were called up in support. The *Vengeance* landed a naval demolition party and 50 Royal Marines to protect them at 2.30 p.m. The small force came under crossfire but Lieutenant-Commander E. G. Robinson, RN, pressed ahead to destroy the guns at Orkanie, winning the VC. On the European side the *Irresistible* landed 45 marines and 30 bluejackets of a demolition party to attack the Sedd el Bahr guns: four out of six heavy guns were found to be intact amid the rubble. Guncotton charges rammed into their barrels destroyed them. The raiding party tried to move on to the Helles fort but was halted by enemy infantry and artillery fire. A pair of medium field guns were destroyed as the party withdrew. Only a few men had received minor wounds. Carden resolved to continue these productive raids the next day,

27 February, but was once again foiled by the weather, which produced heavy squalls in the morning. In the afternoon *Irresistible* landed a naval demolition party covered by some 80 marines at Sedd el Bahr to disable a battery of six German 15-centimetre mortars. Despite a counter-attack the British party achieved its objective without loss and was safely re-embarked under the battleship's booming heavy guns.

The weather on 28 February was so wild that no operations, whether minesweeping, bombardment or landings, were possible. Snow now masked both shores of the strait, and gales turned into blizzards. Planned landings were cancelled, but Carden ordered de Robeck on 1 March to take four battleships as far as was safe up the strait (the four miles that had been swept for mines) to check and if necessary renew the bombardment of the forts battered by the Allied navies earlier. Even so the defenders managed to play cat and mouse with the attackers. Two battleships fired on Fort Dardanos and another in the vicinity. Two others searched for mobile guns and the positions behind Sedd el Bahr from which the resistance to the landing there had come. Having silenced guns firing on them near Kum Kale on the Asian side, the second pair moved on – and promptly came under heavy fire from howitzers as they passed Erenkeui Bay. De Robeck, his flag transferred to the *Irresistible*, crossed over from the European shore to support them. The three ships imposed silence on the local defence in half an hour and de Robeck ordered the first pair of battleships to make a sweep up the European shore. The Turkish guns on that side now laid down a fierce curtain of fire, forcing a temporary withdrawal until naval fire could be concentrated on the new threat. A quarter of an hour later, at 1.15 p.m., *Albion* and *Triumph* moved in slowly to attack Dardanos again. Obstructed by their own destroyers escorting the minesweepers, the two ships came under the most intense and accurate fire yet from the European shore. Forced to take evasive action, they could not hope to mount an accurate bombardment of Dardanos, so they switched their attentions to the European littoral. Having imposed silence on that side, the Allied ships came under a truly withering fire from many well-dispersed and hidden guns on the Asian side, which the circling attackers could not silence. So they withdrew, baffled, for the day.

De Robeck, noting a considerable improvement in the weather, decided to send a large landing party to complete the destruction of the Kum Kale fort. The result was both good news – and bad. The navy demolition men, covered by the usual 50 marines, made a successful landing in which they destroyed eight heavy guns in the fort and half a dozen medium field guns positioned to the west. As the party withdrew to its boats it destroyed four more guns and a mobile searchlight without any casualties. The bad news was that the fort itself had only had nine heavy guns; all the shelling had done was to wreck one of them, leaving seven untouched and one dismounted but still usable.

The minesweepers carried on after dark on 1 March, at least until 11 p.m., when a powerful searchlight came on as they were about a mile and a half short of Kephez Point, followed by massed fire from the mobile batteries on both sides placed there to cover the minefields. The trawlers cut their sweeping cables and retired as their escorting destroyers fired blind and hastily put up a smokescreen. After 40 minutes the navy knocked out the searchlight and the trawlers withdrew undamaged. Here was more food for thought for Carden: to add to the evidence that big naval guns were not much use against shore batteries (far more damage was done to them by the landing parties), he had been shown that minesweeping, at least in its current form, lay somewhere between difficult and downright impossible. An impossible dilemma or what would now be called a 'Catch 22' was developing: the battleships could not silence the guns unless the mines were swept, but the mines could not be swept until the guns were silenced. This is how Admiral Wemyss, commanding at Mudros, saw the situation at the time:

> The battleships could not force the straits until the minefield had been cleared – the minefield could not be cleared until the concealed guns which defended them [*sic*] were destroyed – they could not be destroyed until the peninsula was in our hands, hence we should have to seize it with the army.

The only way to resolve this was indeed to send troops ashore to take the guns in the rear, which is why almost everyone at the Admiralty and the War Office had always believed that a combined operation was the only way to break through the Dardanelles. A landing on the Gallipoli peninsula and the seizure of its guns would enable them to be turned on the less well-hidden artillery on the lower-lying Asian shore.

The 2nd of March began with another storm, making landings impossible. Carden's force meanwhile had reached peak strength, with 18 battleships organised in three divisions: the first consisting of the four most modern British vessels in two subdivisions, the second comprising the older British ships in three subdivisions, and the third was the French quartet. Two seaplane-carriers, four light cruisers, destroyers and submarines completed the fighting fleet. The fourth subdivision, led by HMS *Canopus*, back in action after her Falklands efforts, entered the strait in the afternoon and concentrated on reducing the Dardanos fort from positions off the European shore. After about two hours the fort suddenly fired back with considerable effect, hitting *Canopus* three times in short order and causing minor damage. Keeping on the move to minimise damage, the three ships came under fire from positions on both sides, but kept up the pressure on Dardanos, where one gun was reported to have been hit. Mobile batteries were a major irritant for the attackers, who withdrew before dusk. After dark, another attempt to clear mines was started but there was such heavy gunfire from howitzers and field guns that the trawlers and destroyers soon fell back. Meanwhile, in a useful diversion, the French battleships sailed up the western side of the Gallipoli peninsula to reconnoitre possible landing places and shell military installations in the Bulair area – the northern neck of the peninsula. Accompanying minesweepers found nothing.

The weather was good enough on the afternoon of the 3rd for landing another raiding party from *Irresistible*, which destroyed a hidden battery of six field guns near Sedd el Bahr without injury. The fifth subdivision of three battleships engaged in further bouts of inconclusive bombardment against both coasts. The European side was the more active this time in shooting back. The battleships retired unhurt, and the minesweepers moved up for another attempt to complete phase two after dark.

The seaplanes were still unable to contribute very much in their would-be role observing the fall of shot. The only apparent solution to this crippling difficulty was Carden's idea of seizing Achi Baba heights near the end of the peninsula. But two battalions of marines at Lemnos and the raw Australian brigade about to arrive from Alexandria, the only troops within Carden's immediate reach, were by no means enough to take and hold the position. Carden's pedestrian leadership, soon to come to an end, has often been criticised and was doubted at the time, but he clearly saw the need for accurate observation and the means for obtaining it. He proposed landing 10,000 troops to do it – and was turned down in London by army and navy alike. Naval officers who had observed the Russo-Japanese War of 1904–5 and the slow progress of the Japanese siege of the Russian naval base at Port Arthur, and others who had taken part in the capture of Tsingtao, the German base on the northern Chinese coast, late in 1914, supported

Carden's idea, to no avail. Even General Birdwood, who arrived to see the situation for himself and conferred with Carden on 3 March, failed to appreciate the navy's specific need for a good observation post. But he did realise that the concealed and mobile batteries were a major problem and therefore recommended an immediate landing on the peninsula to take the defence guns in the rear. He wanted to deploy all 30,000 infantrymen in ANZAC, who could not be fully available before 18 March. Birdwood did not believe the navy could succeed alone and proposed a landing at Cape Helles with a simultaneous feint in strength against Bulair at the other end of the peninsula. He believed Achi Baba could be taken in three days.

Although the British could not know this, the Turkish Army appears at this stage to have had no more than a single infantry division in the peninsula. They blindly estimated there were two or three, up to 40,000 troops. The offer from Premier Venizelos of Greece to provide three divisions (up to 60,000 men) for an invasion of Gallipoli on 1 March was formally vetoed by a suspicious and grudging Russia on the 3rd.

But optimism prevailed at the War Council when it met in London that day; ministers busied themselves counting chickens before they hatched. A message arrived from Russia saying that Admiral Eberhard was readying the Black Sea Fleet to deliver an army corps to attack the Bosporus and Constantinople in two to three weeks, as soon as Carden's fleet broke through, which was expected to happen by 20 March. A Russian naval liaison officer was already attached to Carden's staff. Three monitors were even detailed to prepare for operations in the Danube after sailing up to Constantinople and onward through the Black Sea. The Council decided that there would be no simultaneous invasion by the 60,000 troops expected to be on hand by 20 March; they were to wait for the navy to complete its work, assisted only by small numbers of troops as necessary, and to be landed afterwards to march on Constantinople and join hands with the Russian corps coming from the north. Still no combined operation, even though the army's man on the spot, General Birdwood, had reported more than once that the navy could not succeed alone. Kitchener however was unmoved. Carden was left to his own devices, and planned to attack the main forts guarding the Narrows, using the *Queen Elizabeth*'s 15-inch guns firing 'over the top' of the peninsula.

Delightful early spring weather on 4 March prompted de Robeck to order the third pinprick landing, by two companies of Royal Marines with naval demolition parties, to complete the neutralisation of the Helles and Orkanie subsidiary forts on the European and Asian shores respectively. A subdivision of three battleships covered each shore. As a diversion, *Canopus* was sent north along the Aegean coast to preoccupy any troops in the Bulair area. Brigadier-General C. N. Trotman, commanding the marines, supervised the landings from a destroyer; other destroyers brought the men from the island of Imbros, where they had spent the night.

A company of the Plymouth battalion, RM Light Infantry, went ashore first, on the Asian side, only to discover that the Turks were well prepared this time with shrapnel shells and snipers. The men had to take cover under the battered walls of Kum Kale until the ships closed in and shelled the defenders, who retired despite the best restraining efforts of German officers. But the marines' advance was bitterly contested all the way by snipers and infantry. The marines withdrew after dark at the end of a long, hard day without achieving any of their objectives but with 44 casualties, 17 of them fatal. The other Plymouth company landed a little later on the European side and met a similarly stiff reception. The marines withdrew in the afternoon with three killed and one wounded, again without reaching their objective, and General Trotman abandoned the operation that evening. Only later was it discovered that both objectives had actually been permanently silenced for once by bombardment from the ships on 25 February. The time had clearly expired for using troops in penny-packets for pinprick raids: the Turks might have retired when attacked from the sea, but this did not mean they would not regroup and fight back from another position. In the same spirit, they were evacuating the forts for trenches during bombardments and returning to their guns when the ships turned their attention elsewhere.

Carden's next target was the inner defences of the Narrows, inevitably the strongest in the Dardanelles. The European side boasted three main forts centred on Kilid Bahr, equipped with the heaviest cannon of up to 14-inch calibre. Opposite, at Chanak, were two main forts, one of which, the strongest of them all, had two 14-inch pieces that could reach 17,000 yards plus seven 9.4-inch (15,000 yards) and the latest German rangefinders, all of quite recent manufacture. This fort, Hamidieh I, was reported to be manned entirely by Germans. The fixed positions, as usual, were supported by movable field guns, howitzers and heavy machine-guns. To attack the European forts at the Narrows the *Queen Elizabeth* took up a position south of Gaba Tepe previously swept for her on the Aegean side of the peninsula, some 15,000 yards from her targets. As seaplanes were still generally too feeble to be reliable spotters, usually unable to rise above rifle range, three old battleships were to take it in turns at 12-minute intervals to observe the fall of shot from inside the strait, where however they had to keep on the move to evade enemy artillery fire. They could get no closer than seven or eight miles from the target because of the minefields and their covering guns. The super-dreadnought fired her first shot at noon on 5 March. Two seaplanes went up but one crashed and the other's pilot was hit by a rifle bullet but survived. The *Queen Elizabeth* shrugged off no fewer than 17 hits from the mobile artillery, which did no notable damage but were a considerable nuisance, causing a fire at one stage. She set off an ammunition store with one of the 33 15-inch shells she fired but had to stop for bad light.

Rotating fire-spotting was abandoned as unreliable. On 6 March one ship was used, though constantly on the move, to provide the greater reliability of 'one pair of eyes'. Carden asked for land-based (i.e. army) aircraft, of which none was available to him. He also asked the Admiralty to change its mind and let him send the *Queen Elizabeth* into the strait for direct shooting. This was approved but Carden decided to wait awhile. On the 6th, one more attempt at an indirect bombardment was made, the target this time the second fort on the Asian side, Çemenlik. If anything, this experiment worked even less well than the previous day's. The big battleship was forced to pull back half a mile by accurate coastal artillery fire and started shooting only at 12.30 p.m. She managed just five rounds in an hour before being forced to move again, opening the range to ten miles. After only two more shots, de Robeck ordered her to cease fire while deploying his five older battleships in a direct barrage against various forts inside the strait from about six miles.

That night the minesweepers made another attempt to sweep as far as Kephez but were driven back by a torrent of fire aided by searchlights. On 7 March Carden tried a new approach: the French squadron volunteered to tackle a number of mobile batteries that had just been located, while the most modern pre-dreadnoughts, *Agamemnon* and *Lord Nelson*, fired on the Narrows forts from seven to six miles off. A very heavy, possibly 14-inch, shell plunged on to the *Agamemnon* at one p.m. and caused considerable damage aft. Her partner scored direct hits on magazines in two Asian forts, which exploded. More and more shells hit the attacking pair before they withdrew in mid-afternoon. But for the intense fire kept up by the French battleships, the damage would have been worse. The *Lord Nelson* was holed below the waterline, the *Agamemnon* set off a floating mine, but both ships retired safely with only minor casualties. Meanwhile, at the other end of the Sea of Marmara, the Russian fleet put in a rare appearance to shell ports near the Bosporus. British light cruisers bombarded military installations in the Bulair area from the Aegean. That night it was the turn of the French minesweepers to enter the strait, but they could make no headway against the current.

By now Carden and his staff were deeply frustrated by the lack of progress, while the Turks and their German advisers could justifiably congratulate each other on a supple, spirited and well-directed defence; their shooting and their tactics alike were clearly improving. On 8 March Carden moved his flag to the *Queen Elizabeth* and ordered her into the strait, inside a cordon of four older battleships, to shell all five Narrows forts in turn. It was an embarrassingly hesitant operation, inhibited by a chronic shortage of heavy ammunition. And the weather closed in; the super-dreadnought got off just 11 shots at one of the forts, all of which stayed silent while mobile batteries once again laid down an irritating curtain of fire. The big ship may – or may not – have scored one hit. The British and French battleships withdrew at 3.30 p.m., foiled once again after 18 fruitless days.

At the meeting of the War Council in London on 10 March, Field Marshal the Earl Kitchener of Khartoum, His Majesty's Secretary of State for War, announced that he had changed his mind.

CHAPTER 7

Crescendo

The situation on both western and eastern fronts against Germany, said Kitchener, was now sufficiently stable to enable him to release the 29th Division, of 18,000 men, for dispatch to the Aegean. The BEF launched a four-division attack on German positions at Neuve Chapelle in Flanders that very morning of 10 March, a qualified success. With ANZAC (now 34,000 infantry and cavalry), a French division (18,000), the RN Division (11,000) and eventually a Russian corps of 47,000 (only available once the Anglo-French force had reached Constantinople) there were more than 125,000 troops on hand for land operations against western Turkey, 80,000 for the Gallipoli peninsula. But even now Kitchener did not think in terms of a combined operation. In his view the troops were there to intervene if the naval assault failed. Despite his 'U-turn' on the 29th Division, he had not changed his underlying attitude since early February, when he said that if the navy needed army support, 'that assistance would be forthcoming'. His earlier idea that the attack on the strait could simply be abandoned if it did not work was no longer relevant. So much effort and precious ammunition had been expended that British prestige was at stake, and not just that of the Royal Navy. Kitchener had vacillated for three weeks before committing just one British Army division, resisting Churchill's most passionate pleas. By 10 March it was too little, too late: the Turks had not only added many guns to their mobile artillery but already increased their infantry strength in the peninsula from one division to three, with more to come.

An important witness to, and participant in, the naval attack on the Dardanelles was Commodore Roger Keyes, who was appointed Carden's chief of staff just before the bombardments began. Previously commodore in command of submarines at Harwich, he was a relative rarity in the upper reaches of the contemporary Royal Navy – a leader with a generous, not to say over-generous, supply of attacking spirit. The future admiral of the fleet and hero of the Zeebrugge Raid in 1918, Keyes, described elsewhere as 'all gung-ho and no staffwork', was acutely disappointed by Carden's lack of inspiration and angered by the poor performance of the mine-sweepers. His prolific letters to his wife present a vivid account of events before, during and after the naval campaign against the forts, supplemented by volumes of post-war memoirs.

Keyes, determined that something drastic should be done about the minefields, had a major row with Carden on the evening of 9 March. The admiral planned to sail to Mudros on the 10th to inspect the expanding base there, taking the *Queen Elizabeth* and *Inflexible* with him, the latter to be sent back to Malta to replace two of her gun barrels while Carden transferred his flag to the former. He also let his deputy, Rear-Admiral de Robeck, prepare to sail up the Aegean to reconnoitre the Bulair area at the northern neck of the peninsula at the same time. This meant that a mere captain RN, Arthur Hayes-Sadler, commanding HMS *Ocean*, would temporarily be the senior officer at the Dardanelles.

This filled me with consternation [Keyes wrote]; it was vital and essential to clear the minefields without further delay. How could the captain of the *Ocean* be expected to initiate new and perhaps rather desperate methods in the absence of the two admirals ...

We *must* attack the minefields vigorously, and I wished to satisfy myself that we were going to do so. For instance that night all that was proposed was a reconnaissance by two picket boats – when we had 35 sweepers – that was not acting vigorously ...

The position of commodore, signified by a single broad gold stripe on the sleeve, is not a true rank in the Royal Navy but only a mark of special responsibility for an officer who remains a substantive captain (the next step up the ladder of rank being rear-admiral). As Keyes was lower down the captains' list than Hayes-Sadler, he was not entitled to give the latter orders unless at the behest of Carden or de Robeck. Carden accepted Keyes's argument at 11 p.m. and signalled de Robeck to stay put. Keyes next won over the second-in-command to the idea of a sweep as near the Narrows as possible, but with an important difference. One battleship, the *Canopus*, one light cruiser, destroyers and picket boats would accompany seven trawlers (allowing for the 500-yard minesweeping wires, two and a half inches thick, such was all there was sea-room for) up the strait as near to Chanak as possible. The wires, each supported not only by a mine-sweeper at each end but also by a large wooden kite in the middle to help maintain the correct depth, were to be deployed only when the trawlers put about. This time they would sail downstream with the current instead of having to fight it with their inadequate power. Fewer than half of the 21 trawlers available on 18 March could make 14 knots. If a pair snared a mine, they had to encircle it with the cable, tow it away and set it off by rifle fire. The technique was hopelessly inadequate in calm waters with no enemy fire; in the often choppy strait, especially under shellfire and searchlights, it was impossible. Keyes asked Captain Heathcote Grant of *Canopus* (also senior to him) for permission to accompany him and observe. He requested from the Admiralty permission to give the trawlermen a bonus if they were successful: 'they were not supposed to sweep under fire, and had not joined for that'. He also wanted to stiffen the crews with volunteer junior naval officers and ratings, but permission did not arrive in time.

The escorts blazed away at the five searchlights that lit up the scene but failed to douse them. Guns ashore put up the customary wild barrage. The trawlers formed three pairs with the seventh as leader, but the nervous crews of two of the pairs failed to maintain the requisite 500-yard distance apart, which meant they did not sweep at sufficient depth, making their efforts pointless. The third pair did better, catching and exploding two mines – only to run on to a third, which exploded under one of them. She sank, her crew all rescued by the other trawler's. The accompanying picket boats proved slightly more effective, using grapnels to snag the mine cables and setting them off with small explosive charges. It was by far the best haul of mines so far, but it still only scratched the surface of the problem. Only two men were wounded that night. The next sweep, on the night of the 11th, was a complete fiasco: the trawlers simply fled when the Turks opened fire. Keyes was furious: 'How could they talk about being stopped by a heavy fire if they were not hit?' Churchill could not understand this either, signalling to Carden more than once that reasonable losses were both acceptable and expected. But neither he nor Keyes had ever been a civilian trawlerman suddenly exposed to blazing searchlights and murderous cannonades in the dark. On the 12th, permission arrived for putting a naval lieutenant as skipper aboard each trawler with three senior ratings to support him. There were scores of volunteers, enabling each battleship to part-man a trawler in this way. There was also another verbose signal, drafted by Churchill himself, to Carden, which ended: 'We will support you in well-conceived action for forcing a decision even if regrettable losses [are] entailed.' Keyes read this and at once commandeered a destroyer to take it personally to Mudros and hand it to Carden, who then returned to the Dardanelles. The French minesweepers had no success at all on the night of 12 March. De Robeck put the minesweeper problem down to inexperience among the fishermen manning the adapted trawlers. They did not seem to have any fear of mines 'though they do not seem to like working under gunfire, which is a new element in their calling'.

Carden and his staff decided on one more try on the night of the 13th, with navy men in direct command of the trawlers. The performance of the minesweepers was much more determined, but so was the gunfire from both shores, as the sweepers struggled against the current, as they turned and tried to put out their equipment and as they tried to sweep downstream. Battleships, cruisers and destroyers fired back copiously, to no noticeable effect. Only two out of seven sweepers were able to start work. One trawler was hit 84 times, though not by heavy shell, her crew saved by the steel-plate screens fitted as part of the conversion for sweeping. The five picket boats did better, cutting many mines loose which were later set off by rifle fire in daylight. The light cruiser *Amethyst* of the escort, however, deliberately drawing fire away from the trawlers, was hit by a heavy shell and suffered 24 dead and 36 wounded. Aboard the trawlers, the toll ran to just five killed and four wounded, but there was considerable damage: four minesweepers and one picket boat were put out of action. Carden decided to give up night sweeps. On 14 March Churchill, obviously still unaware that the trawlermen and their naval colleagues had put up their best performance so far, signalled to the admiral: 'I do not understand why minesweepers should be interfered with by firing which causes no casualties.' The First Lord, in a misguided attempt to lift Carden's spirits, added that the Admiralty had heard the forts were running out of ammunition and in 'despondent reports' German officers were asking for more. It was time to press on: 'The unavoidable losses must be accepted. The enemy is harassed and anxious now.' The last sentence contained at best an element of truth but read more like wishful thinking.

Carden responded stoutly enough to the signals urging him on by telling the Admiralty that he proposed to initiate an all-out attack, including a massive bombardment as well as minesweeping, by daylight on 17 March, weather permitting. He apparently remained confident that he could break through into the Sea of Marmara and requested fleet minesweepers (purpose-built or adapted naval vessels) to support his subsequent operations in the Marmara. Meanwhile he decided to use destroyers for the purpose temporarily, since more than a quarter of the trawlers had been sunk or knocked out. The Admiralty earmarked 30 more Suffolk trawlers as an interim reinforcement and ordered torpedo-boats from Suez to join Carden's fleet as minesweepers. Two old battleships he had detached for operations off Smyrna were called back to join him, raising his force back to its maximum of 18 battleships (including the four French) by 16 March. Two more from the Channel Fleet were ordered to stand by for detachment to the Aegean as possible reinforcements, in anticipation of losses. Commander C. R. Samson, RN, the distinguished naval air pioneer, was ordered with a squadron of 14 new, land-based naval aeroplanes to the Aegean via Marseilles to solve the observation problem that had plagued the whole Dardanelles operation; he and his aircraft would sail with General Hamilton on the *Phaeton* (see below). All these positive developments would have been of rather greater benefit had they been decided earlier. Carden's renewed suggestion that troops should land in strength on the peninsula at the same time as he mounted his great attack was met with the instruction to confer with the general who was coming out to take command of a force that would amount to 60,000 by 18 March (Kitchener's vacillation had ensured that the 29th Division would not be present in time).

Sir Ian Standish Monteith Hamilton, General Officer Commanding Home Forces, was working in his room at Horse Guards, London, on 12 March 1915 when a messenger arrived with a summons to Kitchener's office. The general was 62 years old, tall, slender, elegant and erudite, not the most useful attributes for popularity in the officers' mess. He had nevertheless distinguished himself in one of the British Army's many inconclusive entanglements in Afghanistan in 1878 and rose to be Kitchener's chief of staff at the end of the Boer War in 1901. His photographs give an effete impression. He was regarded by his peers as both passive and over-confident.

'We are sending a military force to support the fleet now at the Dardanelles, and you are to have command,' Kitchener told him, without preamble. In his *Gallipoli Diary* Hamilton drily noted: 'At that moment Kitchener wished me to bow, leave the room and make a start ... My knowledge of the Dardanelles was nil; of the Turk nil; of the strength of our own forces next to nil.' There had been no previous hint of the appointment. Kitchener looked up and barked, 'Well?' A reticent man, Kitchener was reluctant and curt when Hamilton started asking questions, but then opened up and became almost garrulous. Hamilton was told that he would have under command ANZAC (General Birdwood), the 29th (Major-General Hunter-Weston) and RN (Major-General Paris) divisions and a French division (*Général de division* d'Amade). Hamilton asked for four territorial divisions as well and was answered in the negative, with expletives. He also asked for submarines to stop the Turks supplying their forts by sea: a good idea but they were not in his chief's gift. He was told that his chief of staff would be Major-General W. P. Braithwaite.

When the latter joined other generals (who were as amazed as Hamilton by the appointments) in Kitchener's office, he asked for some of the latest army aircraft, to which Kitchener snapped: 'Not one!' The army's role in the Aegean, the field marshal said, was to be a 'second string', on the assumption that the navy would succeed: 'But if the admiral fails, then we will have to go in.' There were to be no piecemeal operations: the Mediterranean Expeditionary Force (MEF) was to be used as a whole and only on the European side of the strait. It would have no reserves of manpower (the normal practice on the Western Front was an initial extra allowance of 10 per cent for the inevitable casualties). Kitchener believed that once the fleet broke through and threatened Constantinople, there would hardly be any need to land troops anyway. The French and the Russians could be left to get on with occupying the city while British imperial troops controlled the railways and strategic points to south and west while the fleet dominated the Marmara, so that the 29th and RN divisions could be sent to France. Kitchener was a one-man band, unable to delegate yet with no interest in organised staffwork. His 'plans' for the MEF were vague to non-existent. At least Hamilton was able to dissuade him from tempting fate by naming the new command the Constantinople Expeditionary Force ... The Secretary for War, indulging his penchant for oracular pronouncements, terminated the interview with the words: 'If the fleet gets through, Constantinople will fall of itself and you will have won, not a battle but the war.'

Hamilton left London's Victoria station for Dover on a special train at five p.m. the next day. Churchill himself came to see him off. In his pack the general had a textbook on the Turkish Army dated 1912; a pre-war report on the Dardanelles defences from the late British naval mission; an out-of-date map; and two small guidebooks. He had no staff yet, apart from Braithwaite. Waiting at Dover was a destroyer with the unintentionally ironic name of HMS *Foresight* to take him to Calais. The port was, not inappropriately, fogbound for hours. Hamilton finally reached Calais at 10.30 p.m. and entrained for Marseilles, where the light cruiser *Phaeton* was waiting to take him on to the Aegean. He arrived at Tenedos, the small island between Lemnos and the Dardanelles used by the Allies as a forward base, at three p.m. on 17 March. Earlier in the day the *Phaeton* had passed another British cruiser conveying Vice-Admiral Carden in the opposite direction, to Malta.

The two commanders never met. Vice-Admiral Carden had been in pain for some days, and on 16 March doctors advised him to give up the command and take sick leave as a matter of urgency. The symptoms were similar to those of duodenal ulcers, their presence hardly surprising after the unaccustomed strain on an administrator of protracted and unsuccessful command of a very large fighting force. The problem of the succession was quickly resolved. There were two rear-admirals on hand: the senior, Rosslyn Wemyss, was in command at Mudros, the main base for Dardanelles operations, and could not be spared from a complex task; John de Robeck was however the obvious choice because he had been Carden's deputy, knew the plans, understood the problems and was well known in the fleet. Wemyss gracefully stood back as de Robeck was promoted over his head to acting vice-admiral on 17 March and ordered to take over, with Wemyss as his deputy, though remaining in charge of the vital task to expand the Mudros base as swiftly as possible. De Robeck was asked by the Admiralty if he approved of Carden's plan and was expressly given the choice to reject or amend it. He replied that it would go ahead unaltered and as intended on 18 March if the weather was suitable.

John Michael de Robeck was a scion of the Anglo-Irish nobility who joined the navy as an officer cadet at the usual age of 13 in 1875. A rear-admiral since 1911, he had begun the war as flag officer of the Cape Verde and Canary Islands station before his assignment as Carden's deputy in January 1915. Unlike his predecessor he was an imposing figure, tall and broad, popular with both superiors and inferiors and noted for his charm and resolve. He was younger than Hamilton. Keyes stayed on as chief of staff, a happier man now that a rather more convincing commander was in charge.

Vice-Admiral de Robeck implemented the reorganisation of the fleet prepared by Carden. The 18 battleships were once again in three divisions, but the second and third were enlarged. The First consisted as before of the four strongest ships, *Queen Elizabeth* (fleet flag) and *Inflexible*, the two dreadnoughts, in the first subdivision, and *Agamemnon* and *Lord Nelson* in the second. The Second Division now included eight older British battleships in three subdivisions of four, two and two, led by Captain Hayes-Sadler in HMS *Ocean*. The Third Division was led by Rear-Admiral Émile Paul Aimable Guépratte in *Suffren* (flag), and the three other French ships in the sixth subdivision, supported by two further British battleships in the seventh, placed under his flag. Carden's plan called for the attack to be opened by the First Division in Line A, starting some 14,000 yards from the Narrows forts, while Line B was formed by the French quartet. The seventh subdivision pair moved to flanking positions to cover both lines as they took it in turn to bombard the forts, the French advancing through the British line to fire at closer range from the limit of the swept area, so from about 8,000 yards. The minesweepers were ordered to start work under the big guns at the same time, after the first two hours of bombardment. The Second Division's third and fourth subdivisions plus the two flanking ships would relieve the French for the closest shelling. Picket boats were to dance attendance on the battleships, always on the lookout for floating mines. Planes would take off every hour to observe the fall of shot: their wireless sets could transmit but not receive. Troops from the RN Division were loaded on to seven transports to give the appearance of an imminent landing at the northern end of the Aegean coast of the peninsula. This feint was meant to draw enemy troops away from the scene of the attack.

The ships were to fire at six main forts which between them housed 42 guns of eight-inch or greater calibres, including six 14-inch. There was an unknown but doubtless profuse number of mobile batteries of howitzers and field guns on either side of the strait. All this and more was set out at a captains' conference chaired by de Robeck aboard his flagship, *Queen Elizabeth*, on the afternoon of 16 March. That night and the next, minesweepers swept the previously cleared area and found nothing new. Since Erenkeui Bay, a feature on the Asian side which offered extra sea-room for manoeuvre and turning, lay south of the innermost limit of sweeping it was not searched thoroughly. As far as the trawlermen were concerned, there were no mines in the Dardanelles before the notional 8,000-yard line chosen for the second stage of the bombardment.

General Hamilton managed to put together a staff of nine from army and marine officers on the 17th, when he was also conveyed to what he called 'that lovely sea monster, the *Queen Elizabeth*', anchored off Tenedos, for a meeting in the afternoon with de Robeck, Wemyss, Keyes, Guépratte, d'Amade, Braithwaite and an army staff captain, all of whom were junior in rank to the general. Hamilton thought de Robeck 'a fine-looking man with great charm', whose main worry was the concealed and mobile artillery which had frustrated the minesweepers. Other pressing concerns were the minefields themselves, and the anticipated arrival of German or Austrian submarines, whose potential had been so vividly illustrated by Norman Holbrook, VC, in *B11*. Although no notable activity had been seen ashore since the small-scale marine landings against the guns, it was quite clear that the Turks were working very hard on the defences during darkness: the results were plain to see each morning. Seaplanes were still having difficulty rising above extreme rifle range (800–1,000 yards): 'actually the d****d things can barely rise off the water'.

Hamilton went on to write in his diary:

[De Robeck] gave us ... to understand that German thoroughness and forethought have gripped the old go-as-you-please Turk and are making him march to the *Parade-Schritt* [Prussian goose-step] ...

The admiral would prefer to force a passage on his own, and is sure he can do so ... He has no wish to call us [troops] in until he has had a real good try.

Ironically, this of course reflected precisely Kitchener's assessment thus far of the role of the army at the Dardanelles. De Robeck asked to see Hamilton's orders. When Braithwaite, the army chief of staff, read out Kitchener's instructions to Hamilton with their vague generalisations and reservations, an astonished Commodore Keyes blurted: 'Is that all?' Hamilton admitted he had no means yet of landing a significant force – no transports, no lorries, no pack-horses, no mules. It would take weeks to assemble them. 'Here, the peninsula looks a tougher nut to crack than it did on Lord Kitchener's small and featureless map.' Keyes wrote that the recital of Kitchener's orders 'acted on us rather like a cold douche'.

Hamilton spent the night at Tenedos on HMS *Phaeton*. She left there for Mudros harbour, Lemnos, at four a.m. on 18 March, the day appointed for the great naval attack. The general inspected the shore facilities at daybreak – and found them gravely wanting for a force of 50,000 or more men. Offshore, however, 'I never saw so many ships collected together in my life.' He sent a message to Kitchener, saying that Alexandria would have to be the army's main base: the RN Division transports 'have been loaded up as in peacetime and they must be completely discharged and every ship reloaded in war fashion'. Lemnos could not cope with such a task. The cruiser then took Hamilton on a fast 60-mile run along the Aegean coast of the peninsula so he could see the terrain and possible landing sites. He noted the tangle of trenches already dug at key points on the coast before the ship put about:

> Sailing southwards we are becoming more and more conscious of the tremendous bombardment going on in the straits ... everyone excited and trying to look calm.

Captain Cameron of the *Phaeton* took his ship as close as he dared to the bombarding ships:

> We found ourselves on the outskirts of – dream of my life – a naval battle! ... The world had gone mad ... the elephant and the whale of Bismarckian parable were at it tooth and nail! Shells of all sizes flew hissing through the skies. Before my very eyes the graves of those old gods whom Christ had risen from the dead to destroy were shaking to the shock of Messrs Armstrong's patent thunderbolts!

A less exalted recollection of the Allied bombardment, probably the loudest noise heard in the Aegean since the volcanic explosion on the island of Thera (Santorini) in 1500 BC, was provided by Marine William Jones of the battleship *Prince George* to the Sound Archive of the Imperial War Museum in London. His ship, of the seventh subdivision, was flanking the French battleships as they attacked the forts:

> We got part way up the Dardanelles; the first ship that got sunk was the French ... *Bouvet* – she got struck by a mine, turned over and within minutes she was sunk.
>
> Carrying on further up the Dardanelles, we were getting shot at, missed quite a lot engaging guns, batteries and the like on the European and the Asiatic side. Further ahead of us was the *Ocean*, and the *Irresistible* ...
>
> All of a sudden, and ahead of us, there was this big explosion which caused the *Ocean* and the *Irresistible* to sink.

Marine Jones's memory tended to accelerate and telescope events, as we shall see. Engine Room Artificer Gilbert Adshead served aboard the *Lord Nelson* (he was below deck in the aft dynamo room which supplied the ship's electricity, but it had a ventilation shaft with an internal ladder leading up to the quarter-deck and was topped with a 'mushroom' cap offering slits to look through):

> To see that bombardment, never having seen demolition like that before, well, it seemed terrible to me at any rate because the forts seemed to be knocked completely down and we did silence most of the guns. And on our last operation when they had an all-out attack – every ship available – to see if we could definitely finish off the forts and make them surrender, we carried on but we lost about half a dozen ships that day. We lost … the *Bouvet* – I actually saw that, it was a terrible sight …
>
> We made very good progress and we stopped the forts firing, and we were astonished when … the Admiralty said that the naval ships were to no longer attack in the Dardanelles because we'd lost too many ships on this final operation … If we'd only carried on for a little while longer the Turks with their German assistants would have run up a white flag because we'd put so many guns out of action and they were very short of ammunition and they couldn't have carried on for much longer.

The future Captain Henry Mangles Denham, RN, was a newly promoted sub-lieutenant aboard HMS *Agamemnon*. He told one of the most bizarre stories of the bombardment: how Commander St Clair, the battleship's executive officer, ordered ratings to descend on ropes to paint the side of the ship facing away from the direction of fire.

> They were quite safe, the men who were painting, because they were on the disengaged side and they couldn't be hit, and at the time we didn't think it particularly unusual. We had to take the opportunity, and we only wanted half the armament manned, so it was quite logical for the other half, the safe side of the ship, to be painted.

Denham thought that Keyes, rather than Carden or even de Robeck, had been the driving force during the campaign. The 18-year-old was on the lookout in the crow's nest on 18 March and felt the impact of the hits on the ship below; he was profoundly shocked to witness the sudden death of the *Bouvet*.

The fleet had got on the move from Mudros from 8.15 a.m. It was a perfect early spring day with a gentle breeze, a little early haze that soon cleared and a cloudless sky. The minesweepers reported finding nothing new in the cleared zone up to four miles short of the Narrows. At 10.30 the *Agamemnon*, behind a destroyer screen, led the way for the First Division, which was flanked by the seventh subdivision, *Prince George* and *Triumph* on either side. Half an hour later the first Turkish howitzers opened up from north of Kum Kale on the Asian side. At 11.30 the battleships took up their initial firing positions seven miles short of the Narrows and started the bombardment. By this time mobile guns and howitzers were blazing away at the heavily armoured ships, which were in line abreast: *Queen Elizabeth* (flag) with de Robeck aboard nearest the European shore, next *Agamemnon*, then *Lord Nelson* and finally *Inflexible*. The flagship first targeted the fort Hamidieh I on the Asian shore, firing across her partners, which attacked various positions on the European side. All four were in action within ten minutes, laying down a deliberate fire, the forts apparently remaining silent while the hidden and movable guns did their irritating worst. At Çemenlik just below Chanak at the Narrows there was a great explosion at about noon as an ammunition store was hit. The fort was abandoned for the time being, as was Dardanos near by, a seaplane pilot reported.

Stand on the ramparts of the Çemenlik fort (now incorporated into an excellent naval museum) today and look across the Narrows and you are bound to see a few of the ships that make a total of about 60,000 passages per year through the straits – one every ten minutes. Many of them are huge tankers, sailing in ballast high out of the water towards the Black Sea or lying low as they return fully laden with oil or liquid gas towards the Mediterranean. The tankers, the bulk carriers for grain or minerals, the ugly container ships and the like are often much bulkier than any First World War battleship, yet they look manageably small at a distance of a mile or less against the cliffs on the European side. The bombarding warships four or more miles to the south-west therefore may not have appeared particularly fearsome as clouds of black smoke were thrown up by their funnels and their guns – until the shells roared in with a noise like an express train and detonated, usually harmlessly in earth but occasionally to more dramatic effect. Within the fort there lies an undetonated heavy naval shell, rusting away in front of the hole it bored into the stone of a thick wall. Many of the guns used in the defence are also on display, some with their breeches blown out.

At sea the gunnery directors and gunlayers found their view obscured by their own smoke, blown back upon them by the north-easterly breeze. But just after noon de Robeck called on the French squadron to pass through Line A as planned, to fire on the forts and batteries at closer range. By this time *Agamemnon* had taken a dozen hits from a six-inch howitzer battery of four guns firing accurately from the Asian shore behind her. The superstructure was badly damaged, causing the ship to turn full circle to throw off the Turks' aim, but she did not withdraw. At the other end of Line A the *Inflexible* was also taking half a dozen hits from a battery of four six-inch cannon, losing her wireless and suffering fierce fires in her upperworks all the way up to the foretop. So as not to throw out the French Line B as it passed by, the battlecruiser remained in position and maintained fire. De Robeck then ordered her out of the line.

Meanwhile the French *Suffren* and *Bouvet* moved up the Asian side, with *Gaulois* and *Charlemagne* advancing up the European, leaving the British in the middle of the strait, still firing at 14,000 yards. The French soon came under heavy fire in their turn as they advanced to 10,000 yards, then 9,000. By now the forts had joined in and were scoring hits on the French squadron: the *Gaulois* was badly damaged by an armour-piercing shell near her bow, causing Guépratte to ask a British light cruiser to stand by her. She slowed down, listed to starboard and started to go down by the bow but withdrew under her own power. The *Bouvet* had targeted the Namazieh fort opposite Chanak on the European side until the battered French flagship *Suffren* led her back out of the line at about 1.40 p.m.

Five minutes later the *Bouvet* was rocked by a great explosion that threw up a column of ochre and black smoke. Moments later there was another explosion aboard, presumably from a magazine. Destroyers raced to the rescue but she listed heavily, then turned turtle and sank out of sight within two minutes. More than 600 men were lost; *Agamemnon* took two score survivors aboard. Both British and French assumed the ship had succumbed to a lucky shot from a heavy shell, or even a shore-based torpedo. The forts were clearly not disabled; from time to time they fired, then ceased fire, then fired again, as if taunting their attackers. Several mines were spotted in the waters, some swept by the trawlers, two probably released by the *Bouvet* explosions, others apparently free-floating. Like periscopes in faraway northern waters, they seemed to be everywhere. Still the trawlers could not press forward under the hail of mobile artillery fire.

Meanwhile Hayes-Sadler in *Ocean* led the third subdivision of four battleships to relieve the withdrawing French. He took the right-hand station towards the Asian side, the *Vengeance* the left-hand, European side with *Albion* and *Irresistible* between them. *Swiftsure* and *Majestic* moved up on the flanks to relieve *Prince George* and *Triumph*. At about 3.15 p.m., however, an explosion was heard and seen alongside *Irresistible*, which began to list slowly. The third subdivision may have sailed too close to the Narrows and struck the last transverse line of mines, the tenth, or she may have been caught by the same, last-minute parallel line, the eleventh, laid by the *Nusret*, which accounted for the *Bouvet*. Hayes-Sadler pulled his line back; at just after four p.m. the *Inflexible*, still manoeuvring in her place at the right of Line A, struck another of *Nusret*'s mines in Erenkeui Bay with her starboard bow and began quite quickly to go down by the head. She made for Tenedos under her own power, the wounded taken off in a cutter. Ten minutes later the helplessly drifting *Irresistible*, dead in the water, hit a moored mine and began to list to starboard and go down by the stern. De Robeck ordered *Ocean* to stand by her as the bulk of the crew were rescued by a destroyer and a picket boat, Captain D. L. Dent, RN, having issued the order to abandon ship. Despite an unrelenting hail of fire, the destroyer *Wear* (Captain Christopher Metcalfe, RN) lifted 610 officers and men and delivered them to the flagship. Admiral de Robeck sent the *Wear* back with a message to Hayes-Sadler on the *Ocean*: he was to withdraw if he could not get a tow-line aboard the *Irresistible*. This failed, so the ship was left to drift in the hope she could be towed away after dark. De Robeck issued the general recall just after 5.30 p.m.

Obeying under heavy fire from the Asian forts, HMS *Ocean* hit a *Nusret* mine when she was about one mile from the hulk of the *Irresistible*. Water poured in through the hole on the starboard side and her steering jammed. A shell from shore also struck the starboard side, compounding the damage. An attempt to return to an even keel by flooding compartments on the port side failed to forestall or correct a list of 15 degrees to starboard. Three destroyers closed in, ignoring the shelling from both shores, and rescued the crew. The *Ocean* too was now abandoned. After dark, Hayes-Sadler returned to his crippled ship to rescue four men still trapped aboard and left her to float in mid-channel. Later in the evening the destroyers and minesweepers went back to try to clear a path and take the two old battleships in tow. Keyes went with them. No trace of either was found.

The tally for the day was 6 battleships knocked out of a fleet of 18 – a startling loss rate of 33 per cent, even higher if regarded as a part of the total of 16 battleships that had actually gone forward to bombard. The *Bouvet*, *Irresistible* and *Ocean* were sunk. The *Gaulois* was beached in a sinking condition. The *Suffren*, the gallant Guépratte's flagship, was badly damaged by shellfire and definitely *hors de combat* for the foreseeable future; the French *Charlemagne* had also been damaged by gunfire but needed no immediate help. The *Inflexible*, patched up by her crew as best they could, made it to Tenedos thanks to the brilliant seamanship of Captain R. F. Phillimore, RN. She was pumped out and more temporary repairs were effected before she limped to a shipyard at Malta under escort for a complete overhaul. This was surely a remarkable harvest for a last-minute afterthought of a minefield laid ten days before the great naval attack. 'It changed the course of history,' said Keyes. The six trawlers sent forward to sweep towards the Kephez Point line under the guns all turned and fled; only two managed to get their sweep out. The Allies had no idea what had done the main damage. Nor did they realise until after the war how little significant damage they had done themselves: two 14-inch guns and perhaps three other large guns had been knocked out; not one howitzer or mobile field gun of the minefield defences was damaged.

Such was the turning point of the struggle for the Dardanelles.

CHAPTER 8

Heads Roll

The Turks and Germans assumed that the attack had merely been broken off for the night. Proud, dazed yet relieved that they had almost all survived, the defenders surveyed the spectacular but militarily mostly ineffectual damage – the craters, the mounds of earth, the battered ramparts, the smashed buildings – caused by the unprecedented bombardment and wondered what the next day would bring. They immediately started work on shoring up and repairing such defences as they could. Ammunition was short, but almost certainly not as deficient as British naval intelligence liked to think at the time. The armour-piercing shells most capable of doing damage to ships were more depleted than other categories. The various historical sources – British, German, Turkish – disagree on how much was left. The widely accepted ironic legend that, had the Allied ships renewed their bombardment within hours or days, the Turks and Germans would soon have been completely out of armour-piercing ammunition is clearly false. Many ashore however believed it was only a matter of time, perhaps days, before the fleet came back and broke through. They also believed that it was the batteries that had inflicted the brunt of the damage on the attackers (true for two of the three French casualties): hardly anyone knew of the *Nusret*'s decisive contribution.

Major-General Jevad Pasha, Turkish commander of the straits forts, said shortly after the war:

> The morale of the troops was excellent after the bombardment of March 18. They were prepared for and expected another attack. If the fleet had got through, I do not consider they [*sic*] could have done any good. They could have got through to Constantinople but we had an army there and we could have closed the straits behind them.

Just before the great bombardment, morale in Constantinople had been rather lower. A British informant in the city reported early in March that the government was preparing to move to Konya, a town on the Baghdad

Railway, some 250 miles (400 km) south-east of Constantinople in central southern Anatolia. Ministry archives had been transferred there. The Ottoman and German commercial banks evacuated their gold and cash reserves. Rich Turkish families had left the city or sought protection from German or Austrian friends. The Central Powers' ambassadors sent the families of their staff home by rail. Special trains and boats were on standby to evacuate the Sultan, ministers and other key officials. Ambassador Wangenheim had a plan to withdraw to Berlin if the Dardanelles were forced. In the other direction new guns and ammunition were pouring into the city by train from Germany via neutral Romania and Bulgaria and the Danube from the Czech munitions factories. The German crews of *Yavuz* and *Midilli* were confined to their ships, which were on short notice to move against an intrusion into the Marmara, despite the mine damage to the former. Two torpedo-boats nervously patrolled the Bosporus and the waters round the city for submarines.

Vice-Admiral de Robeck was understandably depressed on the evening of 18 March; he had lost three capital ships and another three had been incapacitated. He expected to be dismissed at once. After describing the day's events in his first report to the Admiralty on 19 March he wrote:

> It therefore appears damage inflicted was due to drifting mines.
> With the exception of ships lost and damaged, squadron is ready for immediate action but the plan of attack must be reconsidered and means found to deal with floating mines …

But: British casualties were fewer than 150 men (50 killed) out of some 15,000 engaged; two more old battleships, HMSs *Queen* and *Implacable* from the Channel Fleet, superior to the lost ships they would replace, were already on their way, approaching Malta; two more veterans, *London* and *Prince of Wales*, would follow; the French were sending the *Henri IV*, already at Suez, to replace the *Bouvet*. The Admiralty, Churchill to the fore, was still optimistic, even though (or perhaps even because) Fisher had once predicted the loss of a dozen battleships if the navy acted alone. Churchill sent the First Sea Lord a comforting message saying, 'As long as the crews are saved, there is no cause for serious regret.' Keyes still believed a breakthrough was possible. The 'only' obstacle was the minefield, which could surely be dealt with by a reorganisation of sweeping and more powerful and suitable sweepers – specifically adapted destroyers.

But Generals Hamilton and Birdwood, both of whom had witnessed the naval assault, were less sanguine about the navy's prospects. Hamilton telegraphed to Kitchener on the 19th:

> I am being most reluctantly driven to the conclusion that the straits are not likely to be forced by battleships as at one time seemed probable and that, if my troops are to take part, it will not take the subsidiary form anticipated. The Army's part will be more than mere landings of parties to destroy forts, it must be a deliberate and progressive military operation carried out at full strength so as to open a passage for the Navy.

Churchill reported on developments at the Dardanelles to the War Council on 19 March, on the basis of the first telegram from de Robeck. It was too soon for a final assessment, he said, but he was willing, if the Council agreed, to instruct the admiral 'to use his discretion in continuing the operations'. He had been informed that the Turks were running out of ammunition and mines, he added. The 29th Division was due in Alexandria on 2 April.

Kitchener summarised what he had been told by Hamilton. He agreed with his commander on the spot that Alexandria would have to be used as the British Army's main base as it had all the facilities lacking at Mudros. The French division could use the facilities of Port Said on the Suez Canal before being shipped to Mudros. All this implied a wait of at least a month for the army to get ready. The meeting agreed that Churchill should inform de Robeck that he could continue the operations at the Dardanelles if he thought fit. The admiral's subsequent telegrams on the 20th and as late as the afternoon of the 21st showed him willing, even eager, to renew the assault as soon as possible, weather permitting. The weather however was not in permissive mood as persistent north-easterly gales blew from the 19th every day to the 24th.

On the morning of 22 March de Robeck and his staff invited Hamilton and his staff to a conference in his stateroom on the *Queen Elizabeth*. Hamilton recalled:

> The moment we sat down de Robeck told us he was now quite clear he could not get through without the help of all my troops ... So there was no discussion. At once we turned our faces to the land scheme.

As the army needed time to prepare and reorganise at Alexandria, and pending the arrival of the 29th Division at the beginning of the month, there could be no full-scale land operation before 14 April.

Why had de Robeck changed his mind overnight? According to his evidence to the Dardanelles Commission, there were two factors behind his decision: the mines; and Hamilton's uncompromising advice on 22 March that success would simply not be possible unless by means of a combined operation. It is fair to add that he was profoundly affected by the losses of ships under his flag. He reported his decision to the Admiralty on 23 March: 'Having met General Hamilton ... I consider a combined operation essential.'

Predictably Keyes, who missed some of the meeting because he was visiting the minesweepers, was distraught. He implored his chief to renew the attack as soon as the minesweeping had been reorganised around eight 'Beagle'-class coal-burning destroyers (which however would not be ready for their new role until 4 April). There were volunteers aplenty from the crews of the lost battleships. The trawlermen were being sent home. He thought the mines could be swept on or about 4 April, whereupon the Allied fleet could enter the Sea of Marmara, destroy the Turkish fleet, stop the seaborne supplies to the forts and artillery (there being no roads worthy of the name on the peninsula) ... The fiery commodore did not indicate how the navy could dispose of the mobile batteries at the Narrows that had been covering the minefields so effectively. De Robeck had concluded that he could not safely land troops in enough strength inside the strait to tackle the peninsular artillery directly: this would have to be done from the southern and western coasts of the peninsula by an advance overland. But the admiral was generous enough to allow Keyes to return to London as late as October to plead for a renewed naval attack, even though the two men had disagreed fundamentally about the way forward after 18 March.

Back in London in March, Churchill, still calling for a continuation of the navy-only assault, was all but isolated. The fact that the men on the spot – admiral and general – regarded a combined operation as the only way to proceed was decisive for everyone at the Admiralty except the First Lord (and his loyal Naval Secretary, Commodore Charles de Bartolomé). Fisher, the admirals in the War Group, the Sea Lords and the staff were now totally and outspokenly opposed to the continuation of the unsupported naval assault. Even Asquith, who knew nothing at all about strategy or naval warfare, and the other ministers were opposed. Kitchener of course now supported his man Hamilton and the latter's plan for a combined operation with the army in the lead.

Churchill tried to persuade de Robeck to press ahead without waiting for the army, but his notorious overbearing style did not work as well by wireless as it did in person. (Fisher, not a shy figure, complained that he would take a clear, well-buttressed opinion into a meeting with Churchill and emerge with his mind changed, a fact which he usually rued afterwards. In his *Room 40* Patrick Beesly cites a revealing anecdote from Admiral Sir Reginald Hall, Director of Naval Intelligence in 1914–18, about Churchill's power of persuasion, so extraordinary 'that again and again tired Admiralty officials were hypnotised … into accepting opinions which differed vastly from those they normally held'. Hall dealt with this as follows: 'I began to mutter to myself, "my name is Hall, my name is Hall …"' Challenged by Churchill to explain, Hall replied: 'I am saying to myself that my name is Hall because if I listen to you much longer, I shall be convinced it's Brown.')

Hall had taken a direct hand in the Dardanelles campaign by sending two agents to Bulgaria in January 1915 to try to bribe Talaat Bey, the CUP Minister of the Interior and close ally of Enver, through intermediaries to break the German connection and give the Royal Navy free passage through the Dardanelles. The agents were empowered to offer £3 million, with leeway to go up to £4 million (multiply by about 65 for today's values). The Turks politely strung the agents along and made encouraging noises; but when Hall told Churchill and Fisher what he was doing, Fisher ordered him to desist. After the defeat of 18 March the Cabinet suggested Hall try again, but Albion, thief of dreadnoughts, was now classified as incurably perfidious by the Turks and it was too late.

The First Lord wrote a lengthy memorandum to de Robeck which amounted to an order to continue, rather than an argument in favour, but given the general opinion of the War Council, the unanimous opposition of both commanders on the spot and all senior naval officers concerned (except Keyes), he did not send it. On 28 March Churchill (unintentionally prophetic) asked de Robeck what would happen if the army failed. The admiral had no answer beyond saying that the fleet would still be very much in being and could mount another attack: he could not however afford to let the strait be closed behind him by the Turks and therefore needed the army to keep it open by suppressing enemy artillery.

Kitchener and Hamilton were henceforward in charge of both strategy and timetable. The army was calling the shots, and de Robeck accepted that the fleet would fulfil only a secondary, supporting role until further notice. The War Council met briefly on 6 April to hear Churchill read from de Robeck's full report; the First Lord again pressed for an early resumption by the fleet without waiting for the soldiers. Five weeks later, on 9 May, de Robeck reported in effect that the army had failed: should the fleet try again? Nobody in London said yes, not even Churchill, who finally gave up on the navy-only approach. The War Council's next full meeting was only on 15 May, the first in two months. Churchill announced that he and Fisher had sent de Robeck a message (their last jointly signed telegram) on the 13th saying that 'the moment for a renewal of a naval attempt to force the Dardanelles had past [*sic*] and was not likely to arise again'. Such was Churchill's personal admission of defeat. He told the Council:

> If we had known three months ago that an army of from 80 to 100,000 men would now be available for the attack on the Dardanelles, the naval attack would never have been undertaken. Three months ago, however, it was impossible to foresee this.

Kitchener was both defensive and disingenuous in his reply:

> When the Admiralty proposed to force the passage of the Dardanelles by means of the fleet alone, I doubted whether the attempt would succeed, but was led to believe it possible by the First Lord's statements of the power of the *Queen Elizabeth* and the Admiralty staff paper showing how the operations were to be conducted ...
>
> I considered that, though there was undoubtedly risk, the political advantages to be gained by forcing the Dardanelles were commensurate ... I realised that if the fleet failed ... the army would have to be employed to help the navy through. I regret I was led to agree in [*sic*] the enterprise by the statements made, particularly as to the power of the *Queen Elizabeth*, of [*sic*] which I had no means of judging.

By this time, the army was already bogged down on the Gallipoli peninsula. Kitchener complained that the Admiralty had withdrawn the *Queen Elizabeth* to her allotted place in the Grand Fleet some weeks after 18 March: 'I never for a moment thought it possible that, if the army was employed on the Gallipoli Peninsula to help them, the Admiralty would withdraw the principal naval unit on which they and we relied.' This was a strange complaint, given that the army was ashore precisely because the biggest naval guns of their time had proved incapable of doing the job! But we are getting ahead of ourselves.

The immediate cause of the defeat of the Royal Navy and its loyal French ally in their attempt to break into the Sea of Marmara was the defensive minefield system combined with the artillery and searchlights protecting it, and the impotence of the sweepers deployed against it. The idea of using powerfully engined destroyers with disciplined sailors and guns instead of unarmed wooden trawlers with civilian crews came too late. The mine as a weapon had been grievously underestimated despite its successes in the Russo-Japanese War of 1904–5, which several Royal Navy officers present at the Dardanelles had witnessed as observers. Fear of the torpedo was much greater in the fleet, despite the fact that U-boats did not take a hand in the campaign until several weeks after the climactic naval bombardment. The well-protected minefield proved to be a much more intractable defence than the fixed guns in the forts or even the mobile batteries directed at the ships.

Admiral Wemyss at Mudros was not alone in regarding those running the war in London as a bunch of ill-informed amateurs. There was no proper staffwork at Admiralty or War Office, both run by strong-willed personalities. There had been no proper planning or discussion or co-ordination between navy and army. Hamilton ruefully acknowledged this pervasive spirit of shambolic amateurism in his *Gallipoli Diary*:

> On the German system plans for a landing on Gallipoli would have been in my pocket, up to date and worked out to a ball cartridge and a pail of water. By the British system (?) I have been obliged to concoct my own plans in a brace of shakes almost under fire ... in matters of supply, transport, organisation and administration our way is the way of Colney Hatch.

The sardonic question mark in the above is Hamilton's own; Colney Hatch was a notorious lunatic asylum north of London, reclassified in 1918 as a mental hospital. We noted above the pathetic collection of 'intelligence material' the general carried in his kit on the way from London to the Aegean.

As Tim Travers puts it in *Gallipoli 1915*, the war leadership 'simply indulged in a Darwinian struggle for control of operations'. Asquith was a weak and passive leader. Hankey, the Secretary of the War Council, was in many ways the most acute member of it but even he produced his own plans without consultation. Even so, the idea of the flank attack on Turkey via the Dardanelles, generally accepted as the best strategic idea of the war, originated with him rather than Churchill, who immediately saw its worth, took it up with enthusiasm and unfortunately chose the wrong way to implement it.

It is not mere hindsight that enables us to conclude that the whole idea of relying on the battleships to force the strait without full army support was a fundamental blunder: all the authorities, naval, military, strategic, believed from the lesson of Duckworth's expedition in 1807 onwards that the only way to do it was through a combined operation. There were also the more recent lessons provided by the Japanese siege of Port Arthur in 1904 and the attack on German Tsingtao ten years later. Even Churchill believed in a combined operation until Kitchener insisted there were no troops available, whereupon the First Lord lost patience and almost single-handedly forced through his navy-only strategy. Kitchener's U-turn after three weeks of dithering over the dispatch of the 29th infantry division also came too late: in the end the army was not ready until 24 April 1915. And when it was, the idea of a full-blown combined operation against the Dardanelles, if it had even been seriously considered after the naval failure, was abandoned as the navy fell back into a subsidiary role, providing escort, delivery and shore-bombardment services for the army. The failure from the outset to opt for a combined operation, or to wait until one became possible, and the consequent separation of the naval attack from the be-lated army invasion of the peninsula entitles us to see the Gallipoli military disaster as the first *consequence* of the failure of the fleet.

But before taking our narrative ashore on to the peninsula we need to consider the political consequences of the navy's failure to deliver Chur-chill's undertaking to break through the Dardanelles into the Sea of Mar-mara with a fleet unsupported on land. They were profound: Turkish morale soared; by their own assessment and Churchill's, the Germans gained two years' extra capacity to endure in what turned out to be a four-year war; several states in southern Europe decided which side they were on; in London heads rolled and the government was reconstructed; and a normally deferential, unquestioningly patriotic British press began to complain of 'bungling in high places'. These trends would only be strengthened by the course of the Gallipoli land campaign which began on 25 April 1915 and had stalled by 9 May, though it would endure for many months yet as a smaller-scale but even more intense offshoot of the Western Front.

Fisher, who had never been wholly convinced by Churchill's advocacy of a navy-only attack but supported his chief out of loyalty and gratitude for his reappointment in 1914, reverted to his main concern, the Germans in the North Sea, after the failure of 18 March. Britain had declared a total maritime blockade of Germany on 1 March in response to the increased U-boat threat, even though goods for Germany could still be delivered to neutral Scandinavian and Dutch ports: neither side wanted to provoke the non-belligerent United States. For the old admiral, when it came to the British margin of superiority over the Imperial High Seas Fleet there was no such thing as enough, and he felt increasingly uneasy about the fleet of 16 battleships, 4 light cruisers and 24 destroyers, the latter of greatest value, still sitting in the Aegean with an array of auxiliary vessels. The battleships were mostly elderly but were the bulk of Britain's naval reserve of last resort against the Germans; Fisher tried to ensure that de Robeck's most modern ships, the *Queen Elizabeth, Lord Nelson* and *Agamemnon*, were kept out of operations inside the strait. Nervousness at the Admiralty about the North Sea was exacerbated by signs at the end of March that the German fleet was about to come out, a plan abandoned when a sharp increase in British naval wireless traffic indicated to the Germans that the Grand Fleet was itself preparing a foray. British diplomats and spies in The Hague learned at about this time that Germany was exerting enormous pressure on her Dutch neighbour to enter the war on the side of the Central Powers. The War Office considered landing troops at the Hook of Holland and the Admiralty looked at establishing a destroyer and submarine base on the Dutch Frisian island of Terschelling; the Dutch scare however faded by mid-April.

But by the end of March the Germans had set up their U-boat flotilla at Zeebrugge with their first small coastal and new mine-laying types of submarines, shipped in sections to the Belgian coast by rail and assembled at Antwerp. Elsewhere U-boats sank 29 merchant ships totalling 90,000 tons around Britain in March, more in a single month than in the whole of the war so far – an uncomfortable portent.

The navy's failure to break through the Dardanelles and its military consequences cost its political and operational chiefs their jobs. But whereas the former had to be pushed, the latter defenestrated himself, and rather messily at that, bringing a sad end to a unique career.

It is difficult to keep track of the number of occasions on which the excitable and emotional John Arbuthnot Fisher threatened to resign after the First World War broke out, but there were at least seven before the great setback of 18 March: we saw how Kitchener had to persuade him not to walk out of the War Council. He had risen from the lowest to the highest in his beloved Royal Navy, a fighting admiral with extraordinary courage, administrative ability and energy – a rare combination indeed. He was 40 when appointed captain of the most powerful battleship of the day, HMS *Inflexible* (not to be confused with the Dardanelles casualty), in 1881. He distinguished himself in action in China and Egypt. A rear-admiral in 1892, he joined the Board of Admiralty as Third Sea Lord and *ex officio* Controller of the Navy, responsible for the design and construction of ships. In his five years in the post Fisher introduced the water-tube boiler and the destroyer (originally known as the 'torpedo-boat destroyer') to the fleet, and initiated a large ship-construction programme. A rare career failure was his appointment as naval delegate to the first Hague Peace Conference in 1899, where he most undiplomatically spoke his mind: 'moderation in war is imbecility' was just one of his blunt 'sound-bites'. This did not prevent him from becoming commander-in-chief of the Mediterranean Fleet, the navy's plum command, later the same year for three years, during which he introduced far-reaching, modernising reforms that were spread across the entire navy when he became First Sea Lord in 1904, aged 63.

The leitmotiv of his six hectic years in this supreme office was preparation for what he correctly foresaw (remarkable foresight was another of his many gifts) as the inevitable war with Germany, which was expanding its navy at an alarming rate. Among his innovations were the 'all-big-gun ship' (HMS *Dreadnought*, built in a year and armed with ten 12-inch guns), making all other battleships in the world, including Britain's, obsolete at a stroke in 1906; its faster but less well-armoured sister, the battlecruiser (HMS *Invincible* with eight 12-inch guns was the prototype), to scout for the battlefleet and lead it into action; a ruthlessly pruned reserve fleet with core crews of 40 per cent strength to be filled out in time of war; concentration of Britain's naval power against Germany; a rapid switch to oil propulsion from coal; better gunnery training; submarines; the Royal Naval Air Service. Fees were abolished at officer-cadet schools; conditions were markedly improved for the lower deck; merit began to displace privilege as ground for promotion.

Fisher's reforms mostly kept pace with the speed and scope of advances in naval technology and weapons but aroused a powerful conservative opposition within the upper reaches of the navy, led by Admiral Lord Charles Beresford, commander-in-chief of the Channel Fleet from 1907, no match for Fisher in professional attainment but a charmer with a taste for office politics writ large. This is not the place to go into the details of a complicated dispute which split the service and in which Fisher's own conduct was arrogant, ruthless and devious: suffice it to say that as a result of the constant feuding he resigned as First Sea Lord in January 1910, aged 69 and with a barony. He had been the driving force behind the strengthened fleet that eventually overcame the unprecedented maritime threat from Germany, a priceless legacy overriding his many faults and failures. Churchill thought that Fisher had been right in nine-tenths of what he fought for and brought him back in 1914 in the hope of more of the same from an admiral of the fleet who, however, was now 74.

Churchill was 33 years younger but had already built up an impressive record. Grandson of a duke and son of a Cabinet minister, he served in Africa as a cavalry subaltern and was a press correspondent in the South African War at the end of the century, when he escaped from Boer captivity with a price on his head, before entering parliament as a Conservative in 1900. He 'crossed the floor' to join the ruling Liberals in 1906 and was rewarded with a junior ministry before advancing to President of the Board of Trade and the Cabinet in 1908, then to Home Secretary aged 36 in 1910. In late October of the following year he became First Lord of the Admiralty – a post he had declined in 1908. He had got to know Fisher in 1907 and began as a result to take a real interest in naval affairs, sharing the admiral's certainty about war with Germany but falling out with him early in 1911 over the mounting cost of the dreadnought programme, which was drawing funds away from the social reforms the Liberal Cabinet wanted to introduce. At the Admiralty however he strove for a further strengthening of the navy against the German challenge, introduced a rudimentary naval staff and proved as keen as Fisher had been on technical innovation, especially aviation, and improvements in conditions of service.

His single greatest contribution to the welfare of the nation by the time war broke out lay in working with First Sea Lord Battenberg to ensure the navy was ready for war, by sending the Grand Fleet to Scapa Flow just before it began and keeping the reserve fleet fully manned after the providential naval review at the end of July 1914. Though ridiculed for his intervention in the abortive attempt to save Antwerp, Churchill's efforts helped to delay the Germans long enough to enable the Allied line in Flanders to stabilise itself. His stamina, energy, self-confidence and persuasive powers led him to intervene in the tiniest matters of operational detail at the Admiralty. Unable to delegate and unabashed by his own technical ignorance, he poured out an endless stream of ideas and initiatives in memoranda and telegrams which in the end drove Fisher and many others to distraction. He was intolerant of fools, whose number clearly included most of his ministerial colleagues, and appeared to believe that he should be in charge of the entire conduct of the war. He seized upon Maurice Hankey's suggestion of a flanking strategy, using Britain's maritime strength, which he controlled, against the weak point in the position of the Central Powers that Turkey represented. The mediocrity of its execution and consequent failure was a disaster for Churchill as well as the Allied cause, and would have destroyed the career of anyone else.

The two men at the top of the Admiralty formed a mutual admiration society but could hardly have been more different. Fisher's formidable energy was waning through age and had to be husbanded by an early-to-bed, early-to-rise regime; he did his best work in the morning. The much younger Churchill already had the self-indulgent habits that became famous during the Second World War, rising late, snoozing after lunch, eating a convivial, daunting dinner washed down with copious quantities of alcohol and working until the early hours. The flow of ideas often peaked just when most people had gone to bed after a tiring day, which meant that Fisher found challenging notes from his chief on his desk when he got to his office, often before dawn. It is mildly surprising that they managed to meet so often as their working days barely overlapped. Fisher was particularly annoyed by Churchill's pre-emptive habits. The First Lord clearly regarded 'consultation' as a process that took place between a decision and its implementation, as so many modern politicians do. Fisher, who was constitutionally entitled to initiate operational proposals and put them to the First Lord for approval, found himself faced with a *fait accompli* almost on a daily basis, with which he felt he had to concur out of loyalty. This went against nature for a natural autocrat with far better and deeper technical knowledge of naval matters than his political chief, who did not shrink from firing off long and detailed orders to admirals like the passive Carden. Fisher was frequently driven to thoughts, and not infrequently threats, of resignation. In the end Churchill's impetuosity precipitated both men out of office.

By the second week of May 1915 the army had incurred nearly 20,000 casualties at Gallipoli, the equivalent of an entire division and more. Hamilton wanted reinforcements and extra ammunition. De Robeck cautiously signalled the Admiralty that he was contemplating another major naval effort. But he was about to lose a squadron of four old battleships to counter the Austrians in the Adriatic. Churchill and Fisher on 11 May discussed a limited operation to clear a new section of the Dardanelles minefield and provoke the defence into wasting its ammunition. Fisher suspected Churchill still wanted to rush the strait and opposed any major naval initiative. The result was a compromise: de Robeck was ordered on 13 May to seek express permission from London before undertaking any new operation. The night before the final abandonment of a leading role for the navy at the Dardanelles, the old battleship *Goliath* was sunk in a fog by a Turkish torpedo-boat with a largely German crew. Some 570 sailors drowned in the kind of tragedy Fisher was most concerned to avoid: the loss of an entire trained crew. This was a reminder of the vulnerability of battleships to torpedoes, whether fired by surface vessels or U-boats: they struck the hull below the heavy belt of armour round a ship's vitals, the same lightly protected area beneath which mines detonated. The Allies were aware that U-boats were on their way or already in the eastern basin of the Mediterranean and the Adriatic. On land the British Army suffered more losses in abortive attacks on the Western Front – and a new crisis was developing over the acute shortage of shells (and high proportion of duds), which now became a major scandal prompting more attacks on the 'bunglers in high places'.

At this bleak juncture Fisher, shocked by the *Goliath* catastrophe, announced the withdrawal from the Aegean of the *Queen Elizabeth*, to be replaced by two more old battleships plus two of the new monitors, each equipped with 14-inch guns. Kitchener went to the Admiralty on the 12th and objected to the recall of the super-dreadnought, describing it as a desertion. Fisher exploded: he threatened to walk out of the Admiralty never to return unless the ship left for home and the North Sea that very night. Churchill consented, without enthusiasm, and that evening de Robeck ordered her out of the Aegean in response to the Admiralty's telegram. It was a purely operational decision, and Fisher had every right to make it, and indeed to expect the First Lord's unconditional consent, if not approval.

Two evenings later, Churchill paid a brief visit to Fisher's office before dinner. As the two men normally got on very well, it was an amiable half-hour's conversation on routine questions of supply and replacements in the Aegean. As usual the admiral went to bed early. When he returned to his office at about dawn on 15 May, there were no fewer than four notes from Churchill, containing decisions on operational matters. He wanted to send two of the latest submarines to the Aegean, then two big 15-inch howitzers, extra 9.2-inch guns and more monitors. This was too much for the First Sea Lord, who had gone to bed thinking everything had been settled, only to find, as so often, that one could never be sure when it came to Churchill and the Dardanelles. For the ninth time Fisher announced his resignation, and this time he was going to make it stick. He told the Chancellor of the Exchequer, David Lloyd George, of his intention; the Chancellor told Asquith, who immediately sent a note to the admiral, ordering him in the King's name to stay in place. Fisher went to see him and said he would not be dissuaded. Churchill himself could not talk him out of it this time. In a note on the 16th even more excitable than usual, littered with capital letters and underlinings and exclamations, Fisher accused his chief of still being intent on driving the fleet through the Dardanelles: 'I know you so well ... *You will remain.* I SHALL GO. It is better so.' He stayed in his official apartments at Admiralty Arch, determined this time to keep out of reach of Churchill's overwhelming persuasiveness and planning to get away to his friend the Duke of Hamilton's estate in Scotland.

The Prime Minister and the Foreign Secretary, Grey, urged him to sit tight and say nothing. The shell crisis was about to bring down the Liberal government and Asquith felt obliged to form a coalition Cabinet with the Conservatives in order to stay in power. Could this mean that Churchill would not be in the new administration, or at least not at the Admiralty? Fisher seemed to weaken: he might stay on, he indicated, if neither Churchill nor Balfour, whom he disliked intensely, became First Lord. Meanwhile Churchill on 17 May chose the excessively malleable Admiral of the Fleet Sir Arthur Wilson to replace Fisher, a choice which appalled Jellicoe, the Grand Fleet commander, who described Churchill as a 'danger to the empire' (Wilson accepted the offer but changed his mind on the 19th). Later on the 17th, Room 40 discovered that the High Seas Fleet was about to deploy in the North Sea arena. Fisher was told but still refused to return to duty, believing that the Germans were not about to make a major foray (in fact some battlecruisers came out, but only as distant cover for a large mine-laying operation near the Dogger Bank; the Grand Fleet came out too, but the Germans very soon turned for home). The Second Sea Lord,

Admiral Sir Frederick Hamilton, stood in at the operations room. The King, the Prime Minister and his government and the Admiralty classed Fisher's absence as desertion because his resignation had not yet been accepted. Some spluttered that he should be taken out and shot; but they all still wanted him to stay.

The news of the resignation leaked into the public domain on 18 May, and the entire national press urged him to remain: he should be made First Lord himself, on the model of Kitchener and the War Office. Most admirals wanted him to stay as the only man who could at least stand up to Churchill, if not restrain his wilder ideas. Buoyed up by the great breadth and depth of sympathy and support for him, Fisher finally overreached himself, setting out six imperious conditions for staying on in a long memorandum to Asquith on 19 May. No Churchill, no Balfour, no Wilson; the new First Lord to be kept out of operational matters, which must be wholly reserved to Fisher, along with appointments, dockyards and establishments; disband the RN Division, bring the two 'Nelsons' back from the Aegean; more mines, more aircraft …

Asquith simply concluded that the old admiral was out of his mind, at least temporarily, but still refused to accept his resignation. He let Fisher know through an intermediary on 22 May that Churchill would not be First Lord in the new Cabinet. Sympathisers including Hankey advised the admiral to go away on leave before he completely destroyed himself. Asquith let him go to Scotland, even though he had still not accepted the admiral's resignation. But when Arthur Balfour was appointed First Lord of the Admiralty that very day, everybody in the know recognised that this would be the last straw for Fisher, who would never work under the Tory veteran. Asquith therefore finally accepted his resignation later on 22 May. It was a sad and embarrassing ending to the glorious career of the Royal Navy's greatest modern leader.

Winston Churchill was informed on 17 May of Asquith's plan to form a coalition government, preferably without him. The Conservatives expressly wanted the turncoat Churchill excluded from the Admiralty, especially if Fisher was not going to be there as a restraining influence. The King favoured the appointment of Balfour. Churchill held out for the War Office if he could not keep the Admiralty; he tried to persuade Fisher to stay on with a seat in the Cabinet if he could only stay on at the head of the navy, behaving as if he and not Asquith were forming a government. Fisher, still avoiding a direct encounter with his old chief, said no three times: he was not coming back in any capacity unless his arrogant conditions were accepted (which he must have known could not happen; indeed it is possible that he produced them as a way of burning his boats, to ensure that his resignation was accepted). On 21 May Churchill conceded defeat and recognised that Asquith would not reappoint him. Retaining his dignity, he condescended to accept the post of Chancellor of the Duchy of Lancaster, a Cabinet sinecure. The press and the admirals were openly delighted with the fall of the pushy young minister: only the *Observer* predicted that he would be back, that 'his hour of triumph will come'.

Admiral Sir Henry Jackson, aged 60, was appointed First Sea Lord.

CHAPTER 9

The Gallipoli Campaign

Hamilton, on his arrival in the Aegean, was contemplating a landing on the western side of the neck of the Gallipoli peninsula, at the Bulair line. As the *Phaeton* conveyed him along the coast of the peninsula and up the Gulf of Xeros towards Bulair at its neck, he could not fail to notice that every part of a generally difficult coastline where the ground was even remotely suitable for a landing had already been fortified, at least by trenches and barbed wire. He soon concluded that Kitchener's theory of a landing at Bulair, forcing the Turks to evacuate the peninsula and retire towards Constantinople, was baseless: their infantry and artillery were being supplied by sea on the Marmara side. If the peninsula is viewed as a pistol pointing at Constantinople, Suvla on the Aegean coast is the point at which the stock turns into the handle. Below Bulair and above Suvla Point there was almost nowhere suitable for a large-scale landing; below it there were several beaches open enough for invasion, particularly at the end of the 'butt' from Tekke Burnu round Cape Helles to Morto Bay on the strait side.

Apart from the two battalions of Royal Marines and the 3rd Australian Brigade, already camping out at Mudros, Hamilton decided that all troops were to assemble at Alexandria (the French at Port Said), where their supply ships would be emptied and refilled or, in modern parlance, 'combat-loaded', so that their contents were stored in the correct order – last in, first out – for supporting an opposed landing by troops. This was a logistical and logical principle new to the Admiralty's Director of Transport, Graeme Thomson, a civilian shipping expert appointed by Churchill against the advice of his admirals and the Secretary to the Admiralty, Sir Graham Greene. The Aegean Squadron also had to prepare for its new role of supporting operations on land, all of which meant that the enemy had several more weeks to get ready and that there was no possibility of strategic, and not much of tactical, surprise.

As Turkish Minister of War and commander-in-chief, Enver Pasha expected the Allied fleet to return as soon after 18 March as the weather allowed. So did the inspector-general of the army, Otto Liman von Sanders. Soon after the withdrawal of the enemy ships on the 18th Enver asked Liman to his office and appointed him commander of the forces defending the Dardanelles – the Turkish Fifth Army. The two men had been at serious odds over Enver's dispositions, which had placed penny-packets of troops on each side of the strait under separate European and Asian commands. Until February there had been only one infantry division in the vicinity, divided into small detachments based at Bulair, Gaba Tepe on the Aegean coast south of Suvla, Maidos (now Eçeabat) opposite Chanak at the Narrows, Cape Helles at the southern tip of the peninsula and at Kum Kale, facing Helles on the Asian shore. On 19 February a second division arrived, so that there could now be one division on each side of the strait. If the Allies were indeed coming ashore, it was highly likely that they would land simultaneously on both sides. Liman had been arguing for drawing a line *across* the waterway rather than along it, with an integrated single command for the whole area under threat of invasion, and the autocratic Enver wanted to get rid of him. But the situation had become much more urgent in the light of the great bombardment and the apparent likelihood of its renewal. Given the command, Liman determined to do it his way and was given the go-ahead on 24 March. The German general immediately requested and was granted extra divisions, raising his total to six, and departed by sea on 25 March to the little town of Gallipoli (now Gelibolu) that gave its name to the peninsula. On the same day, as it happened, General Hamilton left for Alexandria to supervise his army's preparations.

Liman set up his headquarters in the abandoned French vice-consulate on the 26th. Like Hamilton, he had arrived in post in a rush and without a staff, but this was soon remedied: he had plenty of German officers already stationed in Turkey to choose from, although he relied in the main on Turkish staff officers, with a German artillery commander. He was also receiving detailed intelligence about enemy preparations at Mudros on Lemnos, at Tenedos island, just off the Asian side of the Dardanelles, and in Egypt. The general's dispositions were straightforward. Discounting a landing from inside the strait, he placed two divisions (the 11th and 3rd) to the south-west on the Asian shore where landing conditions were good; two – the 5th and 7th – at the north-eastern end of the peninsula near Bulair (Liman believed for a dangerously long time that this must be the main target); one, the 9th, to the south-west, covering Cape Helles, and one inland in the south under his direct command as a mobile reserve, ready to move to the most threatened area when the main thrust of the enemy attack became clear. The head of this under-strength, newly formed reserve division, the 19th, was a certain Lieutenant-Colonel (later Lieutenant-General, finally Marshal) Mustafa Kemal. Divisional commanders, usually holding the rank of full colonel, were warned to be ready to move units to specially threatened areas: the chosen strategy was forward but not fixed defence with a mobile reserve, although as many as five lines of trenches had been dug, Western Front-style, complete with sandbags and wire, at the most likely landing areas. Apart from a small handful of aircraft based at Chanak, the defenders had no aeroplanes or seaplanes. By the beginning of April, Liman had some 60,000 infantry under command, plus about 25,000 support troops, including artillerymen. Cavalry was of no use on the peninsula's tortuous terrain.

General Hamilton and his staff left Alexandria on a requisitioned Cunard liner on 8 April and arrived at Mudros on the 10th, when a conference was held on de Robeck's flagship, the *Queen Elizabeth*. The overall plan for a main landing at the southern tip of the peninsula was agreed by the naval and army officers as the most useful for the navy's ultimate objective of breaking through the straits; it was also agreed that if naval fire support was to be of any use, the initial landings would have to be made in daylight, and from warships with landing vessels, mainly rowed cutters, in tow until the final approach, rather than from mercantile transports, which would have to stay out of range of enemy fire until beachheads had been secured. Once the first wave, known as the covering force, had established beachheads, the main body would be rowed ashore as soon as their troopships had closed up. The landing beaches V, W and X were small, enabling a combined maximum of 18 towed and rowed cutters at a time to unload, amounting to a first wave of 2,200 troops. Some 45 minutes would elapse before a second wave could be landed in this way; to increase substantially the size of the covering force, therefore, an ingenious variation on the theme of the Trojan horse, which had turned the trick for the besieging Greeks on the other side of the Dardanelles 3,000 years earlier, was proposed by the captain of a destroyer, Commander Edward Unwin, RN. His idea was to cram another 2,000 troops on an inconspicuous-looking collier, the SS *River Clyde*, and run her ashore on V beach as soon as the first troop-tows had arrived. She was equipped with a shielded machine-gun nest on the foredeck and would tow a steam barge, which was to run itself aground in turn in the shallower water ahead of the collier. Also in tow were flat-bottomed lighters to be used with the grounded barge as a pontoon bridge from the *River Clyde*'s bows to help the soldiers get ashore. Plates were cut from her sides near the bows, and plank walkways were suspended from them forward, to enable the troops to reach the bridge. Unwin retained command.

One of two further late additions to the plan of attack was the decision to land French troops on the Asian shore near the entrance fort of Kum Kale for a short period, instead of keeping the French division back as army reserve. V beach was most exposed to shellfire from the Asian side, which the French were to neutralise before withdrawing in due course. The other amendment was Hamilton's decision to add Y beach to the plan as an extra landing spot for 2,000 men. With them, and those going ashore at S beach, the covering force was increased to 4,900 troops plus the 2,000 on the *River Clyde*. Feint landings were mounted against Bulair by the RN Division and against Besika Bay on the Asian side opposite Tenedos by the French, each covered by battleships. A separate strong thrust would be made by a covering force of 4,000 ANZAC troops at Z beach some 12 miles to the north of the main assault; the balance of General Birdwood's corps of two divisions would follow them ashore.

For its part, the Allied navy planned to assist the army, not only by ferrying its troops ashore and supplying them, but also by attacking the Dardanelles again with a view to entering the Sea of Marmara within days of a successful landing. De Robeck recalled the great success of HM Submarine *B11* in December 1914 and decided, if either or both of these enterprises failed or stalled, to send another boat into the Dardanelles. The day before, however, on 16 April, a Turkish torpedo-boat, the *Demir Hissar*, mounted a bold attack on one of the last troopships bringing the 29th Division to the Aegean, the SS *Manitou*, with about 650 soldiers and 600 horses aboard. The 100-tonne boat had a Turkish crew with German officers and had already crippled a British seaplane-carrier in the Gulf of Smyrna. She slipped away from there on the night of 15–16 April without being noticed by British ships in the area and made for the Alexandria–Mudros transport route. Unusually for a troopship, even in those earliest days of the U-boat menace, the *Manitou* was unescorted and incapable of defending herself as there was no ammunition aboard. The German commander, observing prize rules, ordered the master to abandon ship in three minutes before issuing the order to sink her by torpedo; but she had enough boats for only a third of those on board. They were therefore given an extra ten minutes to jump overboard, but chaos reigned. The troops had been doing boat drill when the torpedo-boat arrived, and began launching lifeboats independently, overloading and capsizing some. Two torpedoes were fired; both missed, and the *Demir Hissar* made off when British destroyers approached from north and south, eventually beaching herself on the neutral Greek island of Chios, where the crew was interned. Fifty-one men died in the confusion on the *Manitou*. Another stable door was closed when the handful of ships still to come from Alexandria were henceforward provided with naval escorts.

Lieutenant-Commander Theodore Brodie, RN, took one of the newest submarines in British service, *E15*, into the Dardanelles on 17 April. A naval aeroplane circled overhead, with Brodie's twin brother aboard as observer. The eternal current got the better of the submarine, which went aground near Kephez Point on the Asian shore on the 20th. The Turks and Germans promptly opened fire with their artillery, killing Brodie and 6 others and taking 24 sailors prisoner. A Turkish destroyer tried to tow the wreck clear but withdrew when British planes dropped bombs; the small British submarine *B6* came up the strait and tried to torpedo the *E15* but had to withdraw under heavy enemy fire. Two British destroyers were the next to try but were also driven off by heavy shelling. On the morning of the 18th Holbrook's famous submarine, *B11*, tried her luck but was foiled by a typical Dardanelles fog. Next two old battleships came up but could get no closer than six miles from the wreck under fierce enemy fire and withdrew without hitting it.

De Robeck was determined to prevent the enemy from learning the stranded boat's secrets, so on the next night Lieutenant-Commander E. G. Robinson, who had won the VC for leading gun-demolition parties ashore in February, led two picket boats, each carrying a single torpedo in a deck launcher, in a stealthy advance towards Kephez. They too came under heavy shellfire when caught in Turkish searchlights, which however also conveniently lit up their target. Both torpedoes were fired at the submarine, but as the two boats withdrew one was hit below the waterline by a Turkish shell and began to go under. Robinson's boat rescued the men on the other and withdrew; just one man was lost. It was only on the morning of the 18th, when an aeroplane flew over the scene, that the gallant raiders learned that their attack had succeeded and the *E15* had been destroyed. For the moment, submarine forays were suspended.

Among those captured from the *E15* was a Lieutenant Palmer of the Royal Naval Volunteer Reserve, until recently the British vice-consul at Chanak, who was on de Robeck's staff as an intelligence officer and became the subject of a tantalising rumour. He was personally interrogated by the Turkish commander of the Dardanelles forts, Colonel (later Major-General) Jevad, and apparently took the highly dangerous decision to provide some disinformation: talking freely about the Allied invasion plans in an apparent bid to save his neck, he said that the main focus would be the neck of the peninsula – Bulair and the Gulf of Saros. There is no proof, but this 'revelation' may well have influenced Liman von Sanders's dispositions in the five days before the invasion (which included an elaborate feint against Bulair).

Meanwhile the largest fleet in terms of tonnage ever seen in the Mediterranean was gathering at Mudros: warships and naval auxiliaries, troop transports, supply ships and attendant vessels, more than 200 in all. Mudros, a capacious bay which normally had room to spare for the Allied naval forces, was not big enough for the whole of the invasion fleet, obliging the RND's and the French transports temporarily to make for Trebuki on the island of Skyros to the south-west, while those of the 29th and ANZAC divisions filled Mudros along with the warships. These numbered 59; strength had not declined since the losses incurred in the defeat of 18 March – on the contrary. There were once again 18 battleships, including 3 French, 12 cruisers (4 French) and 29 destroyers (5 French). These were supported by a dozen submarines (4 French), 5 French torpedo-boats, 6 fleet minesweepers and 20 trawlers, a seaplane-carrier, a submarine depot-ship – and one balloon ship with which naval gunfire could be observed.

The naval forces were organised into seven squadrons (one French under the irrepressible Guépratte). Admiral Wemyss, de Robeck's second-in-command and still acting governor of the Mudros base, was entrusted with the direction of the southern landings as flag officer of the First Squadron, by far the largest with 6 battleships, 4 cruisers and 6 fleet minesweepers – the Fourth Squadron of just 2 cruisers and 12 trawlers was also attached to his flag, which he flew on the cruiser *Euryalus*, more manoeuvrable than a battleship and able to go closer inshore. Rear-Admiral Stuart Nicholson was his second-in-command, leading the battleships and flying his flag on the *Swiftsure*. Rear-Admiral Cecil Thursby commanded the Second Squadron of 5 battleships, a cruiser and 8 destroyers, the seaplane-carrier and the balloon ship, which were to cover the ANZAC landing. A small Third Squadron (one battleship, and 2 each of cruisers, destroyers and trawlers) conducted the feint against Bulair. The Fifth consisted of the battleship *Agamemnon*, 10 destroyers, three minesweepers and two trawlers: their task was to sweep the mouth of the strait for mines and to lay nets against enemy submarines. Admiral Guépratte's Sixth Squadron of three battleships (plus one British) and four cruisers (one of them Russian), seven destroyers and five torpedo-boats, covered the temporary landing on the Asian shore. A Seventh Squadron of just four destroyers was detached to blockade the port of Smyrna (now Izmir) against sallies by torpedo-boats like the *Demir Hissar*.

These units in all their complexity were ready for battle on 19 April. All first-wave troops sailing on warships and the *River Clyde* had rehearsed an opposed landing by then and 23 April was chosen as what would now be called D-Day. For this to be achieved, the first vessels would need to move out of Mudros on the 20th, but as so often in the history of the Dardanelles campaign the weather dictated otherwise and de Robeck had to order a 24-hour delay on the 19th and again on the 20th. Troops on ships exposed to the rough swell suffered miserably from seasickness. Only at midday on the 23rd did the weather turn fair, and vessels began to leave Mudros in their predetermined order. Seaplanes reconnoitred enemy defences and five aeroplanes took off from Tenedos to bomb Maidos on the European side of the Narrows. This had the unhelpful effect of driving up to 2,000 Turkish troops westward out of the village to positions one and a half miles closer to Anzac Cove.

The first wave of the Mediterranean Expeditionary Force, the covering units for the subsequent main landings, went ashore after dawn on 25 April 1915 at seven places more or less simultaneously. French troops landed in the vicinity of Kum Kale on the Asian side, while British units landed on five beaches at the Aegean end of the Gallipoli peninsula south of Suvla, earmarked clockwise and from east to west as S beach in Morto Bay, V and W (on either side of Cape Helles), X and Y to the north. S and Y beaches were last-minute embellishments of the plan of attack, broadening the front. The objective for 25 April was the high ground at Achi Baba, just over 700 feet above sea level. The invaders never reached it, still less their ultimate objective, the Kilid Bahr plateau overlooking the Narrows from the west.

ANZAC units landed a little before the others a dozen miles to the north of the Cape Helles landing places – *on the wrong beach*. What was to be immortalised as 'Anzac Cove' is a small indentation on the Aegean shore of the peninsula with a narrow beach, overlooked by sheer cliffs. Between there and the promontory of Gaba Tepe to the south is the rather longer and gentler shore of what was labelled Brighton Beach by the Allies. This is where they were meant to land; but in the dark Admiral Thursby's Second Squadron overshot and herded them ashore too far to the north. Their objective was the high ground of Chunuk Bair, less than two miles to the north-east as the crow flies. But between the impossibly difficult landing place and the targeted height (850 feet) lies a tortured landscape of ridges and ravines covered in scrub and small trees. Walking across it in peacetime is a daunting, ankle-breaking prospect; fighting over it (in both senses) could only be a very bloody business. This objective too was never secured.

General Hamilton, who moved his headquarters to the *Queen Elizabeth* on 24 April, disposed of an invasion force for the southern tip of the peninsula consisting of three divisions: the British 29th under Major-General Aylmer Hunter-Weston, the French 1st Division under *Général de division* Masnou and a scratch composite division under Major-General A. Paris, the commander of the Royal Naval Division, elements of which were added to the 29th, French and composite divisions. The French troops, six battalions of colonials and six from Metropolitan France, were the bulk of General Albert d'Amade's French Expeditionary Force. The 29th included three British brigades and one Indian (Sikhs, Punjabis and Gurkhas), totalling 20 infantry battalions; the composite was made up of one Australian, one New Zealand and one naval brigade, ten battalions in all. Divisional troops variously attached to the three divisions included artillery, signals and engineer units, the RND's Motor Machine-Gun Squad, a battalion of the French Foreign Legion, an RND Cyclist company and Algerian Zouaves.

At sunset on 23 April there assembled, at an anchorage north of the island of Tenedos, the cruiser *Euryalus* with Admiral Wemyss aboard, two battleships, three transports carrying a battalion each for W, V and S beaches and towing between them a dozen lighters to take them ashore, the *River Clyde* weighed down with troops, and tugs pulling extra pontoons. To carry out their elaborate feint, the bulk of the RND and its transports and escorts were the first to move on the 24th, at dawn, as they had the furthest to go: from their anchorage at Skyros to a position off the tiny island of Xeros at the head of the eponymous gulf, due north of Bulair. The French ships had left Skyros three days earlier to take up temporary station off Mudros, where their admiral took the opportunity to organise unpromising landing rehearsals for the unpractised troops. The French moved on to an anchorage off Tenedos. The bulk of the 29th Division in their transports congregated on the open sea off the mouth of the strait, while the ANZAC units bound for Z beach collected five miles offshore on three of Admiral Thursby's ships, with their supplies in four transports; the main ANZAC force assembled off Cape Kephalo on the island of Imbros. The two British battalions bound for Y beach, escorted by two cruisers and sailing on two transports, gathered off Tekke Burnu, at the south-western tip of the peninsula.

What followed was, in too many places, a classic demonstration of the workings of what is known in polite circles as Murphy's law: anything that can go wrong will go wrong. We have already noted that the ANZACs were delivered to the wrong beach. The Bulair feint appeared to be a waste of time and effort, provoking almost no reaction from what appeared to be unmanned defences. One small gun opened fire. In fact the effect was quite useful to the attackers in that Liman von Sanders was prompted to shift a whole division to the purportedly threatened area, and to move his own command post temporarily to a hill overlooking the central portion of the Bulair lines, where he stayed for more than 24 hours. Thus there was only one Turkish battalion at Gaba Tepe to face the ANZACs when they came ashore in the first Allied landing. The leading 1,500 men of the 3rd Australian Brigade were in position aboard three battleships five miles offshore at midnight; the remaining 2,500 troops, completing the covering force for the corps, arrived in six destroyers 90 minutes later. The water was calm and the sky all too clear, lit up by the moon until it set at about three a.m., when the warships crept towards the shore in two echelons, each towing a train of four boats to be released two to three miles offshore. Three more battleships lay further out, ready to provide covering fire. The disadvantages of landing in the dark soon manifested themselves: the naval officers commanding the motorised picket boats escorting the boatloads of troops could not pick out any landmarks and some towlines became entangled. The landing craft drifted too far north as a result.

It was only well after the real landings had taken place far to the south that the German commander accepted that the battleship *Canopus* (Captain Heathcoat Grant, RN) had been leading a dummy run and sent his troops back southward, vacating the area himself.

From Z beach the Australians pushed inland towards their objective, the heights of Chunuk Bair. The few Turkish troops facing them with their single-shot Mauser rifles began to withdraw when they ran out of ammunition – just as a lieutenant-colonel arrived to spy out the ground. It was Kemal, the divisional commander, who told them to stay put, fix bayonets and lie down facing the enemy. The Australian advance party did the same, halting their advance towards the top of the hill 1,000 yards off, providing the defenders with just enough time to reinforce decisively. Kemal happened to have a regiment on exercise on the far side of the heights and ordered it to advance to the top, leading the first 200 men himself. The main Australian column was now 400 yards away, but the rapid Turkish build-up at the top held them in check as the first Turkish field artillery pieces arrived, Kemal joining in manhandling the guns into place. Three more Turkish regiments were called in, and the Australians, now supported by the New Zealand Brigade, were held in check two-thirds of the way to the crest. The fighting lasted all day in the heat and casualties piled up on both sides in the withering fire of machine-guns. Neither side would yield. General Birdwood asked Hamilton for permission to withdraw his troops but was told to wait for the advance from the southern end of the peninsula the next day.

Down at Cape Helles, however, a machine-gun nest on the cliff overlooking V beach cut great swathes through the three battalions emerging from the beached *River Clyde* as they tottered ashore along their gimcrack, wobbly landing walkways and temporary bridges. Liman's artillery commander, Lieutenant-Colonel Wehrle, had placed one of his mobile batteries in the ruins of the exploded Sedd-ul-Bahr fort, which caused more havoc among the invaders. More were cut down as they came ashore from oar-propelled cutters. Others drowned under their own kit of heavy pack, rifle and ammunition. Landings had to be interrupted until dark, when the *River Clyde* completed its unloading. By that time casualties among the covering force had passed 50 per cent.

At W beach a battalion of Lancashire Fusiliers approached an apparently deserted shore tightly packed in their cutters – only to come under heavy fire at the psychological moment from machine-guns and rifles fired by Turks in hidden slit trenches. Naval shelling had made no impression on the barbed-wire entanglements. Casualties surpassed 57 per cent.

The beaches codenamed S, X and Y were defended hardly or not at all. Troops who landed at S brushed aside a dozen Turks and turned to help the Lancashires at W. All in all, however, sufficient numbers had landed to acquire a solid beachhead across the south-western triangle of the Gallipoli peninsula. When Turkish prisoners stated that there were only about 1,000 defenders between the landing beaches and the objective, Achi Baba hill, they were not believed, and the British dug in, Western Front-style, instead of advancing northward. By dark on the second day, over 30,000 men had got ashore; but dead and wounded amounted to 20,000 and the beachhead looked like a slaughterhouse. A fleet of hospital ships took the wounded away to Skyros, and eventually Egypt for the worst cases. Liman rushed reinforcements southward against the Cape Helles landings; they formed a defensive line before Achi Baba under the command of Colonel Hans Kannengiesser. Eight machine-gun teams of marines detached from the two German ships arrived in support. British troops could not even get as far as the village of Krithia, half-way between the beachhead and Achi Baba. Within a few days of the landings on 25 April a stalemate had developed at Cape Helles and another at Anzac Cove. During the first landings six sailors and six soldiers won the VC. The French forces had not been badly mauled in their diversionary attack on the Asian shore opposite Gallipoli and were re-embarked to join the British at Cape Helles.

Three battles were fought at Krithia village, on 28 April, 6 May and 4 June, as the Allies tried to break out of their southern beachhead towards Achi Baba. A few hundred yards of territory were the only gains; the losses on both sides were out of all proportion.

Several bloody battles having failed to change the strategic situation at Cape Helles or at Anzac Cove in three months, Hamilton decided to land IX Corps at Suvla Bay, to the north of the latter, on 6 August 1915. The objective was to link up with the ANZAC beachhead and drive the Turks off Chunuk Bair and beyond. First to go ashore was the 11th Division, soon followed by the 10th. On 7 August 20,000 British troops were ashore in the blazing heat, many having landed in the wrong places, with no shelter, no water and no artillery. The next day, as desperate efforts were made to keep the troops supplied, General Hamilton actually set foot on shore for a change, to urge on his generals.

As a diversion the Australians had launched an attack across the extremely rough ground north of Anzac Cove, penetrating the Turkish defences at the Battle of Lone Pine, one of the worst engagements of a brutal campaign. At some points the opposed trenches were only metres apart; grenades thrown by one side were actually caught and thrown back before they went off (the record was reportedly four throws with the same grenade!); local museums are full of pairs of spent bullets which fused with each other in the lethal hail of shots from both sides. Seven Australian soldiers won the VC.

At Suvla Bay the invaders initially made good progress until the Turks arrived to oppose them in strength. The Allied commanders, brought up on the Western Front, could not believe that they had gained half a mile without serious opposition and called a halt. This and other unnecessary pauses gave the Turks just enough time to rush reinforcements northward, both to Lone Pine and then to cover the high ground to the east. On 8 August a New Zealand battalion reached the top of Chunuk Bair briefly but barely had time to enjoy the view of the straits before the troops came under heavy fire from adjacent high ground. The next day a small force of British and Gurkha troops got to the top of the ridge and engaged in hand-to-hand fighting and bayonet charges, but they too were driven off – by mistimed British naval gunfire. The New Zealanders hung on and counter-attacked a Turkish force sent to dislodge them. But on 9 August Liman von Sanders gave Kemal the 12th Turkish Division as a reinforcement. The counter-attack by his corps on 10 August proved decisive: he personally led them over the top. By that time the New Zealanders had been relieved by two unblooded British battalions: six Turkish battalions put one of them to flight and killed every man in the other with their bayonets – nearly 1,000 men. Both sides were exhausted and the survivors pulled back, the Turks to the heights and the Allies towards the coast. Kemal, having saved the day in the struggle for Gallipoli for a second time, was raised to general rank with the Ottoman title of Pasha.

Liman von Sanders and the British official military historian alike concluded that the surprise achieved by the Suvla landing had been frittered away by unnecessary delays on the part of poorly trained troops led by poor commanders – donkeys led by donkeys. Kitchener sacked one corps and two divisional commanders (a third resigned). The root of the problem, complete lack of initiative, was a fatal by-product of trench warfare as learned on the Western Front. The possibility of a war of movement, of marching across open country unopposed to reach a position further forward or to turn the flank of the enemy were now alien concepts, especially for the men of the New Armies, and outside the experience of all but the oldest officers. The same had applied to the ANZACs, but they were healthier, with better physique and higher morale, unaccustomed to blind obedience. A third beachhead brought a third stalemate, as costly as the first two. Another landing was planned none the less, for which the French offered a whole army and the British earmarked two more divisions. It was postponed until November, by which time opinion in London had changed fundamentally.

The War Council had spawned a Dardanelles Committee which met for the first time on 7 June. Churchill was a member: on 19 August, obviously having lost faith in the enterprise he had initiated, he suggested trying for a separate peace with Turkey, but was told that the Russians would never consent. Criticism of the conduct of the campaign mounted in the London press and (especially) in Australia. General Hamilton, who hardly ever left his command ship, was finally recalled in October 1915, to be replaced initially by Lieutenant-General Sir Charles Monro from France, who promptly advised Kitchener to withdraw the army from the peninsula. Monro was diverted to the Salonica front shortly afterwards, leaving General Sir William Birdwood in command; on 23 November Monro was appointed commander-in-chief in the eastern Mediterranean while Birdwood was named commander at Gallipoli. Around this time, when Keyes went to London to press yet again for another naval assault on the Dardanelles, he saw Kitchener, who decided to go and see for himself. At the end of November another kind of disaster struck the hapless Mediterranean Expeditionary Force: the worst and most prolonged snowstorm in living memory reduced Allied strength by 10 per cent in a few days. Kitchener accepted Monro's advice and made one of his oracular pronouncements: nobody would die in the withdrawal.

The War Council in London decided to evacuate the Gallipoli peninsula on 7 December 1915. Anzac Cove and Suvla Bay were evacuated in stages by de Robeck's fleet without loss by 20 December, to the astonishment of Liman and his Turkish troops (and no doubt of their opponents, who had predicted losses as high as 50 per cent). Just 3 men were wounded as 83,000 troops were taken off the beaches in less than two weeks – without alerting the Turks. A quarter of them were taken off on the last two nights. The extraordinarily successful evacuation was led by Commodore Keyes, using 37 of the new motor lighters ('beetles') ordered as landing craft in Churchill's days at the Admiralty. Thus encouraged, the Dardanelles Committee decided on 27 December to clear Cape Helles as well.

Some 35,000 men of four divisions were still dug in; the French Expeditionary Force was withdrawn without loss on New Year's Day 1916, leaving 19,000 British. Men of the gallant 29th Division were moved by boat to plug the gap left by the French in the last landing of the Gallipoli campaign. Liman ordered an attack on 7 January; fortunately for the British Kemal was ill, and the attack was beaten off with such a hail of fire that no

Turk reached the attenuated British line, where the British Army's famed musketry skills enabled the veterans of the 29th to give the impression that their numbers were much greater than was the case. Finally, on the night of 8–9 January, the rump of the Mediterranean Expeditionary Force was withdrawn by the Royal Navy, again without loss. The last to go left rifles on the parapets of their trenches and planted helmets on sticks to give the impression that the abandoned positions were still occupied. The last man to leave was probably Major-General F. S. Maude, who had also been at the Suvla evacuation: he had forgotten his valise and just made the last boat out from W beach.

The vain struggle for the accursed peninsula had gone on for 259 days, involving a total of a million men, half of whom became casualties – dead, wounded or sick. Twenty Turkish divisions were released for other fronts; the Allies had to find another million men to fight the Turks and Central Powers in campaigns in the Balkans and the Middle East consequent on the failure in 1915 to knock Turkey out of the war.

The Royal Navy and its French ally did not confine their operations in the Aegean to supporting the troops with landings, supply, medical care and shore bombardments. Submarines featured prominently in Allied naval activity in the Dardanelles and the Sea of Marmara, while German U-boats scored several spectacular successes in the Aegean. When the *E15* was grounded in mid-April, her sister boat *E14* got through into the Marmara at the same time, to lurk until the end of the month. The first submarine of the Royal Australian Navy, *AE2*, was however the first to score there, sinking a Turkish gunboat on 25 April as the landings were proceeding. On the same day Lieutenant-Commander Hersing, IGN, took the first German oceangoing submarine, *U21*, out of Wilhelmshaven to begin an adventurous voyage to the eastern Mediterranean. Two days later *E14* struck at last, sinking a Turkish gunboat and a transport; but also on the 27th *AE2* was damaged by a Turkish torpedo-boat and forced to scuttle: her crew of 32 went into captivity. But submarine successes forced the Turks to stop sending troops by sea on the hitherto safe internal route to Gallipoli: for a while they were forced to march over the unhelpful ground of the peninsula, especially when the *Queen Elizabeth* sent a transport to the bottom at the Narrows with four shells fired from seven miles off. On 1 May *E14* sank another transport with 6,000 Turkish troops aboard in the Marmara. But on the same day the French, much less lucky in this form of warfare, lost their submarine *Joule* to a mine with all hands.

On 11 May the cryptanalysts at Room 40 warned de Robeck that U-boats were approaching. Two days later HMS *Goliath* was sunk with the loss of 570 men by a small Turkish torpedo-boat, the *Muavenet-i-Millet*, commanded by a German lieutenant. On the 17th the small submarine *UB8* got to Smyrna: shortly afterwards she lay off Mudros and on the 30th she sank a curious victim – the steamship *Merion*, which was decked out with plywood and canvas, plus poles for 'guns', to look like the battlecruiser HMS *Tiger*. By then Lieutenant-Commander Nasmith's *E11* had sunk eight enemy vessels, including a torpedo-boat, in the waters off Constantinople during her latest patrol. But it was a U-boat, Hersing's *U21*, that brought off the most dramatic coup by any submarine in the underwater campaign, on 25 May. Hersing sank two old battleships, HMSs *Triumph* and *Majestic*, within a few hours. The former went down off Gaba Tepe near Anzac Cove with the loss of just 73 men, the latter turned turtle off Cape Helles in seven minutes with the loss of only 43 crew. *U21* then proceeded to complete her long voyage to Constantinople, having evaded three Allied attacks and had her tanks filled with the wrong fuel off Spain. Two smaller submarines, *UB8* and *UB7*, joined her in June.

While sinking a French ammunition ship off Cape Helles on 4 July, *U21* was damaged and had to be docked at Constantinople. But two large replacements were about to set off from the Baltic: *U34* and *U35*. The British *E7* surfaced to fire her single gun at the Berlin–Baghdad railway on the coast of the Gulf of Ismid on 17 July, blocking it. Ten days later the French submarine *Mariotte* got caught in the Turkish anti-submarine nets in the Dardanelles and was lost with all hands. The same fate was meted out to *E7* on 4 August; trying to free herself from the nets she set off a mine and was lost. After torpedoing a 5,000-ton Turkish steamer on 7 August, forcing it to beach, *E14* was joined by *E11* to shell Turkish troops marching along the road south from Bulair – who were there because of earlier submarine attacks. The next day *E11* sank the old Turkish battleship *Heireddin Barbarossa* and went on to sink two transports and two ammunition ships, all south of Bulair on the Aegean coast of Gallipoli. *E14*'s beached victim had the dubious honour on 12 August of being hit by the first torpedo to be launched by air, from a British seaplane. Two other ships in the Marmara were subjected to the same indignity; one of them sank.

A day later *UB14* sank the British troopship *Royal Edward*, an 11,000-ton converted ferry off the island of Cos: 865 troops out of 1,366 aboard drowned. On 2 September the same U-boat sank the SS *Southland*, another transport, but with few casualties. On the 3rd *E11* returned from her spectacular second patrol, during which she sank 2 warships, 27 steamships and 57 sailing vessels, nearly all by gunfire. But the *E7* was trapped in nets off Nagara on 5 September; the ever-busy *UB14* arrived and set explosive charges to send her to the bottom. In the broader Mediterranean, through which ships bound for the Aegean had to pass, two U-boats, *U33* and *U39*, sank a total of 16 larger steamships totalling 62,000 tons in September.

It was not until 30 October that the French succeeded in getting a submarine into the Marmara proper, but the *Turquoise* was spotted, shelled, forced ashore and captured. On searching through her papers, the enemy found a plan for a rendezvous with the British *E20*. The ubiquitous *UB14* turned up instead and sank the British boat on 6 November. But during the month and into December, Nasmith's *E11* completed a record patrol during which he sank 46 vessels in 48 days: his last victim was a Turkish destroyer. On 9 December 1915 *E2* set off from Mudros and entered the Dardanelles. On 2 January 1916 she was recalled, the last Allied submarine to penetrate the strait. The campaign had not only sunk half the Turkish merchant fleet; it had also caused a severe coal shortage in the Ottoman Navy.

De Robeck's surface warships were mainly preoccupied with supporting the army, but every now and again there would be a separate operation against the enemy coast. Battleships shelled the Turkish naval base of Smyrna on 6 April, and HMS *Lord Nelson* bombarded Chanak from a safe distance on 30 April, setting the town ablaze. Two months later, on 25 June, she did it again, this time assisted by a spotter in a captive balloon.

After the army's withdrawal from the Gallipoli peninsula, naval activity in the eastern Aegean faded away. But a residual naval guard force remained as insurance against an enemy foray out of the Dardanelles. The possibility was dismissed as highly unlikely, with the result that, in January 1918, the Royal Navy was caught out – by SMSs *Goeben* and *Breslau*. Again …

CHAPTER 10

The Inquest

The escape of the *Goeben*, the detonator of the struggle for the Dardanelles, led to the extreme rarity of a court martial in wartime of an admiral on a charge of failing to attack the enemy: he was acquitted, to the chagrin of many of his peers, but the least that can be said about the result is that there was a powerful element of doubt in the case against him and he was entitled to the benefit thereof. The double failure of the Royal Navy and then the British Army to force a passage through the strait led to the Dardanelles Commission, set up by parliament in August 1916, which began hearing witnesses in September and delivered an interim report in April 1917, to which the final report added very little in essence, while giving much extra detail on such matters as medical provision. It would be facile to dismiss the Commission's work as whitewash, as so many official inquiries have been in Britain: compare the wartime inquiry into the 'Channel Dash' by three enemy heavy ships from Brest to Germany via the Channel in broad daylight in February 1942; or more recently the inquiry into the Falklands War of 1982, to say nothing of the second Northern Ireland 'Bloody Sunday' inquiry, in its twelfth year at time of writing, with the bill approaching £200 million. But the Dardanelles Commission, although it delivered a number of strictures about the conduct of this part of the First World War and the leading individuals involved in it, clearly pulled punches too as it analysed witness statements, which were usually anything but spontaneous and sometimes very carefully prepared. The Commission could have been a lot harsher in its judgements; but it is fair to say that it did not – could not – shy away altogether from the many embarrassing failures by the war leadership. It is possible to discern, despite the emollient prose, clear elements of scepticism and even disapproval. In a sentence, the Commission concluded that the whole undertaking had been a ghastly mistake resulting from poor preparation and execution, a less than shattering finding in itself but embellished with nuggets of criticism. By summarising and analysing the report in this chapter and stripping the elaborate text to its essentials, it is possible to arrive at a coherent and not uncritical overview of the events described in this book.

The Commission was chaired by Lord Cromer, a scion of the Baring banking family with a distinguished colonial career in India and in Egypt, where he had been Agent and Consul-General – *de facto* ruler – from 1883 to 1907 (the post held by Kitchener from 1911 to 1914). Cromer died in January 1917, before the Commission could produce the second and final part of its findings. He was succeeded by Sir William Pickford, a High Court judge. The secretary throughout was Sir Grimwood Mears, a senior civil servant who was responsible for the text of the report.

Thirty-five witnesses were called, including Churchill – who gave evidence over five days, unlike all the rest (maximum of a single day) – Asquith, Fisher, Hankey, Hamilton, de Robeck and Carden, other admirals, generals, politicians and civil servants. The witness of lowest rank was a mere commander, RN (retired), who had been seconded to the Turkish Navy just before the war. Among those not called were Lord Kitchener, who died at sea in June 1916 (though his private secretary was questioned); Admiral Limpus; General Birdwood; any Australian, New Zealand or other Allied official or officer. But the overriding concern was with the conception, preparation and conduct of the campaign by the civil, naval and military leaderships. 'It is indeed obvious that none but officials could throw any light upon the special subject which has ... engaged our attention', says the report.

All such officials had been working very hard at the time, and as records were not complete, many had to rely on memory in giving evidence, which inevitably produced differing versions of events, it says. What follows is a perfect example of the orotund, spare-no-comma style and careful circumlocutions favoured by the Commission:

> It can, therefore, be no matter for surprise that the evidence given as to the views expressed at the time by some of the leading officials should be, in certain cases, somewhat conflicting.

The English for that is that there are discrepancies among the official accounts. The report goes on to observe, though at rather greater length than this, that some witnesses indulged in hindsight, and that the death of Kitchener, together with his obsession with secrecy, made it impossible to know whether his opinions and objectives had been fairly represented: even the War Council had never been taken fully into his confidence.

Unfortunately the best source on him, his personal military secretary, Colonel Fitzgerald, had also drowned. A convoluted double negative follows:

> We have not thought that we should be justified, in deference to the consideration which is rightly shown to the memory of the illustrious dead, in abstaining from a complete revelation of the action which Lord Kitchener took during the various phases of the events under consideration, nor have we hesitated to express our views on that action. It is necessary to do justice to the living as well as to the dead.

Kitchener's position was historically unique at the time the Dardanelles operations were being planned and carried out; so were his prestige and authority. In effect he was running the war single-handed, without, at his own wish, benefit of staff. Churchill, who quite clearly would have liked to be running the war single-handed himself but was not, said in evidence that he never knew Kitchener to have been overruled by the War Council or anyone else. 'When he gave a decision it was invariably accepted as final … All-powerful, imperturbable, reserved, he dominated absolutely our counsels at this time.' By emphasising the field marshal's crushing burden of responsibility combined with his no less crushing oracular and unchallengeable approach to command, Churchill was clearly shifting as much of the blame as possible for what went wrong on to the late Secretary of State for War, even as he went out of his way to praise the lost leader for much personal kindness to him. Kitchener's persistent refusal, until very late in the day, to commit troops to the enterprise undeniably stoked up Churchill's determination that the navy should go it alone. This does not of course alter the fact that the past and future First Lord with his powerful personality remained entirely responsible for his own actions.

The report next describes the mechanics of the conduct of the war, starting with how the Committee of Imperial Defence, a mainly consultative organ, segued into the War Council, the Cabinet committee with the same initial membership that was to run the war, on 25 November 1914. The CID was mainly but not only advisory: it did make some decisions and passed them on to the relevant department of state for action. This was facilitated by the fact that the Prime Minister himself presided, with several senior ministers also present (usually the Chancellor, the Secretaries for War, Foreign Affairs and India and the First Lord of the Admiralty) along with expert advisers. Both bodies reported to the full Cabinet of 22 ministers, the CID *before* a final decision was taken but the War Council *afterwards*; one advantage of the latter arrangement was to concentrate decision-making upon half a dozen ministers, plus Arthur Balfour, the former Conservative Prime Minister, who served on both bodies in his capacity as elder statesman; the army and navy advisers took no part in decisions, which were made not by voting but by Asquith assessing the mood of the meeting. The CID advised and consulted the Cabinet, a fact which caused much delay in the first four months of the war; the War Council acted for the full Cabinet, which was merely kept informed, and thus worked at a better pace. To speed things up even further, no formal minutes were kept of War Council meetings (unlike the CID's), obviating the need to pass them round to those who had been present for amendment or correction; Hankey, who stayed on as Secretary, merely took a longhand note which, as we saw, remains the only detailed and continuous source on the War Council's meetings. We may note that the efficacy of a small group running the war was offset by the technical ignorance of all the ministers except Kitchener, and the silence at the War Council of the technical experts who could have put them right (see below). If ministers knew what the experts thought, it can only have been made clear to them away from the Council, whose other members perforce remained ignorant of their views.

The War Council in turn was dominated by a triumvirate: Asquith, Kitchener and Churchill, who made all the big decisions about the Dardanelles. Churchill modestly testified: 'I was on a rather different plane. I had not the same weight or authority as those two ministers, nor the same power, and if they said, This is to be done or not to be done, that settled it.' Not having been born yesterday, the Commission noted: 'Mr Churchill probably assigned to himself a more unobtrusive part than that which he actually played.'

One of the aspects of the Dardanelles fiasco that preoccupied the Commission more than most was a question of protocol: the position and rights of the expert advisers. Much was made at the time, and has been ever since, about whether such people as Fisher, other attending admirals and generals were members of the War Council or invited guests, consultants who, like Victorian children, spoke only when spoken to. Kitchener's position was unique as both minister and chief military adviser. The only other general officer who attended regularly was Sir James Wolfe Murray, Chief of the Imperial General Staff from 25 October 1914, who expressly told the

Commission that he had never once been asked for his opinion. Churchill, however, was not his own leading expert or classed as one; the First Sea Lord, Fisher, and Admiral of the Fleet Sir Arthur Wilson, VC, who had no official position but was frequently asked by Churchill and the Admiralty for his views, were the principal naval advisers to the Council, sometimes supported by Vice-Admiral Sir Henry Oliver, the Chief of War Staff at the Admiralty, and/or Admiral Sir Henry Jackson.

A puzzled Lord Cromer asked Fisher for his assessment of the role of the advisers. 'We were not members of the War Council … We were the experts there who were to open our mouths when told to,' the admiral said.

Q (Cromer): Nothing else?
A (Fisher): Nothing else … The members of the Cabinet were members of the Council, and the others were simply there ready to answer questions if asked.
Q: And they never were asked?
A: They were sometimes, because I was asked how many battleships would be lost, and I said twelve.
Q: But they were never asked anything about the Dardanelles?
A: No.

Wilson concurred when his turn came. Churchill was by no means the only politician who completely disagreed. When he had addressed the Council, it was on behalf of the entire Admiralty, he said, incorporating the opinions agreed at its daily meetings.

I was expressing those opinions in the presence of two naval colleagues and friends who had *the right, the knowledge and the power* [author's emphasis] at any moment to correct me or dissent from what I said, and who were fully cognisant of their rights.

Foreign Secretary Grey said the Council went entirely by the opinions of Kitchener and Churchill on military and naval matters. He and Balfour each agreed that when it came to the experts their silence meant consent to, or at least absence of serious disagreement with, their minister's opinion. Lord Crewe, Secretary for India, and Lord Haldane, who succeeded Lloyd George as Chancellor, bluntly admitted that the politicians on the Council talked too much and the experts too little; but they also thought that the silence of the latter meant at least acquiescence. Lloyd George, Chancellor during the relevant period, strongly agreed. Asquith, the Prime Minister of the day, did not agree that the experts should give their opinion only if asked, but also thought that if they did not dissent, then they assented (an inversion of the familiar oversimplification of differences of opinion: if you are not for me, you are against me). Hankey, neither politician nor technical expert although a former Royal Marine officer, came down 'very strongly' on the side of the politicians: silence meant consent. The fault here seems to lie with Asquith, who as chairman could have ensured that each person present was invited to speak, or at least that the military and naval advisers were consulted there and then, at least on crucial professional and technical matters. But he preferred brevity and the appearance of consensus.

One other oddity about the War Council's proceedings, presided over by a Prime Minister who was anything but forceful and decisive, was the subject of complaints from Admiral Wilson and General Murray, who separately testified that they had left key meetings of the Council, such as that of 13 January 1915, with no clear idea, or no idea at all, of what decisions had been taken. Asquith repudiated this, suggesting that some participants might have gone before he recited the conclusions. Hankey supported him in this; but on looking through his notes of Council meetings, one can understand the confusion. The Commission rightly concluded that 'the functions of the experts were, to a great extent, differently understood by the experts themselves and the ministerial members of the Council'. This was an extremely important, not to say disastrous, difference of interpretation, which Asquith could have eradicated at a stroke.

The Commission also explored in detail the changes in the *modus operandi* of both the Admiralty and the War Office on the outbreak of war in 1914, which profoundly affected the conduct of the war in general and the Dardanelles operations in particular. Under letters patent, various acts of parliament and Orders-in-Council, the First Lord of Admiralty was 'solely responsible to the Crown and Parliament for all the business of the Admiralty'. The role of the First Sea Lord was to advise him on large questions of naval policy and operations. Neither First Lord nor First Sea Lord was legally required to consult the rest of the Board of Admiralty – three other sea lords, two civil lords, a permanent secretary (civil servant) and a parliamentary secretary (junior minister). Both leaders were dyed-in-the-wool autocrats and sidelined the Board. The War Staff Group was formed at the very beginning of the war, was strengthened when Fisher returned as First Sea Lord and soon displaced the Board in the direction of the war at sea. It included First Lord and First Sea Lord, Chief of Staff Oliver, Admiral Wilson, Permanent Secretary Sir Graham Greene and Churchill's Naval Secretary, Commodore de Bartolomé. The relegation of the Board caused friction and resentment; it was not formally consulted about the Dardanelles. Churchill later expressed regret about this; Fisher never did. For his part Asquith had no idea of how the Admiralty was run, and was not interested.

The Army was formally run by the Army Council, consisting of four ex-officio military members, a finance member and a civil member. The Secretary of State for War was solely responsible to Crown and parliament for all army business. The Permanent Secretary of the War Office was also secretary to the Army Council, which did not meet very often before or during the war. In fact the army was really administered by the War Office and directed entirely by the Secretary of State until Kitchener's death, after which there was a formal re-separation of powers in favour of the Chief of the Imperial General Staff. The biggest change had come at the beginning of the war, when most senior officers at the War Office were given, by previous arrangement, field or staff positions with the British Expeditionary Force on the Western Front. Their administrative replacements were obviously less experienced, giving even more impetus to Kitchener's assumption of sole and supreme authority. The Commission was unusually emphatic, by its lights, in condemning Kitchener's approach. It was 'much to be regretted that the principles of the devolution of authority and responsibility upon which the War Office system was based were ignored by Lord Kitchener'. The evidence showed that he 'was not in the habit of consulting his subordinates', that he issued orders over the heads of departmental chiefs, sometimes without the knowledge even of the Chief of General Staff, 'and, in fact, that he centralised the whole administration of the War Office in his own hands'.

Add to these habits the awe in which the field marshal was held, even by Churchill, and it becomes clear that it is no exaggeration to say he was running the war single-handed – simultaneously generalissimo and recruiting sergeant, as seen in that immortal poster. His greatest contribution to the outcome of the war was his recognition, almost alone at the outset, that far from being 'over by Christmas', it would last for years, and his consequent, forceful campaign to raise the huge new armies Britain would need to see it through. What he said, went – until the failure at Gallipoli, when even his authority began to slip and the power of the CIGS was restored by a special Order-in-Council. Centralisation had worked well when Kitchener was fighting in the Sudan and bringing an end with an iron hand to the Boer War, but even that campaign was simplicity itself compared with the Western Front, or Gallipoli. The onset of war in August 1914 brought far-reaching changes in governance, the Commission noted. The Cabinet ceded control of the war to the War Council, which replaced the Committee of Imperial Defence; the Board of Admiralty was superseded by the War Staff Group; and the War Office came under the absolute control of a single individual.

The Commission went on to note that an attack on the Dardanelles had always been regarded as a very difficult proposition, by navy and army alike. There could be no question of a naval assault without military support, and naval attacks on forts did not work anyway. But such developments as the revolution in artillery technologies and the deployment of aircraft might be seen as overriding traditional doctrine.

The trial bombardment of the entrance forts at the Dardanelles on 3 November 1914 had been a mistake, serving to alert the enemy without achieving anything much. On the 25th Churchill suggested, as the best means of forestalling an attack on Egypt, a full-blown assault on the Gallipoli peninsula. Kitchener did not dismiss the idea but thought it premature. Then on the second day of the new year came the plea for a 'demonstration' against the Turks from Grand Duke Nicholas, whose Russian armies were under pressure from them in the Caucasus. The Foreign Office relayed Kitchener's positive reply. We have noted that the Prime Minister apparently did not see this rather important telegram before it was sent, but that did not mean he would not have approved had he seen it ... The same applied to the Foreign Secretary, Sir Edward Grey, who said his department had been used merely as a means of communication. Churchill did not see it either but concluded that it was the result of his long talk with Kitchener on the evening of 2 January. The latter told him that he did not believe a demonstration would be a real help to the Russians, although the Dardanelles was the only place where it might just have a positive effect: but no British troops would be available for a new front for months.

At this stage political, naval and military opinions, including Churchill's, were unanimously in favour of a combined operation. His view apparently remained the same as it had been in March 1911, when he told the Cabinet in a memorandum that 'it is no longer possible to force the

Dardanelles, and nobody would expose a modern fleet to such peril'. Kitchener clearly envisaged a demonstration by the fleet alone because he could spare no troops, but in no sense an attempt to force the strait by the navy on its own. He also claimed to have been strongly influenced by Churchill's enthusiastic description of the latest battleship, HMS *Queen Elizabeth*, the most powerful in the world at the time, and her dispatch to the Aegean. By the same token Kitchener was very upset when she was withdrawn to the North Sea in May 1915.

Even so, Churchill asked Admiral Carden on 3 January 1915 whether he thought that it was 'a practicable operation to force the Dardanelles by the use of ships alone'. The rest of the telegram made it clear that the question was virtually rhetorical, one that students of Latin would recognise as a *nonne* question – one expecting the answer yes. And indeed that was Carden's answer, albeit a qualified one: yes, given time and lots of ships, the Dardanelles 'might be forced'. In his evidence to the Commission he tried to hedge: 'I did not mean distinctly that they *could* be forced.' What he really thought was that one needed to destroy the entrance forts and enter the strait to find out whether it could be forced. The Commission noted: 'No reservation of this sort was made in [Carden's] telegram ... [of] January 5.' Churchill's reply the next day was dubiously worded: 'High authorities here concur in your opinion', followed by an invitation to send a shopping list of ships required and a plan of attack.

This sentence, the Commission felt, suggested that Admiralty opinion was generally in favour, leading Carden not unreasonably to assume that Lord Fisher, the highest authority under Churchill, and such advisers as Admiral Sir Henry Jackson, Fisher's eventual successor as First Sea Lord, approved. Fisher said in evidence he did not think he had been shown this message before it was sent, because he would have objected. Churchill disingenuously testified, stretching his text to the limit, that he never meant to suggest Fisher approved: the 'high authorities' he had in mind were admirals Jackson and Oliver (chief of staff). In fact Jackson had been working on an appraisal of a solely naval attack, which he wrote on 5 January but which did not reach Churchill until after the 'high authorities' signal had been sent. Jackson's assessment was anything but enthusiastic, pointing out that a fleet passing up the strait into the Sea of Marmara, and more particularly its supply ships that would have to follow, would come under fire from shore-based artillery, infantry and torpedo tubes: there would be no point in threatening or even capturing Constantinople with the fleet 'unless there were a large military force to occupy the town'.

Boiled down to its essentials, Jackson's opinion was neither for nor against, but since he was opposed to an attempt to 'reach the Straits', anything beyond shelling the outer forts would not meet with his approval unless it was absolutely clear that advantage would result, as he told the Commission. With that serious proviso he went along with Carden's four-step plan, wirelessed on 11 January, in a memorandum dated the 15th. Besides, he added, it was not his place to interfere with naval policy except if invited to do so by a superior ...

We also know Fisher had his doubts all along, which he managed to suppress some of the time out of loyalty and gratitude to Churchill for his reappointment in 1914. Admiral Oliver testified that he only went along with the Carden plan on the understanding that if no progress was made it could be called off at any time. Not unreasonably, the Commission concluded that the Admiralty at large would have preferred a combined operation but nobody objected to a bombardment of the outer forts. This was accepted reluctantly, but accepted it was, on the understanding, also expressed by Kitchener, that it could be abandoned if unsuccessful. Therefore in signalling to Carden that 'high authorities here concur' Churchill was not so much being economical with the truth as profligate with a half-truth, and in so doing gave a misleading impression. Coming as it did from a master of the English language, that could not have been an accident.

The War Council had met on 13 January 1915 against a backdrop of stalemate on the Western Front. The Austrians had suffered defeats but the Russians and the Serbs were both in a bad way and the Balkan neutrals were immune to diplomatic persuasion as long as the Allies were unable to produce a victory. How could Britain deliver a blow against the Central Powers? An attack on the Dardanelles seemed, except to Fisher, to be the only practicable proposition at the time, and the potential results of success verged on the dazzling: Russia massively relieved in every sense, Bulgaria won over, the flank of the Central Powers turned, even the 'Turkish Question' definitively answered after centuries of doubt ... But the only germane question was whether or not a purely naval attempt was the right course. Churchill spelt out Carden's stage-by-stage plan to use modern naval guns against the allegedly antiquated enemy artillery and neglected fortifications; there were plenty of old battleships to spare, plus the *Queen Elizabeth*; in a matter of weeks the fleet could enter the Marmara and sink the *Goeben*; field guns and rifles ashore would be no more than an inconvenience. Hankey noted: 'Lord Kitchener thought the plan was worth trying. We could leave off the bombardment if it did not prove effective.'

Fisher did not speak up. The political witnesses were agreed that had he objected, the project would almost certainly have been cancelled. But Asquith also thought that the old admiral's unspoken objection was based mainly on the fact that he wanted to use the fleet differently, in an operation in the Baltic, the other flank of the Central Powers, rather than on his belief that a solely naval attack was too risky. As the Commission was working in wartime, the Baltic option was not mentioned in its first report; but its conclusion that the real reason for Fisher's resignation was because the Dardanelles had blocked his pet project is a misleading over-simplification, not to say bizarre. Fisher told the Commission he believed from the outset that the solely naval attack was doomed to failure and was therefore opposed to it, but no witness said he had mentioned this misgiving at the time. Churchill's evidence makes it clear that as far as he was concerned Fisher's silence meant consent. The 13 January meeting ended with the decision to prepare for a naval expedition to 'bombard and take the Gallipoli peninsula with Constantinople as its objective'. That this apparent, albeit misleading, clarity was rare is shown by the very next paragraph of the report, which says that nobody could review the mass of evidence given to the Commission 'without being struck with the atmosphere of vagueness and want of precision which seems to have characterised the proceedings of the War Council'. Some, such as Churchill, read the conclusion of the 13 January meeting as tantamount to a go-ahead for a solely naval attack, while Asquith said it merely told the Admiralty to *prepare* for one: he understood the matter would be discussed again when it had done so. All witnesses agreed that the decision related to a naval attack without troops. The 'demonstration' of 3 January had been superseded ten days later by 'preparations for a purely naval attack' with the ultimate objective of Constantinople, which everybody knew could not be attained without a large army.

On being given his 'mandate to prepare' an attack on the Dardanelles, Churchill lost no time in contacting the French government to ask for active support. M. Victor Augagneur, the Minister of Marine, came over to London to discuss the matter. His predecessor, Dr Gauthier, had resigned on health grounds (he suffered a breakdown when the Germans declared war) on the day Britain went to war (4 August 1914). Even so the ministry, as we saw, had failed to force Admiral Boué de Lapeyrère, commanding the fleet, to obey the war orders he had himself played a major part in drawing up, a large contribution to the escape of the *Goeben*. Augagneur, who would himself leave office in the wake of the double failure at the Dardanelles in 1915, was no student of Clausewitz, having once delivered himself of the not very *bon mot* that 'in war one does not improvise'. The French government agreed to leave the command in the Aegean to the British while retaining supremacy in the Adriatic and the rest of the Mediterranean, in accordance with the Anglo-French naval understanding that left the British in charge in the Channel and North Sea. Augagneur agreed to place a squadron at the disposal and under the flag of Admiral Carden, and also echoed Kitchener, Hankey and the rest by saying that the enterprise could always be abandoned if it did not make progress.

But as the Commission observed, amid patronising remarks about the oriental mind, if a serious attack was made and it failed, 'the result would be to give a shattering blow to British prestige and influence throughout the East'. The inquiry report however goes on to note, with some complacency, that at time of writing (early 1917) the attack had indeed failed, and had even been followed by serious British setbacks in the Mesopotamian campaign against the Turks, 'but, so far as can at present be judged, the political consequences ... have been so slight as to be almost inappreciable'. But not even Kitchener with all his experience of 'the Eastern mind' could have foreseen this. Those who thought on these lines had in mind a purely naval attack on the outer forts and a withdrawal if this did not produce a result that could be exploited: they were not thinking of the far more damaging idea of abandoning a serious military landing once made. The politicians, Kitchener and Admiral Wilson were all confident, until the solely naval approach was dropped, that British prestige could be preserved, yet the failure of the fleet in March 1915 was followed by the invasion of Gallipoli in great part to *salvage* British prestige, like a losing gambler trying a 'double or quits' bet. The result of the second failure was a much bigger loss of prestige, which could be offset (but never quite eradicated) only by the eventual overall Allied defeat of the Turks on all their other fronts. The effect on the many participating Indian troops, for example, of witnessing at first hand the inability of their colonial masters to carry all before them (to put it no higher) would start the long process of undermining the authority of the British Empire.

The Commission next turned to the seductive argument about the efficacy of modern artillery, in particular the power and enormous range of naval guns, seen by many on the War Council as vitiating Nelson's advice against ships attacking forts: *vide* Liège and Namur or Antwerp, said Churchill. But this was misleading because of the high, 'lobbing' trajectory of the heavy German howitzers, their use of aircraft for spotting the fall of shot and their massive armies, on hand to exploit immediately the effect of the guns. Naval guns had almost flat trajectories except at extreme range, and needed to score direct hits on shore-based cannon to disable them, a well-nigh impossible feat at long distance. The best a naval gun could do was to achieve a downward trajectory of 21 degrees with a reduced propellant charge; a howitzer shell could be fired to fall at an angle much closer to 90 degrees, like a bomb from an aircraft. Naval guns in short were not appropriate for dealing with land fortifications, hidden and/or mobile batteries, or shore-based torpedo tubes which were believed (to an exaggerated extent) to exist in the strait. The fleet also faced the problem of minefields (effectively covered by searchlights and the elusive shore artillery) and eventually the threat of submarines; and seaplanes were not sufficiently powered at the time to rise above ground fire or even the prevalent strong winds – always assuming they could take off at all in the choppy waters. Outside the strait ships could observe the fall of each other's shot whereas inside they could not, for lack of sea-room; on 18 March they barely bothered to try. The fall of the Belgian forts, the inquiry in effect concluded, had been a false analogy: a snare and a delusion.

After the War Council meeting of 13 January the views of Churchill and Fisher on the Dardanelles diverged more and more, with the admiral wanting to drop it not just because it overrode his Baltic idea but because it was not a combined operation and would therefore fail. Asquith was just one War Council witness to this generally recognised difference of opinion: he received a dissenting memorandum from Fisher on 25 January. Churchill claimed he was unaware of the extent of Fisher's misgivings before this. Fisher had wanted to absent himself henceforward from War Council meetings but attended with his chief a private meeting in Asquith's office before the 28 January triple session. When Churchill briskly reported that the Russians and the French were pleased with the Dardanelles plan which would go ahead in the middle of February, Fisher protested that he understood the matter would not be raised in Council that day. He got up to leave but was headed off by Kitchener, who persuaded him not to resign and to resume his seat – the admiral was after all the only one present who disagreed with the Dardanelles operation, Kitchener told him. Yet Wilson too was sceptical, if not as strongly as Fisher, but also kept silent. At the hearings, Wilson said Churchill had 'passed over' dissent at the Admiralty: 'He was very keen on his own views.' He repeatedly said he could do it without the army; 'he only wanted the Army to come in and reap the fruits, I think was his expression.' Churchill had minimised the risk from mobile guns and talked as if armoured ships were immune from damage. Churchill's response was that in so far as Wilson was opposed, he too favoured a strategic alternative, like Fisher. Nobody had ever argued to him that the operation was something that could not work.

Churchill invited Fisher to see him in the First Lord's office after the first session of the day, and the admiral 'definitely consented' to undertake the operation. At the second session in the evening Churchill announced to the War Council that the Admiralty, with the agreement of Lord Fisher, had 'decided to undertake the task with which the War Council had charged us so urgently' (it will be recalled that the 13 January meeting called for *preparations*, and that no urgency had been attached). Churchill told the Commission, presumably with a rhetorical flourish:

> This I take as the point of final decision. After it, I never looked back. We had left the region of discussion and consultation, of balancings and misgivings. The matter had passed into the domain of action.

The purely naval 'demonstration' which 15 days earlier had passed into 'preparation' had now reached its third degree: 'action' by the fleet. The fleet would attack the Dardanelles unaided, with Constantinople as its objective.

The Commission chided Fisher and Wilson for keeping silent and concealing their misgivings. 'They must have ... been aware that none of the ministerial members of the Council had any expert naval knowledge' – not excluding Churchill. The latter was also very much at fault for concealing the two admirals' doubts instead of inviting them to speak to the Council, which could have enabled its members to reach a conclusion in full possession of all the facts and arguments. Instead he pressed his case very strongly: 'he was carried away by his sanguine temperament and his firm belief in the success of the undertaking which he advocated.' He had deluded himself about the degree of support he had won from his naval advisers and suppressed their misgivings, about which, in the psychological jargon of today, he was obviously 'in denial'. The other politicians on the Council should also have sought the express advice of the silent experts; a short adjournment to seek the opinion of more experts from outside could then have been called, the Commission said. But the Council, dazzled by the potential rewards of success, gave insufficient attention to the disadvantages that would accrue 'in the not improbable case of failure'. There is no mention of Churchill's widely attested rhetorical persuasiveness, but it must now be clear that it played the leading part in bringing about a commitment by Britain's war leadership to the solely naval attack on the Dardanelles.

Neither the Admiralty nor Carden, nor of course the politicians, gave much thought to what else would need to be done if the fleet forced its way into the Sea of Marmara. Turkish resistance was arrogantly discounted: they would withdraw once the fleet got in; there would be a revolution in Constantinople. But doubt did begin to creep into some minds, particularly in the military. The question of Britain's prestige in the event of a setback was by no means dead, giving rise to growing unease, but the Commission could not put its collective finger on a single moment or event that marked the palpable shift of opinion towards a military intervention. Major-General Charles Callwell, Director of Military Operations at the War Office at the material time, said simply: 'We drifted into the big military attack.'

Kitchener had promised as early as 9 February 1915 that if the navy needed help from the army at a later stage, it would be forthcoming. Jackson advised Carden on 15 February to keep in mind the likely need for a large military intervention as the fleet progressed, and to collect transports to deliver it: a naval bombardment was not to be recommended 'unless a strong military force is ready to assist'. On 16 February ministers met informally (no Hankey present to take a note) and initiated the movement of the 29th Division to the Aegean, of more troops from Egypt, of Royal Marines and of horse boats and landing craft, while the Admiralty was to organise the construction of transports and lighters sufficient for 50,000 men. All this was endorsed by the War Council proper, and Hankey said that the 16 February meeting was the 'all-important decision from which sprang the joint naval and military enterprise against the Gallipoli peninsula'. Callwell's concept of drift seems entirely appropriate: Kitchener's reluctance to release troops had prevented, before spring 1915, the combined operation which the received wisdom had unanimously recommended – but so had Churchill's impatience. As a result, the naval and military attacks were not combined at all, allowing the enemy to fend them off one after the other. Had the army gone in first, closely followed by the fleet, the outcome could and should have been entirely different – provided of course that the military side of operations had been executed rather more efficiently than was the case.

The first serious bombardment of the outer forts took place on 19 February 1915. Carden said in evidence that 'the result of the day's action ... showed apparently that the effect of long-range bombardment by direct fire on modern earthwork forts is slight'. Guns that seemed to have taken hits opened fire when the ships came within range. The demolition parties had found that some 70 per cent of the targeted guns were still in working order when they landed, even though the forts were in a terrible state. Admiral Sir Reginald Bacon, a gunnery specialist and flag officer of the Dover Patrol, told the Commission that 'if they actually destroyed 30 per cent in the short time they did very well'. Even this modest and conjectural figure was too high.

Around the time of the first major bombardment Kitchener underwent a change of heart. He told the War Council on 24 February that if the navy did not get through unaided, 'the army ought to see the business through'. He recognised that Britain's prestige would be badly damaged in the East after all by a withdrawal that would be seen as a failure. Churchill told the same meeting that he was not contemplating a land attack, but the naval one might be held up by mines, making a 'local military operation' necessary. The Admiralty had prepared to start moving the 29th Division to the Aegean on 22 February, but on the 20th Kitchener said it would not be leaving, provoking a row with Churchill, who all but begged for its release and warned that it would not be his fault if a disaster resulted from the lack of sufficient troops. Was this a disguised acknowledgement that a purely naval assault was not going to be a pushover after all? But the War Council, as usual, took Kitchener's side on 26 February; yet he told General Birdwood that very evening to consult with the navy as to how best the ANZAC and RN divisions and Royal Marines might be used if needed. Clearly at this confused juncture the viability of a solely naval assault was generally in doubt and the deployment of as many as three divisions of troops, some 50,000 men, was regarded as an option, though not yet decided. On 5 and 6 March Birdwood told Kitchener at some length that he did not believe the navy could break through on its own; these messages and better news from Russia and the Western Front prompted Kitchener to announce on 10 March that he would release the 29th to the Aegean after all. The

Commission agreed with Churchill that his long delay had been a major contribution to the failure of the entire enterprise.

We may note that three valuable weeks had indeed been thrown away, and the troopships could not start to leave until 16 March. Had they left on 22 February they might have been on hand for the navy's 'big push' on 18 March; but surely not ready for an invasion, because their supply ships would still have been wrongly loaded and a regrouping in Egypt would have been no less necessary. This suggests the army could have been ready at the earliest on about 24 March rather than the actual date of 14 April. No doubt the fleet could have waited a mere extra week until the troops were ready; but *there is no indication that de Robeck and Hamilton would therefore have changed their strategy in favour of a combined operation* – simultaneous and co-ordinated attacks by navy and army – or that their chiefs in London, Kitchener and Churchill, would have done so either. The interval between the rebuff to the navy and the ensuing army attack might well have been much shorter, but Kitchener's long-standing view preceded and outlasted his vacillations over the 29th Division: *only* if the fleet could not do it alone would the army come to its aid. In that way he was entirely consistent. So was his insistence that he would not let the 29th go until general war conditions permitted. Perhaps he was over-cautious, as the Commission concluded; but it was Churchill who lost patience and went ahead without him. By drifting along with this piecemeal approach the British government allowed the bold Churchillian strategy of a flank attack on the Central Powers via Turkey to fall between the two stools of early withdrawal after a naval demonstration and a full-scale combined assault. This was an unwise course anyway, but especially when the defence was in the hands of the disciples of Clausewitz. After all, the advice of that great evangelist of Prussian militarism was to 'Pursue one great decisive aim with force and determination'.

The hurried dispatch of General Hamilton and his orders from Kitchener dated 13 March 1915 did not portend a change of strategy. His orders were vague. The army would go in only if the fleet attack failed; it would go in *en bloc*; there could be no question of abandoning the project after that; yet minor military operations ashore were not excluded. Hamilton fairly emphasised to the Commission that no plan of operations had been drawn up and he had left for the Aegean without information or arrangements for a water supply or staff preparation. Only on 19 March, the day after the navy

failed, did Kitchener expressly order him to capture the Gallipoli peninsula. Just before his illness forced the handover to de Robeck, Admiral
Carden had signalled that he expected a major army landing immediately
after he had broken through the strait. He would confer with Hamilton on
his arrival. De Robeck testified that he took over Carden's plan, did not
alter it and decided to carry it out as ordered: he would have preferred a
combined operation but he understood he was under orders to force the
strait with the fleet regardless, so he tried to do so. In effect the problem of
supply, assuming he overcame the minefields and got through to Constantinople, was discounted because it was assumed that the Turks would
surrender under the guns of the Royal Navy. 'That was what we were
always given to understand.' But if that had not occurred, 'we should
have had to come down again. Yes, like Admiral Duckworth ...' To the
causes of the Dardanelles disaster we can therefore add to Asquith's
indecisiveness, Kitchener's vacillation and Churchill's over-optimism a
general underestimation of the enemy.

Having caused so much delay himself, Kitchener chided Hamilton on
23 March, the day de Robeck advised that the army should be called in for
a combined operation, for saying that the troops would not be ready to land
until 14 April: 'I regard any such postponement as far too long. I should
like to know how soon you could act on shore.' Until de Robeck's recom-
mendation, the consensus at the Admiralty and the War Council was that
the fleet should carry on despite the losses of 18 March. De Robeck agreed
until he changed his mind after meeting Hamilton on 22 March, so advising
London the next day; from then on Churchill alone wanted to press on
without the army, whereas Fisher, Wilson and Jackson disagreed, believing that they should heed the advice of the commanders on the spot. 'I
bowed to their decision,' said Churchill, 'but with regret and anxiety.'

The Commission looked for crumbs of comfort amid the ruination of
British hopes at the Dardanelles. The Russians had asked for a diversion,
and they had achieved considerable success in that respect. There had been
no victory to seduce the Balkan neutrals, but Bulgaria's adhesion to the
Central Powers had been delayed for months. And the Turks had been
made to keep 300,000 troops for several months on the Gallipoli peninsula
who might otherwise have been deployed elsewhere against the Allies,
including Russia. Enver Pasha said that if the fleet had pressed ahead
despite its losses on 18 March, it might well have got through; as it was he
had six whole weeks to deploy 200 new artillery pieces from Austria-
Hungary in the peninsula. But the Commission, not unreasonably, took the

view that after three battleships had been sunk and three or four knocked out on a single day, with the minefields uncleared further attempts would have been attended by further serious losses; if the fleet had managed to force a passage in this way, there would not have been much of it left with which to threaten Constantinople.

In the overall conclusions of its first and principal report the Dardanelles Commission focuses on our main concerns, the decision to mount a solely naval attack on the Dardanelles, its preparation and execution (the final report concentrates on the ensuing land campaign at Gallipoli). The main points include the following:

- The War Council was wrong in uncritically accepting Kitchener's statements that no troops were available for a combined operation without investigating them. Had this been done it would have emerged that there were enough troops in the region after all, and that they would have been ready rather sooner.
- Churchill overstated the degree of enthusiasm shown by his expert advisers. These were not asked for their views by the War Council, nor did they proffer any, which was wrong. Churchill, Asquith and the other politicians should have insisted that they speak and give their views to the full Council.
- The potential reward of a successful, surprise combined attack at the Dardanelles was so great that it was a major mistake to throw it away by staging a purely naval assault, which could not possibly have succeeded on its own.
- Once the decision to prepare an attack was taken on 16 February and troops were gathered in the region, it was clear to all the world that abandonment of the project must entail serious damage to British prestige. There could be no compromise between withdrawal after an unsuccessful naval probe and a full-blown combined assault.
- Churchill was not informed of Kitchener's decision on 20 February not to send the 29th Division after all, resulting in the loss of three weeks and much damage to the prospects of the eventual invasion.
- The decision to abandon the purely naval assault after 18 March was inevitable.
- The fact that the War Council did not meet between 19 March and 14 May, despite the invasion on 25 April, was 'a serious omission': it should have met to reconsider the entire project. The Prime Minister, or failing

him the other politicians on the Council, should have pressed for a meeting.

- Kitchener failed to make use of the General Staff, rendering his workload impossible and causing confusion and inefficiency.
- Fisher was wrong to believe that he should remain silent at War Council meetings or resign, if he did not agree with his chief. Such a principle would if adopted cause damage to the public service.
- Some advantage was gained from the overall failure at the Dardanelles, mainly in tying down so many Turkish divisions; but whether this was worth the 'loss of life and treasure involved is, and must always remain, a matter of opinion'.

Casualty figures for the Dardanelles and Gallipoli campaigns vary. The latter accounted for the lion's share. The official Turkish figures give, in round figures, 87,000 dead and 165,000 wounded. Some authorities round up the Turkish casualty total to 300,000. The Allied figures give 46,000 killed by all causes, including disease, drowning and accidents, and some 220,000 wounded or otherwise incapacitated. Roughly speaking we can probably agree on over a quarter of a million casualties on each side, half a million in all. This is a fraction of the butcher's bill on the Western Front; but it is no less horrifying, considering the small area involved and the numbers of men who fought on and over that appalling battlefield – and why.

CHAPTER 11

What Became of Them

Among the principal personalities involved in the Dardanelles campaign two figures stand out, one from each side: Winston Churchill, the initiator and greatest of all political survivors, and Mustafa Kemal, who became known as Atatürk, the father of his country. But in reviewing the fates of leading participants, including the Ottoman Empire itself, and other powers and personalities involved in the events of 1914–15 in the Aegean Sea and the Dardanelles, it seems appropriate to start with the two Germans and the two Turks who initiated those events: Ambassador Wangenheim and Admiral Souchon; War Minister Enver Pasha and Interior Minister Talaat Bey.

Hans Baron von Wangenheim, the larger-than-life diplomat who did not hesitate to use a mailed fist in negotiation but brought off the Turco-German secret pact in 1914 with aplomb, lived long enough to see the Allies rebuffed at the Dardanelles and held in check in the subsequent Gallipoli campaign. But he died on 25 October 1915, reportedly of overwork which probably exacerbated cardiovascular symptoms, before the Allied divisions withdrew. He was only 56 and had just returned from sick leave. To his credit, in July 1915 he delivered an official protest against the indiscriminate massacres of Armenians by the Turks, a genocidal crime which remains officially unacknowledged in Turkey nearly a century later. While expressing German sympathy for Turkish internal security concerns, he warned of the dangers likely to arise from 'these rigorous measures' involving indiscriminate expatriation accompanied by 'acts of violence, such as massacre and pillage'. General Liman von Sanders also protested.

Wilhelm Anton Theodor Souchon, flag officer of the Imperial German Navy's Mediterranean Division in 1914 and subsequently commander-in-chief of the Ottoman fleet, was promoted to vice-admiral in the Imperial Navy in 1915 and was awarded the highest decoration in the Kaiser's gift, the Order *Pour le mérite*, in 1916. He managed to gain and retain maritime supremacy in the Black Sea for Turkey, despite a series of increasingly desperate encounters with the Russian Black Sea fleet in which the *Goeben* and *Breslau* were often damaged, sometimes seriously, and despite the appearance of two new, locally built and heavily armed Russian dreadnought battleships in 1915: fortunately for Souchon they were a touch slower than the *Goeben*. In September 1917 he was recalled to Germany to take command of the Fourth Squadron of battleships in the High Seas Fleet. In August 1918 he was promoted full admiral and appointed the Kaiser's principal naval adviser, by then a sinecure. He retired from the truncated Reichsmarine in March 1919 and died in Bremen at the age of 81, having seen his country's second defeat in a generation, in January 1946.

The word 'feisty' could have been coined for Enver Pasha, the restless revolutionary who took it upon himself to conclude the fateful treaty with Wangenheim. Enver had no compunction about squeezing the Germans financially during the First World War. 'What have they done for us which compares with what we have done for them?' he would ask rhetorically. Turkey (with not inconsiderable help from the Germans) had defeated the British fleet and seen off the Allied armies from Gallipoli, had tied down large numbers of Russian troops in the Caucasus and British imperial troops in Egypt, Mesopotamia and Palestine, all of whom would otherwise have been deployed against the Central Powers. They even scored a few early victories against uninspired British generals, especially in Mesopotamia. But, although the Russians fared badly against the Turks in the last weeks of 1914, prompting the plea from Grand Duke Nicholas to Britain on 2 January 1915 for a demonstration against them, the situation was transformed by a Russian victory as early as 4 January, at the Battle of Sarikamish in Armenia. There Enver, having snatched defeat from the jaws of victory with an ill-judged divisional manoeuvre in the snow, narrowly escaped capture as 70,000 Turks froze to death. But the closure of the Dardanelles had undeniably crippled the Russian war effort and economy alike, increasing enormously the internal pressures that led to revolution in 1917 and military defeat in 1918. Churchill agreed with Ludendorff of the German General Staff that Turkey's intervention in the war had lengthened it by two years, or almost 100 per cent. Without it, Russia would surely have emerged on the winning side, perhaps with the Tsar still on his throne.

As war with Turkey loomed in autumn 1914, the British took steps to safeguard their oil supply, tiny though its contemporary needs seem when compared with those of today. The navy was in the throes of switching from coal to oil while the needs of the army and the two air arms would obviously grow quickly. Their main supply point in the region was the Persian port of Abadan, in the British sphere of influence; on the opposite bank of the Shatt-al-Arab waterway is Basra, then an important Turkish military base. The first British force to arrive in October 1914 consisted of 5,000 troops from the Indian Army, supported by the navy's Persian Gulf flotilla. Basra was captured on 23 November and used as a main base for operations against the Turks in Mesopotamia (modern Iraq). Within a fortnight General Barrett advanced northward to take the junction of the rivers Tigris and Euphrates at Qurna.

The Turks struck back early in 1915 but their major counter-offensive was beaten back at the Battle of Shaiba in April, when Barrett was relieved by General Sir John Nixon, under orders from the Indian (but not the British) government to capture Baghdad. He moved further north to seize Turkish bases on the two great rivers, consolidating the British imperial grip on southern Mesopotamia. But Baghdad was still 250 miles away, supply lines were too long, the climate was unbearable, troops keeled over in droves, and the 'Marsh Arabs' were hostile. Basra was incapable of handling enough supplies, which then had to be forwarded upriver. Nixon, who based himself there, was over-confident and dismissive of the Turks. He sent Major-General Charles Townshend's 6th Indian Division up the Tigris in September 1915, overriding the latter's opposition. At first the Turks retreated but at Ctesiphon, about 25 miles short of Baghdad, Townshend was halted, badly mauled and beaten back at the end of November, taking refuge in Kut, which was besieged by four Turkish divisions early in December. The Indian government and a reluctant London administration mustered three divisions, two from India earmarked for the occupation of Baghdad and a third from Gallipoli, for the relief of Kut. But General Nur-ud-Din, the Turkish commander, defeated three Anglo-Indian attacks along the Tigris early in 1916.

General Nixon was relieved on health grounds by General Sir Percy Lake, who assembled a larger force for a new advance on Kut in April 1916. This too was defeated, and on the last day of the month Townshend surrendered Kut to General Khalil Pasha, the Turkish commander-in-chief in Mesopotamia, in a blow to British military prestige even worse than the failure at Gallipoli. Britain now took direct charge of operations, placing General Sir Stanley Maude (the last British soldier to leave Gallipoli) in command in August. By autumn his reinforced troops numbered 150,000 and more British officers had been brought in to exert control over the chaos affecting supply, transport and medical services. The logistical position was transformed by the end of the year with modern aircraft, better weapons and more and more vehicles. Maude's army expanded to a quarter of a million during 1917, outnumbering local Turkish forces by a margin of five to one. An advance towards Kut took from December 1916 to February 1917, when the siege was broken at the Second Battle of Kut. British troops finally took Baghdad in March. Most of Khalil's troops got away and Maude continued operations to prevent them being reinforced by the Turkish XIII Corps coming from western Persia. Despite a surrender and a number of skirmishes, the Turkish Army in Mesopotamia remained in being thanks to several skilled retreats. When General Maude, probably the best local commander on either side, caught cholera and died in November 1917, British operations were scaled down under General Marshall. But the fighting in Mesopotamia continued until the bitter end – the Allied armistice with Turkey agreed on 30 October 1918, to take effect on 1 November. Another British commission of inquiry into the Mesopotamian imbroglio started work as early as August 1916 and concluded that it too had all been an appalling mistake.

Meanwhile British imperial troops were also engaged in another major campaign against the Turks on the Palestine front. It began with the abortive attack towards the Suez Canal by Turkish troops of the Fourth Army led by Jemal Pasha, now governor of Syria, and the German General Kress von Kressenstein from Liman von Sanders's military mission. Some 30,000 Indian and ANZAC troops prevailed with minimal losses, but Kressenstein formed a small yet effective desert raiding force that caused much disruption on the Egyptian–Palestinian borders, and concomitant concern in London. Troops finally withdrawn from Gallipoli at the beginning of January 1916 were moved to the defence of Egypt under a cautious General Sir Archibald Murray, previously Chief of the Imperial General Staff and Commander-in-Chief, Middle East, from March 1916. His command was reduced to four infantry divisions by mid-year, nine having been sent to France and one to Mesopotamia. A second Turkish push towards Suez was beaten off in August.

Reinforced again to 150,000 men, Murray began an advance northward with half his force along the Palestine coast, relying heavily on cavalry and reconnaissance aircraft from the army's Royal Flying Corps and the Royal Naval Air Service. The Turks set up a defence line from Gaza to Beersheba, which repelled two British thrusts towards Gaza in March and April 1917. German air reconnaissance helped inflict heavy losses on Murray. He was replaced in June by General Sir Edmund Allenby as Britain built up its effort in Palestine, heavily outnumbering the Turkish defence, led from November by General Erich von Falkenhayn, the former German Chief of General Staff, based in Jerusalem. Allenby attacked the Gaza–Beersheba line, forcing Falkenhayn to form a new line 20 miles south-west of Jerusalem: but his counter-attack failed to break Allenby's right wing as the latter advanced northward, rolling up the Turkish Eighth Army along the coast before halting for the winter rainy season. Fighting continued however round Jerusalem (both sides were under strict orders not to attack the city itself), until Allenby entered the holy city, on foot at the head of his troops, on 11 December 1917, a massively symbolic victory.

The Mesopotamian front was run down at the beginning of 1918 in favour of Allenby's, which mustered 112,000 men in February. The British general took care to delude Falkenhayn that he would advance inland on his right while planning his major thrust along the coast to his left. On 1 March Liman von Sanders took over command of the Turkish line from the coast to the River Jordan and of the forces committed to the defensive Operation 'Yilderim' (lightning), down to fewer than 40,000 men in Palestine. The infrastructure of the contested territory of the Ottoman Empire, never robust, was falling to pieces amid widespread Arab revolts fomented by the British, and Enver insisted on transferring troops to the Caucasian front against Russia. But Allenby had his problems too, losing 60,000 infantry to the Western Front between March and August 1918: although Indian reinforcements arrived, he could not mount an offensive until autumn, perilously close to the rainy season. Victory at the Battle of Megiddo (Armageddon) in mid-September and rapid cavalry and motorised thrusts broke up the Turkish defence as Allenby's forces advanced northward on a broad front towards Damascus and Aleppo. The dashing, fighting advance, one of the fastest on record since the invention of the internal-combustion engine, stands in marked contrast with almost the whole of the rest of the First World War, dominated as it was by trench warfare and the superiority of defensive tactics and weaponry over attacking forces. The British took 75,000 prisoners for fewer than 52,000 casualties (6,000 killed) over nearly three years – small change by First World War standards.

In the English-speaking world the Western Front is far better known than the Eastern, not surprisingly; in Australasia the Gallipoli campaign is even better known (its naval prelude rather less so, whether in Britain or the Antipodes); but perhaps the least-known front of all in the history of the First World War outside Turkey is the Caucasian campaign between the Turks and the Russians, the struggle for the region south and west of the Caucasian mountains – today's Armenia, Georgia and Azerbaijan. The Russians as ever had agents among the large Armenian population within eastern Turkey and were fomenting trouble even before war broke out: when it did, Armenian nationalist restlessness behind the lines, seen by the Turks as treachery and constituting a Turkish variation on the German post-war nationalist theme of the stab in the back, helps to explain (but not excuse) Turkish brutality towards this gifted but tragic ethnic minority. After a few border skirmishes, Enver, planning expansion at Russia's expense, assembled two armies, the Second and Third, under his own command north of Erzerum, a slow business without a railway in the area. The opposing Russian commander, General Mishlayevski, could not hope for reinforcement against a larger enemy because of the demands of the conflict with faraway Germany, but supported an incursion into Turkey by a division of Armenian rebels, who themselves massacred over 100,000 people in north-eastern Turkey in the opening months of 1915.

The Turkish two-pronged advance petered out when the Second Army was bogged down and the Third was routed at the Battle of Sarikamish. The victorious but still outnumbered Russians could do no more than send in a corps to occupy a strip of Turkish Armenia, where 30,000 rebels were now under arms. When a provisional government of Armenia was declared on 20 April 1915, the Turks engaged in what is now called ethnic cleansing of Armenians all over Ottoman territory. Even though hundreds of thousands of Turkish troops were engaged at Gallipoli, Enver ordered another advance on the Caucasian front in July, which was crushed by the Russians under the skilled General Yudenich in August, after which military activity declined on both sides. Yudenich was able to send a corps into Persia in November to foil both a threatened local revolt against the Allied cause and a Turkish deployment there. Despite preoccupations and bad news from the Eastern Front against Germany, the Russian army on the Caucasus front expanded to 22 divisions over the winter of 1915–16, not least to counter the release of Turkish divisions from the Gallipoli stalemate abandoned by the frustrated Allies. Yudenich captured Erzerum in February 1916 and Trebizond in April. Careful not to over-extend himself in difficult terrain, the Russian general contented himself with establishing a firm grip on Armenia in 1916. The western Allies would have liked him to advance into Anatolia in 1917 to relieve pressure on their forces in Mesopotamia and Palestine, but the internal unrest in Russia, leading to the October Revolution, led him to stay put and sit tight.

That revolution put an end to the Russian occupation, prompting more anti-Turkish revolts by the Armenians, who were not above some more ethnic cleansing of their own. A 'republic of Transcaucasia', set up by the Armenians, Azeris and Georgians, flashed briefly across the political firmament, collapsing under the competing aims of its constituent peoples when Armenia broke away in May 1918.

The Russian Treaty of Brest-Litovsk with the victorious Germans in March 1918 was accompanied by an armistice between Russia and Turkey, whereupon the former evacuated Armenia altogether. By October 1918 the Turks withdrew from their own unprofitable operations in northern Persia, Baku and Armenia and repossessed much of the territory hitherto under Russian occupation. Enver's last major offensive in this region served only to undermine Turkish resistance in Mesopotamia and Palestine by drawing in troops better left there.

The CUP regime collapsed at this time and the dominant triumvirate fled to Berlin early in October. The new Ottoman government under Izzet Pasha set up a tribunal in summer 1919 which condemned the CUP leaders as war criminals *in absentia*. This brings us back to the last chapters in the story of Enver who, disguised as Ali Bey, managed to link up with German troops leaving Turkey for home via the Ukraine. General Hans von Seeckt, whom Enver knew well, was chief of staff on the German south-eastern front at the end of the war and, handily for Enver, became chief of staff in the rump German defence force, the Reichswehr, in 1919. In May of that year Enver made his first attempt to reach Russia, intent on pursuing his pan-Turkic and pan-Islamic ideas (and his own return to power), from Germany by aircraft but was arrested, unmasked and jailed as a suspected spy following a forced landing in Lithuania. After four months in prison the irrepressible Enver escaped and got back to Germany, where he joined other Young Turk exiles plotting in Berlin. In August 1920 he travelled incognito by train via East Prussia and Lithuania to Moscow, carrying a briefcase of papers from von Seeckt proposing a secret military alliance between Germany and the Soviet Union. That paved the way to the Treaty of Rapallo in 1922, enabling the Germans to train with tanks and aircraft in the vast spaces of Russia. This was a fundamental breach of the Treaty of Versailles, concluded in June 1919 between Germany and the western powers, which forbade the Reichswehr to acquire or use such weapons. Thus Enver, who had so dramatically influenced the course of the First World War, helped to sow one important seed of the Second.

He even worked briefly in the Asiatic department of the Soviet Foreign Ministry in 1920–1. The Russians did not trust him but had designs on Turkey, especially if the new nationalist government of Mustafa Kemal were to be brought down by his war of liberation against the Greeks, who were initially supported by Britain and France. Soviet revolution or no, the Russians still lusted after Constantinople, even if the Bolsheviks had stopped referring to it as Tsargrad. Enver wanted to oust Kemal, whose government had been the first to recognise the new USSR (which returned the compliment), but Kemal had worked out Russia's true motives and identified Moscow as a potential enemy. Meanwhile at the end of 1920 Enver was plotting an invasion of Anatolia at the head of a Muslim army, just as Kemal wrote to him urging him to foment trouble among the Muslims in east and south Asia without telling the Russians. Then the Treaty of Kars settled outstanding territorial differences between Turkey and the Soviet Union, leaving Enver in limbo.

But the Bolsheviks still thought he might be useful as an instrument for stirring up unrest among the Asian Muslims, including those in Persia and British India. Enver tried to play off the anti-revolutionary White Russians against the Bolsheviks, but after breaking away from the latter he placed himself at the head of a pan-Turkic movement in Central Asia. He was killed in a suicidal cavalry charge, brandishing a sword against Bolshevik rifles and machine-guns on 4 August 1922, still aged only 40. There were rumours that he had been assassinated. He was given a rather belated state funeral in Istanbul on the seventy-fourth anniversary of his death in 1996, five years on from the collapse of the Soviet Union, after his remains had been returned from Tajikistan by descendants of his supporters there, who had buried him in a secret grave. He was interred a second time, next to Talaat on Memorial Hill.

When the CUP fell at the end of the First World War, Talaat also got to Berlin – where he was, not altogether inappropriately, shot dead in the street in 1921 by an Armenian student who had appointed himself avenger of his suffering people.

Admiral John de Robeck was created a Knight Commander of the Order of the Bath – KCB – after his brilliantly successful evacuation of the British Army from Gallipoli without loss in January 1916. It is a military cliché that 'evacuations do not win wars' but his feat was surpassed in British history only by Admiral Sir Bertram Ramsay's evacuation of British troops from Dunkirk in 1940. De Robeck took command of the Third, and after that the Second, Battle Squadron in the Grand Fleet in December 1916. In 1917 he was promoted to substantive vice-admiral. After the war he was made baronet (a hereditary knighthood) and, in 1919, a Knight Grand Cross of the Order of St Michael and St George (GCMG). He became commander-in-chief of the Mediterranean Fleet and High Commissioner in Constantinople (it is not known whether he appreciated the irony of this temporary appointment). He became a full admiral in 1920, and in the following year his KCB was upgraded to GCB (Grand Cross). In April 1922 he was appointed to the command of the Atlantic Fleet, the diminished successor to the Grand Fleet. On his resignation in 1924 he was awarded the Grand Cross of the Victorian Order (GCVO) by King George V and in 1925 he became an admiral of the fleet after his retirement. He died in January 1928, weighed down with so many honours that his failure at the Dardanelles cannot be seen to have held him back in any way.

His erstwhile chief of staff, Commodore Roger Keyes, who shared with Fisher a belief that war should be fought wholeheartedly and proved it by his personal drive and gallantry in trying to solve the minesweeping problem at the Dardanelles, surpassed even de Robeck in his subsequent career. He hung on to his belief that the fleet should try again to break through, and was allowed by his chief to go to London to plead, in vain, for this in May 1915 (innocently carrying a sealed letter from de Robeck to the Admiralty which undermined his case in advance). As late as November 1915, when de Robeck was on leave and Admiral Wemyss was temporarily in command, he tried again, but a sympathetic Wemyss could hardly resist the government's decision at that time to evacuate.

Keyes rose to national prominence soon after he succeeded Admiral Bacon in command of the Dover Patrol in January 1918 as a vice-admiral. He drew up a plan to neutralise the Germans' Belgian U-boat and destroyer bases at Zeebrugge and Ostend, and launched a heroic but unsuccessful attack – the Zeebrugge Raid – with old cruisers as blockships, and Royal Marines and bluejackets attempting a *coup de main* on the harbour mole during the night of 22–23 April 1918. Eight VCs were awarded and Keyes was made KCB, although the blocking effort failed and nothing at all was achieved at Ostend, partly the result of Keyes's impatience with the minutiae of planning.

But the dashing execution of the chaotic enterprise lifted national morale in the fourth year of war. After it, Keyes was made a baronet and stayed on in the navy, serving as Commander-in-Chief, Mediterranean, and finally Portsmouth. He was promoted to admiral of the fleet in 1930, retiring in 1931. He was elected MP for Portsmouth North in 1934, a seat he held for nine years. He published two volumes of partisan but lively memoirs in 1934–5. After an impassioned speech in the Commons in the full uniform of an admiral of the fleet (an appointment for life) in the crisis which brought Churchill to power in May 1940, Keyes begged him for an active role in the Second World War and was appointed chief of combined operations in July 1940. As he outranked very nearly every other British officer, he antagonised the chiefs of staff with impractical operational suggestions (once again, 'all gung ho and no staffwork'), and was replaced in October 1941 by Vice-Admiral Lord Louis Mountbatten, who was no better but was younger, royally glamorous and had friends in high places. Keyes returned to the House of Commons until 1943, when he was elevated to the House of Lords as Baron Keyes of Zeebrugge and Dover. He died in 1945 aged 73.

General Sir Ian Standish Monteith Hamilton, having been relieved of command at Gallipoli for his weak leadership in October 1915 and eventually replaced by General Birdwood, did not command troops again. A cordially hated figure in Australia and New Zealand, thanks to dramatic press exposés of the conditions and deadly confusions at Gallipoli, he became Lieutenant of the Tower of London, a sinecure, in 1918–20. On retirement from that post, he wrote his engagingly readable *Gallipoli Diary*. He died in 1947, aged 94.

The reputation of Field Marshal Horatio Herbert, Earl Kitchener of Khartoum, suffered in the wake of the Dardanelles and Gallipoli débâcle, but only among those in the know about the conduct of the war. The first sign of his waning influence was the fact that his opposition to the opening of what was effectively a new front in the Salonica region in autumn 1915 was overridden by the politicians, notably Lloyd George. He had lost his veto over military operations. On 5 June 1916 he lost his life. He was on his way with a small staff to confer with Grand Duke Nicholas, the Russian supreme commander, in the cruiser HMS *Hampshire* when the ship struck a mine which had been laid by *U75* off Orkney and rapidly sank in a storm. Minesweeping by the Grand Fleet in the area had been lackadaisical, and help was inexplicably slow in coming: only a dozen men survived. The Cabinet may have secretly heaved a sigh of relief, but it was a profound shock to the British public and the British Army on the Western Front and elsewhere. A suitably grim stone memorial overlooks in solitary state the scene of the sinking off the Orkney Mainland. There were rumours that he had been somehow whisked to Russia to take charge of a new offensive there ...

German Lieutenant-General and Turkish Marshal Otto Liman von Sanders commanded the Fifth Army in defence of the Dardanelles. After the defeat of the Allied fleet and the withdrawal of enemy troops from the peninsula, Liman joined several other German representatives in objecting to the Armenian massacres, and also failed to influence Enver in his unsuccessful campaigning in the Caucasus in 1916.

In February 1918 he took over from Falkenhayn the command of a Turco-German force in Palestine against General Allenby. Seriously outnumbered, his command was overwhelmed by British cavalry at the Battle of Megiddo in September 1918 and Liman narrowly escaped capture in his tent at Nazareth. He got back to Constantinople and oversaw the repatriation of German forces after the Armistice. He was arrested there by the British on suspicion of war crimes in February 1919 but was released without charge in August. He then went home and retired to write his memoirs. He died in Munich in 1929, aged 74.

Blame for the essentially British naval and military débâcle at the Dardanelles and Gallipoli was laid at the door of Winston Churchill, though it has surely been shown here that others must bear a share of the responsibility. It would be wrong to describe him as the scapegoat because historically he does bear the lion's share of the guilt and was fairly and not over-severely punished for his own sins rather than those of others. Such a setback would surely have ruined any other politician permanently. We need hardly point out that it did not destroy the career of Churchill, who was to become Prime Minister in May 1940 when Britain's cause in the Second World War seemed hopeless. Cometh the hour, cometh the man: he inspired the British nation and empire to stand alone for a year against the Nazis and laid the foundations of Hitler's defeat.

But all that lay far in the future when the rising tide of accusations of 'bungling in high places' lapped at the threshold of his office in the

Admiralty Old Building. After failing to cling to his beloved naval brief in May 1915, Churchill was fobbed off with the minor Cabinet position of Chancellor of the Duchy of Lancaster, one of so many strange sinecures in the gift of a British Prime Minister. After that he served briefly in the trenches in France as a lieutenant-colonel. When David Lloyd George replaced Asquith as Prime Minister of the coalition government late in 1916, he recalled Churchill to the government as Minister of Munitions, still a sensitive post after earlier scandals over dud shells and shortages. Although he fostered the development of the tank, which would break the deadlock on the Western Front, while in that post he also helped to destroy the Royal Naval Air Service which he had built up as First Lord: the creation of the Royal Air Force on the ironic date of 1 April 1918 by amalgamating the RNAS and the RFC is widely held to be the greatest setback suffered by the Royal Navy in the twentieth century – apart from the Dardanelles, that is.

As Chancellor of the Exchequer after the First World War Churchill once again holed the navy below the waterline by formulating a 'ten-year rule' – an annually renewed assumption that there would be no major war for a decade – which stifled the defence estimates and led, *inter alia*, to a dangerous shortage of cruisers and destroyers. Having seen the RAF firmly established as the third armed service, he supported the creation of the Fleet Air Arm of the Royal Navy in 1937, but the RAF was in immediate charge of long-range maritime operations through Coastal Command, and of aircraft development, where the navy was usually last in the queue. The result was that the British navy's aircraft-carriers fell well behind those of America and Japan, flying such antiquated aircraft as the Swordfish biplane, which none the less performed astonishingly well. Most British admirals kept faith with the 'big gun' until 1945 even though the development of the torpedo had already sounded the death-knell of the dreadnought to those who would listen (such as Japanese and American admirals). Japanese naval aircraft crippled the US battlefleet in Pearl Harbor and sank two British dreadnoughts off Malaya with airborne torpedoes during Japan's shock opening moves in the war in the Far East: American torpedo-bombers turned the tables just six months later at the Battle of Midway. Fortunately Hitler lost no sleep over the possibilities of maritime airpower: his navy never completed an aircraft-carrier and was forced to cede control of maritime aircraft to Goering's Luftwaffe. None the less the submarine torpedo brought Germany closer to victory over Britain than any other weapon.

When Churchill was ousted from the Admiralty in May 1915, various admirals fell over themselves to condemn him in terms such as a 'succubus' (Beatty) or a 'danger to the Empire'. Having spent the last years of peace in a political wilderness, constantly warning of the menace of Nazi Germany, Prime Minister Neville Chamberlain could hardly avoid giving him a Cabinet post when his own peace efforts collapsed and war with Germany was once again declared on 3 September 1939. So the now elderly but still very energetic *enfant terrible* (he was 65) was sent back to the Admiralty. Two messages went round the fleet on that date: one said 'total Germany' (i.e. commence hostilities); the other said, joyously, 'Winston is back!' To international astonishment he was heavily defeated in the British general election of July 1945, but returned in 1951 for a second faltering term as Prime Minister. He died in 1965, aged 91, an occasion which prompted a magnificent state funeral in which sailors hauled the gun-carriage carrying his coffin. There was a national outpouring of grief – mixed with nostalgia for Britain's (and his own) 'finest hour'. He was unquestionably a great man, a great writer too, whose triumphs were counterbalanced, and so nearly outweighed, by error. Fortunately his great error over the Dardanelles was more than outweighed by his decision to send the fleet north in time for the outbreak of war in 1914.

Mustafa Kemal Pasha, who took the sobriquet Atatürk, father of the Turks, when as president he imposed surnames on his people in 1934, was the creator of the secular republic of Turkey. He looms over its history just as Lenin, another man who changed his name, did over the Soviet Union's – and he has outlasted the Russian as a national icon. To this day Atatürk's image is to be seen everywhere in Turkey, and places with even the most fleeting connection with his life and career retain the status of shrines, almost always embellished with an outsize Turkish flag, red with a white crescent and star. The surname is reserved by law for him alone in perpetuity. His words too are to be found in many places in bronze or stone, especially in Ankara, the post-Ottoman capital, Istanbul, the former Constantinople and perpetual metropolis, and of course on the Gallipoli peninsula.

His posting as attaché to Sofia had ended in January 1915 and he returned home to be given the task of raising a new division, the 19th, still in the rank of lieutenant-colonel. He was promoted to full colonel when he prevented the ANZACs from advancing inland in April and went on to win three more victories against the Allies at Gallipoli in August 1915. Kemal, having on several occasions intervened decisively in the struggle for the peninsula, emerged a national hero when the Allies gave up. He was transferred to the Edirne area in European Turkey as a corps commander and rose to lieutenant-general in 1916, whereupon he won several engagements with the Russians. He returned to Constantinople in 1917 and was posted to Syria as commander of the Seventh Army, but resigned when Falkenhayn arrived to lead the fight against Allenby – because he would not now be dictated to by a foreign general. He resumed command however when his replacement fell ill. The Seventh 'Army' had a total strength of 7,000, enough in better times for half an infantry division, divided into four 'divisions' in two 'corps'. It was one of three such 'armies' later commanded by Liman von Sanders to face Allenby's northward advance through Palestine towards Syria; even after surrendering whole divisions to the needs of the Western Front in countering the great German spring offensive, Allenby's forces outnumbered the Turks by two to one or more and eventually carried all before them despite difficulties of supply and terrain, until an armistice with Turkey was concluded at the end of October 1918. Kemal relieved Liman von Sanders in command of all remaining Turkish forces in the region on 1 November, officially in order to disband them; within two weeks he was back in Constantinople working in the War Ministry, helping to 'clear up' after the comprehensive defeat of the Ottoman Empire.

CHAPTER 12

The New Turkey and Middle East

At this juncture the personal history of Mustafa Kemal becomes inextricable from the contemporaneous history of his country, which he fundamentally reshaped. No less bound up with post-war developments in and around Turkey is the history of modern Greece. Atatürk's republic would emerge, stripped of the last trappings of the Ottoman Empire, like a phoenix from the fire of war with Greece – a rebirth of Turkish pride nearly 500 years after the Ottomans captured Constantinople in 1453.

King Constantine I of Greece (1868–1923; reigned 1913–17 and 1920–2) was of Danish extraction and married to a sister of Kaiser Wilhelm II. He had undergone German military training and favoured the cause of the Central Powers. Eleutherios Venizelos (1864–1936), a Cretan prominent in detaching his home island from Ottoman rule and uniting it with Greece, was elected Prime Minister of Greece in 1910 and supported the Entente. Leaving aside the complexities of Greek internal politics, Venizelos, who dreamed of expansion at the expense of Turkey, more than doubled the size of his country as a result of the Balkan Wars of 1912–13, gaining Epirus, Macedonia and the Aegean Islands: Salonica in western Thrace (now Thessaloniki) was part of the gains from Turkey, which ceded them permanently in the Treaty of Bucharest, settling the Balkan conflict in 1913.

Venizelos's ambitions did not end there and extended to Constantinople itself. He also wanted to embed the new Greece in a modernising western world. The merest glance at a modern map of the Aegean shows how the Greeks gained land, especially islands, from the waning Ottomans in the Balkan wars and afterwards: the international boundary between Greece and Turkey hugs the Turkish coast, leaving all the larger islands, including Lemnos, Mitylene, Chios, Lesbos, Cos and Rhodes, all just offshore, in Greek hands. Imbros (Imroz), off the mouth of the Dardanelles, is the only large Aegean island that remains Turkish. An estimated 1.5 million ethnic Greeks lived in Constantinople, Smyrna and other parts of Ottoman territory, including the coasts of the Black and Aegean seas and the eastern Balkans; they had established themselves in these areas centuries before the Romans created the Byzantine Empire and a couple of millennia before the Turks moved into Anatolia. Many of the more remote ethnic Greeks spoke unrecognisable dialects (or no Greek at all), even using the Greek alphabet to write in Turkish, their DNA probably only fractionally distinguishable from that of their Turkish neighbours and their ethnicity recognisable only by the fact that they attended the Greek Orthodox Church (whose Patriarch resided in Constantinople, not Athens) rather than the mosque, and sent their children to Christian schools. To this day only the language it is written in distinguishes a Greek menu from a Turkish one; many Turks also lived in Greece. Voluntary Greek migration to Turkey continued in considerable numbers in the years immediately before the First World War. The traditional Ottoman *laissez-faire* attitude to minorities however began to fade under the CUP from 1908 and was further diminished after the Balkan wars, when inter-communal unrest and reprisals began. Both communities turned increasingly to nationalism.

The charismatic Venizelos was lionised by western leaders as a statesman when he attended the negotiations at Versailles from November 1918, which led to the most important peace treaty, with Germany, in June 1919. The conference was intended to settle all issues between all the belligerents but in many respects made a worse fist of it than the Congress of Vienna after the Napoleonic Wars. Venizelos denied that Greece wanted Constantinople but secretly calculated that if the city were removed from Turkish rule, the large and enterprising Greek population there would effectively take the place over. It was, he was wont to say privately, virtually and historically a Greek city already.

But if the Ottoman state and the Turkish nation were prostrate after their defeat in 1918, Greek unity was not much less fragile. The struggle for power between King Constantine and Venizelos deeply, and it seems permanently, split the country and almost led to civil war, with the Prime Minister in and out of office, purging his political opponents in all major institutions when he was in power. In 1917 he brought Greece into the war in the Allied cause – the winning side – whereas Enver had ruined Turkey by choosing the losers. Greece had helped the Allies before that, whether lending them captured Turkish island territory off the Dardanelles or allowing Allied troops into Salonica, with Greek troops fighting alongside. They were also fighting alongside the French against the Bolsheviks in 1919, among the many other foreign military interventions against the revolution.

On 3 February 1919 Venizelos got his opportunity to address the peace conference and seized it with both hands, producing a *tour de force* of passionate, persuasive, utterly reasonable-sounding rhetoric. He wanted Greek possession of the Aegean Islands confirmed, he wanted half of Albania, as well as a great swathe of territory between the Aegean and the Black Sea and a generous coastal slice of Anatolia as far south as Smyrna. Ostentatiously he did not ask for Constantinople. The result would have been a curiously circular rim-state wrapped round Turkish territory and waters, which would arouse not only Turkish but also Bulgarian hostility, against which it would be incapable of defending itself should the highly likely need arise. Even some, though not enough, of his admirers saw that Venizelos was seriously overreaching himself as he exploited the sentimentality of classically educated diplomats, so numerous in the Allied delegations (especially the British), and misrepresented the swarthy modern Greeks as the direct descendants of Homer and Pericles, Herodotus and Praxiteles. Recent history enabled him to set the nobility of the Greek liberation struggle against the brutality and corruption of the Turks whom they had fought for their freedom, for which Lord Byron and other foreigners had actually died. The result was a disaster whose consequences continue to reverberate in the twenty-first century.

The British, keen as ever to maximise protection of the sacred route to India via the Mediterranean and Suez and unable to rely on Turkey for the purpose, saw a stronger Greece as an attractive alternative. Lloyd George, still Prime Minister after 1918, knew Venizelos well, liked him and called him the greatest Greek statesman since Pericles. Of the main western powers, only Italy, which had expansionist ambitions of its own in Albania and Asia Minor (as did Serbia, Montenegro and even France), had strong reservations, not unconnected with its recent island acquisitions from the Turks in the Aegean, which the Greeks regarded as part and parcel of the greater Greece of which they were recklessly dreaming. The Americans, albeit benevolent, were mostly neutral, although President Woodrow Wilson admired Venizelos personally very much.

The caretaker government that supplanted the CUP in October 1918 sent word to Vice-Admiral Sir Arthur Gough-Calthorpe, the British commander-in-chief in the Mediterranean at the time, asking for talks. They began aboard his flagship, HMS *Agamemnon*, at Mudros on 28 October between the admiral and Hussein Rauf, a decorated Turkish naval officer and Minister of Marine. On the flimsy grounds that the Turkish approach had been made specifically to the British, the French were excluded. The talks were swiftly and pleasantly concluded, the two principals toasted each other in champagne and signed an armistice on 30 October. Emollient assurances were given to the Turks that the Allies, having availed themselves of the residue of Ottoman Arab territory in the Near and Middle East, had no interest in occupying Constantinople. The terms included the surrender of all Turkish troops everywhere, Allied control of the railways and telegraph services and access to all Turkish ports for Allied warships. The Allies reserved the right to occupy any 'strategic points' if their security was threatened. Points could hardly be more strategic than Constantinople, which was soon filled with Allied ships, soldiers and diplomats behaving as if they owned the place.

Mustafa Kemal rushed back to the city to urge every Turkish official he could reach to stand up to the *de facto* invaders. The last Sultan of Turkey, Mehmet VI, who had only ascended the hollow throne in summer 1918, adopted a policy of appeasement, dissolving parliament in November and trying to exercise direct rule, but without the necessary governmental infrastructure. The erstwhile heart of the eastern Roman and then Ottoman empires was dirty and neglected, its people desperate for food and coal. Refugees poured in from Russia, Armenia and the dismantled empire; tens of thousands of homeless people slept on the bitterly cold streets. There was an eruption of blue and white Hellenic flags as the large Greek community anticipated territorial and commercial profit for their race. For foreigners from the victorious powers the atmosphere seems to have been very similar to that of Weimar Berlin just a few years later: cafés, nightclubs and brothels flourished and hard currency (or food or tobacco) could buy a great deal of debauchery and valuables for very little. There was even an unofficial foretaste of the division of Berlin into sectors in 1945, with the main powers each taking over and policing a segment of the city. When the occupation of Constantinople became official in March 1920, hardly anyone noticed.

The moment an avid Greece overreached herself came in mid-May 1919, when Venizelos, with the blessing of Britain and France and the concurrence of the United States, sent soldiers to occupy Smyrna (now Izmir), the port city midway along Turkey's western coast. Smyrna was indeed ethnically Greek (including large numbers of recent immigrants) but it was a key part of the Turkish economy and its hinterland was overwhelmingly populated by Turks. The triumphant arrival of Greek troops was marred by inter-communal riots in which hundreds of Greeks and Turks died. The disorder spread to the surrounding countryside and major demonstrations by Turks in Constantinople and other centres followed. This was the nadir of Turkish fortunes in the eyes of Mustafa Kemal and his growing tally of nationalist sympathisers. Alarmed, the British demanded that the Turkish government send out an inspector-general to restore order. Kemal, in Constantinople, angled for the job and, armed with a British *laissez-passer*, set off with a small staff for Samsun, a port half-way along the Black Sea coast of Anatolia. He arrived on 19 May – still a national holiday in Turkey, commemorating the moment when the worm turned. Kemal set out to recruit undemobilised Turkish officers and troops for the nationalist cause, reorganising units in the Anatolian interior without the knowledge of the British and French.

As the powers dithered in Paris, there was talk of separate Kurdish and Armenian states, Italian and French territorial ambitions, mandates in Asia Minor for the Americans, of hiving off Constantinople and the straits – soon Turkey could become the rump of a rump. With total commitment Kemal roamed Anatolia turning pockets of protest into a broad nationalist campaign. In June 1919 he warned the Armenians and foreign intruders that the Turks would fight for their territory to the bitter end, and if they could not win their country back they would destroy it. Under Allied pressure the Sultan recalled Kemal, who refused to come and promptly resigned on 23 June, summoning a national congress at Erzerum which declared that all places, including Constantinople, where Turks lived must stay part of Turkey. Meanwhile in Paris the 'Big Three' – America, Britain and France – carved up the corpse of the Ottoman Empire in blissful ignorance of the significance and strength of Kemal's movement.

In London the Lord Privy Seal in Lloyd George's Cabinet, Curzon, who knew more than most about 'abroad', especially the Ottoman Empire, was deputising at the Foreign Office (he was about to become Foreign Secretary in place of former premier Arthur Balfour, who was in Paris). Lloyd George intensely disliked Curzon, who had become Viceroy of India at the age of 39, from 1898 to 1905, for his privileged and wealthy background and effortless superiority (his detractors quoted a little doggerel: 'My name is George Nathaniel Curzon/And I'm a most superior person'). A know-all as brilliant as Churchill but much less stable, Curzon warned again and again that it would be a disaster to partition Turkey proper, not least because it would antagonise the Muslim world, which extended to British India. Foreign Secretary at last from October 1919, his great ambition achieved, he became Turkey's most important advocate, opposing Lloyd George's strong support for the Greeks in Smyrna. On his promotion he sent as a secret envoy an army colonel, who had previously met Kemal, to sound him out. The nationalist leader declared Ankara, in the middle of Anatolia, as the new capital of Turkey, as it still is, in place of Constantinople, which remained in a state of chaos and want. As the Americans withdrew into isolationism, the British, French and Italians with varying degrees of reluctance officially occupied Constantinople in March to restore order, arresting a number of nationalists and officers. Kemal replied in kind, arresting every Allied officer he could find in the Turkish interior, including Curzon's emissary, Lieutenant-Colonel Alfred Rawlinson. He also founded a new nationalist parliament.

Curzon could not persuade Lloyd George to let the obviously organised and formidable Kemal run with the ball and take charge of Turkey. Instead a draft treaty was drawn up and sent to the Sultan's government. It was extremely humiliating. The Treaty of Sèvres, the settlement between a prostrate Turkey and the Allies negotiated at the Paris Peace Conference, was signed by Mehmet VI on 10 August 1920. It not only formalised the amputation of all former Ottoman provinces outside Turkey itself; it put the Dardanelles and the Bosporus under international control – and ceded Smyrna and Thrace to Greece, despite Italian ambitions to acquire the city as part of a slice of south-western Anatolia (opposite 'their' island of Rhodes). Italy and France got 'spheres of influence' in Anatolia; Kurdistan got home rule; and Armenia independence. Several British army divisions from Mesopotamia and Constantinople were in the Caucasus with an eye to the oilfields. To the north General Denikin's White Russians were trying to oust the Bolsheviks. Losing appetite for this massive military involvement in the Caucasus, Lloyd George and the Cabinet decided to withdraw by the end of 1919, promising material support to Denikin if he laid off Armenia. But the Bolsheviks got the upper hand and, desperate for allies anywhere for their pariah state, they supported Kemal. Armenia was in effect crushed between them after a few shaky months of independence. Kurdistan remained divided among Turkey and its neighbours.

In June 1920, in return for sending troops to support the Allied presence in Constantinople, Lloyd George let Venizelos off the leash and allowed the Greek Army to advance from Smyrna into the country around it on a broad front. The troops pushed 250 miles into the interior by August as thin Turkish nationalist forces withdrew before them. Kemal for the time being concentrated on the north-east and on crushing Armenia, which, shrunk to a scrap of territory, signed an armistice with him, opting to become a republic within the USSR in December. (In

March 1920 the Treaty of Moscow settled the Russo-Turkish border as it stands to this day, with the Soviets formally returning previously occupied territory to Turkey. The Bolshevik representative for both these settlements was a certain Commissar Joseph Stalin.)

The removal of Armenia from his agenda enabled Kemal at last to turn his attention westward to deal with the Greeks. They had been shaken by the defeat of Venizelos in the November 1920 general election. The exiled King Constantine came back and sympathy for Greece among the Allies melted away. Her troops fought on, making a remarkable advance over dreadful terrain worthy of Xenophon and his Ten Thousand, but in the opposite direction. Short of Ankara, and 400 miles from Smyrna, logistical problems proved insurmountable, the Greeks faltered and lost heart, and in August 1922 Kemal at last struck back towards Smyrna, which he entered in triumph on 10 September after roundly defeating the Greeks in the field. Turkish vengeance was terrible, with widespread massacres, rape, pillage and arson which razed the Greek districts of the city. Kemal next turned north along the Anatolian coast. Only the British Army, which had taken up positions at Chanak on the Asian shore of the Dardanelles, stood between him and Constantinople. Lloyd George was ready to go to war, but no other power was interested in supporting him except New Zealand, and common sense (and the arguments of Curzon and British generals) prevailed. An armistice on 11 October gave eastern Thrace back to Turkey, while Kemal undertook not to move into Constantinople pending negotiations for a new Turkish settlement.

Lloyd George's coalition government collapsed under the strain and the Conservative Andrew Bonar Law took over as Prime Minister in November 1922. Curzon remained Foreign Secretary and went to Lausanne for talks on a fairer settlement. Also present were the new French premier, Poincaré, a deflated Venizelos (back in office), an Italian representative called Mussolini, along with Bulgarian and Russian delegates. The Americans limited themselves to sending observers. Kemal's representative, General Ismet, led the Turkish delegation; Kemal had already abolished the sultanate. Ismet did not negotiate but merely repeated like a cracked gramophone record his demand for an independent Turkey freed of all outside interference. Now the defeated enemy had the upper hand, with a victorious army in the field, while the victors of 1918 had little or no stomach for a fight. Sèvres was all but torn up. The Treaty of Lausanne of July 1923 formalised a new Turkey within the borders it now enjoys, apart from the boundary with the new British mandate of Iraq, which was settled by the League of Nations in 1925. The straits remained Turkish but with guarantees for their international use. Constantinople, once Byzantium, became Istanbul.

Greeks in their hundreds of thousands moved out of Turkey towards Greece, including Greeks who had never been there, Greeks who spoke no comprehensible Greek, or any at all – a pre-enactment of the exchange of populations accompanying the partition of India in 1947. In their turn Turks soon started to move out of expanded Greece in the opposite direction under the Treaty of Lausanne, which permitted a small Greek community to remain in Constantinople, and a small Turkish one in western Thrace. Salonica and the birthplace of Mustafa Kemal remained Greek.

Kemal went on to abolish the caliphate in March 1924 and embarked on a series of far-reaching social reforms, including the adoption of the Latin alphabet in place of Arabic script, and of the modern international calendar, rights for women, secularisation of education and the law, agricultural and industrial reforms and cultural innovations. First elected president by the 'Grand Assembly' in 1923, his mandate was renewed every four years until and including 1935. He occupied modest apartments within the vast Dolmabahçe Palace on the Bosporus, the last home of the Sultans, and lived simply, although he was over-fond of women, tobacco and alcohol: his liver failed on 10 November 1938 and he died aged only 57. All the palace clocks still show the time of his death: 9.05 a.m. He was buried at Ankara, and reburied 15 years later in a great mausoleum after a state ceremony on 10 November 1953, a national hero *sans pareil*.

The 'Turkish Question' had at last been answered – by a Turk. Or had it? To leap forward from Atatürk's rule to the present day, there is a new 'Turkish question' which is once again exercising the minds of the European powers, and dividing them: should Turkey, most of which is in Asia, be allowed to join the European Union? Every Turkish number plate today features a small blue tag, the bottom half of which carries the letters TR; the top half is blank. It looks just like the tags on plates in EU member-states – except that the EU motif of a circle of twelve gold stars is missing. At the same time, the Turkish Army stubbornly occupies, ever since 1974 and the 'enosis' scare when Greece appeared poised to absorb Cyprus, some 40 per cent of that island, creating the universally unrecognised 'republic of Northern Cyprus' – a large slice of the territory of a member of the European Union which Turkey purportedly wants to join. With 'Europe' in mind, the Turks have been trying fitfully to improve their human-rights record, but it remains a crime to attack 'Turkishness'. The distinguished writer Orhan Pamuk was even prosecuted for daring to suggest that the Armenians were massacred in large numbers at the time of the First World War (but was acquitted under massive international pressure). One of the greatest legacies of Atatürk was a strictly secular republic with no official role for Islam in its affairs. But amid all the enduring discontent in the Muslim world in general, there are strong pressures within contemporary Turkey for a reversal of this provision. A straw in the wind came in 2008, when the Turkish parliament, with a pro-Islamic majority, voted to allow women to wear veils at university. Atatürk must have been turning in his grave at the time at this first inroad on his secular legacy; but the army was already showing signs of returning to its self-appointed role of defending the secular state. So often the Turks appear to be their own worst enemy, with no trace either of that valuable ability to see themselves as others see them or of understanding the value of public relations. If the mullahs ever took over, that would surely be the end of Turkey's already shaky prospects of joining the EU.

Yet modern Turkey is a lot more stable than most of its Asian neighbours which left, or were taken from, the Ottoman Empire during and after the First World War. The story of the demolition of the Turkish Empire in Asia – which had lasted since before the capture of Constantinople in 1453, longer than the Roman Empire in the west, much longer than the British Empire – is soon told. The British made a protectorate of Transjordan in 1916: it became the independent Hashemite Kingdom of Jordan in 1946. Syria and Lebanon were mandated to France by the League of Nations in 1922 although the French had moved in already in 1919 – their share of the Ottoman spoils. Both territories were wrested from Vichy government control during the Second World War and became independent in 1941 and 1943 respectively. What was left of the Arabian Peninsula (the world's largest) after the territories round its edge (Yemen, Oman, Bahrain, Kuwait, Qatar and the Emirates) went their own way, had been the scene of a spectacular campaign by that mysterious, romanticised figure, Colonel T. E. Lawrence, who fostered a revolt in the desert against the Turks by Arab and Bedouin tribesmen. It was not until 1932 that Ibn Saud completed the unification of the four tribal provinces of Hejaz, Azir, Najd and Al-Hasa into the present-day kingdom of Saudi Arabia. An absolute monarchy, it observes the strictest form of Islam, Wahhabism, as it protects Islam's holiest shrines of

Mecca (the birthplace of the religion) and Medina, and rejoices in the world's largest-known national oil reserve.

Mesopotamia was wrested from Turkish control by British troops after 1916 and was mandated to Britain in 1921 as the new state of Iraq, following a series of rows between the British and French over this, over control of Middle Eastern oil and over Syria. Under the Ottomans Mesopotamia, a geographical expression for the region between and adjacent to the rivers Tigris and Euphrates, had been divided into three very distinct provinces – Mosul in the north (where many Kurds live), Baghdad in the centre and Basra in the south. The new political entity was not a nation but a line on a map, rather like Nigeria or the London Borough of Croydon, drawn for administrative convenience. Arabs rose in revolt in Mosul and the Baghdad region in 1920 against British rule, destroying communications, laying siege to garrisons and killing British officials. The rebels were brutally suppressed by punitive expeditions while the infant RAF introduced a new stratagem, the airborne bombing and strafing of civilians as a means of crushing resistance. In March 1921 Churchill, then Colonial Secretary, decided to turn Iraq into a kingdom under the Hashemite Feisal, who had alongside Lawrence raised the banner of rebellion against Turkish rule in Arabia; his brother Abdullah was made king of Transjordan, still ruled as Jordan by his descendants. Churchill was handing out thrones like chocolate bars, rewards for the support given to Lawrence, whose lavish promises to the Arabs had not been honoured.

The Iraqi monarchy, granted independence in 1932, was overthrown in 1958 and a republic was declared. The emergence of Saddam Hussein from the ruling Ba'ath Party as dictatorial president in 1979 inaugurated a quarter of a century of ruinous war, against Iran, against the Kurdish population, against Kuwait, which was briefly occupied in 1991, against a US-led coalition which liberated Kuwait in that year and finally in 2003, when a second American-led invasion toppled Saddam, who was executed in 2007 after a ramshackle trial. The results of the invasion, openly aimed at regime-change but with underlying commercial motives, based on false or forged 'intelligence' and without an exit strategy, have been an unmitigated disaster for the people of Iraq. So far the cure has been worse than the disease and a stupefying quantity of blood and treasure has been wasted.

Turkey can hardly be blamed for what has become of the constituent parts of the Ottoman Empire since it was dispossessed of them in 1918. This applies above all perhaps to Palestine, which was mandated to Britain in

1920 – three years after the fateful Balfour Declaration promising a Jewish homeland. There had however been a considerable influx of Zionists into Palestine under the Ottomans in the 1880s. Balfour's extraordinary document is a perfect illustration of the principle that the road to hell is paved with good intentions. Arthur (later Earl) Balfour (1848–1930) was Conservative Prime Minister from 1902 to 1905 and was a member of the War Council from 1914, briefly succeeding Churchill as First Lord of the Admiralty until serving as Foreign Secretary from 1916 to 1919. He was nicknamed Bloody Balfour for his enthusiastic suppression of Irish republicans; critics of his declaration regard this as an appropriate nickname for another reason. His notorious promise was contained in a short note to the second Baron Rothschild of the enormously influential, Anglo-German Jewish banking dynasty, the nub of which reads:

> His Majesty's Government view with favour the establishment in Palestine of a national home for the Jewish people ... it being clearly understood that nothing shall be done which may prejudice the civil and religious rights of existing non-Jewish communities.

By 1923 it had been clarified as British official policy which included: encouragement of Jewish immigration to Palestine under the auspices of a special body created for the purpose; protection of the rights of non-Jews; equal status for Hebrew, Arabic and English. All this ignored the mathematical and logical principle that two into one won't go. The Arabs complained that the Jews were being given preference at their expense and the rate of immigration threatened their interests; the Jews claimed that the British were dragging their feet in fulfilling their promise to the Jewish people. Tension mounted in Palestine between the wars as more and more Jews fled the Nazis after 1933; then came the unspeakable Holocaust of six million European Jews. This not only encouraged a new wave of migration to Israel by survivors but also left a legacy of guilt among the western powers, especially in Britain, which retained its mandate after 1945, and the United States, where millions of Jews lived thanks to earlier migrations from Europe and collectively wielded enormous political influence.

But, as many a Palestinian Arab has remarked in recent years: 'Why are we being punished for Auschwitz?' The hapless British were demonised for their efforts to control the Jewish influx, which included several public-relations disasters; Jewish groups in Palestine formed terrorist gangs which perpetrated atrocities; and in 1947 the United Nations, successor-organisation to the League of Nations, supported the establishment of two states in Palestine, one Jewish, one Arab. Britain, which had just given up the core of its empire in the Indian sub-continent, could not wait to be relieved of its mandate, and when a date could not be agreed at the UN, gave unilateral notice of its intention to leave in 1948. The Arabs rejected the two-state solution, so David Ben-Gurion promulgated the state of Israel on 14 May 1948. Challenges from the neighbouring Arab states were beaten off, and Israel became the local superpower in a series of further wars with the Arabs (1956, 1958, 1967, 1973, 1982 and 2007, not to mention aerial bombings of neighbouring states), acquiring nuclear weapons along the way and confining the Palestinians to the teeming Gaza Strip and the West Bank of the River Jordan.

Many millions of Palestinian refugees live miserable lives in countries such as Jordan, Lebanon, Syria and Egypt. Tragically, the Arabs will not absorb them, understandably if cruelly, because that would imply acceptance of the Israeli occupation of Palestine. Ironically, 60 years after the Arabs rejected the idea of two states on the soil of Palestine, Israel's all-powerful protector, the United States, tried to revive the seriously neglected 'peace process' on the basis of a 'two-state solution'. The Palestinians have seen their fragile hopes crumble as the Israelis built a wall across Palestine against Arab suicide bombers and allowed scores of illegal Jewish settlements on the West Bank. The fact that a once-persecuted people has itself turned persecutor is surely one of the bitterest ironies in history.

If Turkey is responsible for none of the foregoing, why mention it? The twin roots of the endless crises that have engulfed the former Ottoman lands since 1918 are first, that Turkey should have remained neutral in 1914 (as it wisely did in 1939) rather than joining the Central Powers, and second, that the Royal Navy squandered the chance to correct this mistake by its great failure at the Dardanelles to mount a combined operation. While this might be dismissed as mere hindsight, it is fair to point out that most of the Turkish Cabinet favoured neutrality in 1914; and that overwhelming *contemporary* opinion in British ruling, naval and military circles had always been that only a combined operation could hope to force the Dardanelles.

To the combined effect of two huge, failed gambles, Enver's in Constantinople and Churchill's in London, must be added Souchon's successful one in delivering the instrument, itself the beneficiary of another blunder by the Royal Navy, to activate the Turco-German alliance that doomed Russia. As Barbara Tuchman wrote in *August 1914*:

Thereafter the red edges of war spread over another half of the world. Turkey's neighbours, Bulgaria, Rumania, Italy and Greece, were eventually drawn in. Thereafter, with her exit to the Mediterranean closed, Russia was left dependent on Archangel, icebound half the year, and on Vladivostok, 8,000 miles from the battlefront. With the Black Sea closed, her exports dropped ninety-eight per cent and her imports by ninety-five per cent. The cutting off of Russia with all its consequences, the vain and sanguinary tragedy of Gallipoli, the diversion of Allied strength in the campaigns of Mesopotamia, Suez and Palestine, the ultimate break-up of the Ottoman Empire, the subsequent history of the Middle East, followed from the voyage of the *Goeben*.

Not only *post hoc*, but also *propter hoc*.

Epilogue
The Tale of Two Ships

After the Russian Revolution there was very little for the Turkish fleet to do. Many of the sailors on the two German ships were farm boys, and they were given some land near their anchorage of Stenia (Istinye) where they could grow maize and rear pigs. Eventually this little enterprise turned a profit in a Constantinople which was close to starvation. From 4 September 1917 their flag officer was Vice-Admiral Hubert von Rebeur-Paschwitz, Souchon's replacement. The Black Sea was quiet after three years of sometimes desperate actions with the Russian Black Sea Fleet, now confined to port. When intelligence indicated in December 1917 that two British divisions were about to be moved from Salonica to reinforce Allenby in Palestine, Paschwitz was reminded that there was another enemy afloat at the other end of the straits with whom the Turco-German fleet had never fought an action. He suggested to Enver that his ships stage a raid on Salonica, 120 miles from the entrance to the Dardanelles, to disrupt the troop movements and raise Turkish morale.

Even Enver could see that this was an extremely risky, not to say crazy, proposition, but preparations for a sortie out of the Dardanelles went ahead. To avoid confusion the two German ships are referred to here by their original names. Enemy naval forces were well known: the last two British pre-dreadnoughts, *Lord Nelson* and *Agamemnon*, which with a combined total of eight 12-inch guns outgunned the *Goeben*; one French heavy and one British light cruiser, both elderly; two monitors (floating gun platforms for coastal bombardment), HMMs *Raglan* and *M28*; a small flotilla of destroyers and miscellaneous vessels.

Paths were quietly cleared in the defensive minefields beyond the Narrows and German aircraft plotted the positions of Allied mines off the entrance on a chart as Paschwitz scaled down his plans to a hit-and-run raid on the Allied guard force which, in one form or another, had been in place off the Dardanelles since August 1914. He hoped to make a surprise attack and get his ships back inside the Narrows long before the pair of battleships could get to the scene from Mudros. The admiral assembled the strongest and most viable squadron available to him: the *Goeben* and *Breslau*, four of the best Turkish destroyers and the German submarine *UC23*, which was detailed to lay mines off Mudros under cover of the raid and lie in wait for torpedo targets.

Hearing of the plan at the last minute, General Liman von Sanders helpfully gave the admiral a British Admiralty chart, seized from a British steamer grounded off Gallipoli, which bore markings interpreted (wrongly) as Allied mine positions. The two charts proved irreconcilable, suggesting that there were no gaps at all between or within the opposed minefields, but Paschwitz metaphorically shut his eyes and pressed on. At 5.10 a.m. on 20 January 1918, after his ships had crept through the Turkish minefields during the night, the *Goeben* at the head of the column struck a British mine. Damage was minor and soon brought under control, so *Goeben* sailed on after a few minutes.

Breslau turned north-west out of the entrance and targeted the monitors at anchor in Kusu Bay, Imbros. The *Goeben* caught up and both ships started shelling the eastern coast of the island. *Raglan* blew up and sank at her moorings, shortly followed to the bottom by *M28*, whose magazine exploded. Remarkably, both monitors had managed to return fire, though only briefly and to no avail: only 132 men out of the two crews totalling 310 survived the double blast.

At 5.20 a.m. the tiny destroyer HMS *Lizard*, which had been on night-patrol duty off the Dardanelles, sent out the signal the guard force had been waiting for these past three and a half years: 'GOBLO … GOBLO …' – *Goeben* and *Breslau* out. She had challenged the unfamiliar light cruiser ahead of her and got no reply; then she sighted a battlecruiser one mile behind. None the less the 780-tonne destroyer (Lieutenant O. A. G. Ohlenschlager, RN) opened fire on the cruiser even as she was shelling the monitors, breaking off to organise help for their crews. *Breslau* opened fire on her as she zigzagged violently, her guns hopelessly outranged. Her patrol partner and sister-ship HMS *Tigress* was the only Allied warship to come to her aid. British naval aircraft based on Imbros heard the GOBLO alert, took off and harassed the Germans as best they could, prompting them too to zigzag as they fired machine-guns in the air. The German pair turned north up the coast of Imbros, looking for new targets, damaging ships and buildings, the pair of destroyers following, even though the *Breslau* had resumed firing on them.

At 7.31 a.m. the *Breslau*, sailing half a mile behind the *Goeben*, pulled out of line to take up station ahead of her – and ran into a British minefield. One blew up under her stern and wrecked her rudder. The *Goeben* turned to help and set off a mine aft. Five minutes later the *Breslau* succumbed to two more mines under her damaged stern, and yet another exploded on her port bow. She went dead in the water, listing to port. A fifth mine went off amidships and Captain Georg von Hippel gave the order to abandon ship. More then 500 men jumped overboard, and their captain led three cheers from the bitterly cold water for their dying ship. The two British destroyers had turned to beat off an attack by the four Turkish ones before it started, driving them back into the Dardanelles and turning back again to rescue more than 150 Germans, including von Hippel, despite the mines all around. *Goeben* took a further mine amidships and began to list, a development which was corrected by yet another mine on the other side as she zigzagged at half speed back into the Dardanelles. With her pumps working flat out she evaded the Turkish minefield inside the Narrows – only to run aground on a sandbank near Nagara Point on the Asian shore. British aircraft circling overhead were met by German aircraft and dogfights developed as Captain Stoelzel, in command for just 16 days, struggled to refloat the *Goeben*. She was a sitting target, open to air and submarine attack and within range of the big guns of the British battleships, listing at an angle that prevented her from using her own main armament. She had never been closer to destruction.

But, as ever, there was a British admiral on hand to ensure that a golden opportunity was missed. Rear-Admiral Arthur Hayes-Sadler had hoisted his flag just eight days before the last foray of the Mediterranean Division. When he found his yacht was out of service and needing to confer with army headquarters at Salonica, he took the *Lord Nelson*, thus ensuring that there were not enough big guns on hand to outshoot the *Goeben*, the very reason why the two pre-dreadnoughts were there together in the first place. The rest of the guard force was scattered, leaving just the pair of little destroyers on watch, a fact which may partly explain why Hayes-Sadler used a battleship as a taxi, but not why his ships were so dispersed. The commander-in-chief in the Mediterranean, Vice-Admiral Sir Arthur Gough-Calthorpe, was furious and slammed another stable door by ordering that the pair of battleships should stay together in future …

As frantic work went on round the clock to save the *Goeben*, more than 250 Allied air sorties failed to cause significant damage with their little bombs, even by rare direct hits. More Allied planes came over from Salonica; seaplanes from the carrier *Ark Royal* tried the new tactic of dropping torpedoes in the water. The beached ship was thus constantly surrounded by columns of water, explosions, smoke from bombs and anti-aircraft fire from Turkish batteries at the biplanes growling overhead as other ships tried to free her. On 26 January, as the German sailors lightened ship and a strong wind grounded Allied aircraft, Turkish warships assembled for an almighty towing effort, freeing the *Goeben* in the afternoon. She sailed slowly under her own power to Constantinople, which she reached on the morning of the 27th, saved by the strength and construction of her hull. But for her at last the war was over. On the same day Hayes-Sadler decided after days of dithering that one of his three submarines on hand might usefully pass up the strait to administer a *coup de grâce* by torpedo to the crippled battlecruiser. *E14* got as far as Nagara Point, where the *Goeben* had lain for the best part of a week, at dawn on 28 January, but of course found nothing. A British aircraft came over at about the same time and reported that the bird had hopped away. On her way out *E14* was detected and sunk by shore batteries and destroyers. Nine men survived and were taken prisoner. The *Goeben* had once again eluded the Royal Navy in acutely embarrassing circumstances. The new First Sea Lord, Admiral Sir Rosslyn Wemyss (formerly in command at Mudros), was no less furious and sacked Hayes-Sadler, the third British admiral after Milne and Troubridge to be removed from seagoing command for missing the *Goeben*:

> The *Goeben* getting away is perfectly damnable and has considerably upset me, since we at the Admiralty were under the happy delusion that there were sufficient brains and sufficient means out there to prevent it: of the latter there were; of the former apparently not.

He could just as well have been talking in August 1914.

The anti-climactic battle of Imbros cost the British 200 men, two monitors, one submarine, two aircraft and a steamer; the Germans and Turks lost some 400 men along with SMS *Breslau*, together with SMS *Emden*, the most successful light cruiser in the history of the Imperial German Navy. Since the war was going badly for the Turks on all remaining fronts, the *Goeben* was given only running repairs because her heavy guns might be needed at any time to defend Constantinople.

On 1 May she sailed out of the Bosporus bound for Sevastopol, where she had helped with her guns to force Russia into the war in 1914, to keep an eye on the naval base which she reached the next day. The victorious German Army had marched into the city and a Russian admiral had led two battleships, ten destroyers and other ships out of harbour to Novoros-siysk, in breach of the Treaty of Brest-Litovsk. The Kaiser's ensign was hoisted on the four remaining battleships and German troops took posses-sion of them. On 6 June the *Goeben* started a week in a naval dry dock, for the first time since well before the war started. The three holes from the Imbros mines were left with temporary plugs for want of time and labour. After various local tasks the *Goeben* arrived back in Constantinople on 12 July for serious repairs. The first hole was closed by the middle of October.

Immediately after the Allied armistice with Turkey, Paschwitz formally handed over the *Yavuz* to the Turkish Navy. The Turks let the German crew go home despite Allied demands for their surrender. They went to Odessa by steamer and got back eventually by train. The Turks refused to hand over the battered ship, which was moored in a little bay on the Asian shore not far from Constantinople. There she rotted until 1927, when a reviving Turkey called in French salvage and repair experts.

In 1930 the gleaming *Yavuz* re-emerged as the imposing flagship of the Turkish Navy and showed the flag in the Mediterranean on many occa-sions, visiting still-British Malta in 1936. In 1938 she had the honour of conveying the body of Mustafa Kemal Atatürk across the water from Istanbul to the railhead from which he was carried to Ankara for burial. She was transferred to the reserve in 1950 and decommissioned in 1954, when she became a floating museum. In 1973 she was sold for scrap, a process, completed in 1976, which marked the disappearance of the last ship of the Kaiser's navy to survive afloat. The Turkish Naval Museum in Istanbul retains one of her secondary 15-cm guns, her emergency bridge and the fixtures and fittings of Admiral Souchon's state cabin.

So much for the great German ship which was the trigger of the Dardan-elles campaign; what of the much more modest vessel that determined its outcome, the Turkish minelayer *Nusret*, with which this story began? When the war ended, the poacher turned gamekeeper: the minelayer was used to look for stray mines in the Sea of Marmara and the Dardanelles from 1918 to 1926, undergoing a refit in 1927. Ten years later she was renamed *Yardim* and put to use as a support ship for divers. Restyled *Nusret* in 1939, she worked with mines again until decommissioned in 1955 and laid up. In 1962 she was sold off and worked as a tramp steamer until 1966. After that she was sold off again, and then again, and gradually rusted her way through the 1980s in the south-eastern Anatolian harbour of Mersin. She was saved by harbour cranes when she turned over, but this did not stop her sinking altogether in 1990 at Mersin when under tow on her way to Magosa in northern Cyprus. She was refloated but beached and left to rot on a mud bank. In 2002 the municipality of Tarsus, a few miles east of Mersin, was given ownership rights by the Turkish Ministry of Culture and announced it would have her restored and placed in a new Gallipoli Park as centrepiece of a display.

Meanwhile she has been cloned; a replica *Nusret* in gleaming warship grey can be explored as she stands proudly ensconced on a special plinth at the excellent Naval Museum at Çannakale, overlooking the Narrows which the original was so successfully deployed to defend – the most devastatingly successful minelayer in history.

A Note on Sources

The main source of information about the Royal Navy's role in the Dardanelles campaign of 1914–15 is, not surprisingly, the National Archives at Kew, Richmond, Surrey. The chief sources for the Germans' role are the Federal Archive at Koblenz and its associated Military Archives at Freiburg-im-Breisgau. Nowadays there is a mass of material, of mixed value, on the Internet. One site deserves special mention: the writings on the Dardanelles campaign of Piotr Nykiel, formerly of the Polish diplomatic service, who was stationed in Ankara from 2000 to 2004 and joined the department of Turkish studies at the Jagiellonian University in Krakow. He provides a neutral and unusual viewpoint and his papers can be reached via www.navyingallipoli@yahoo.com.

At Kew, various files in the huge but not very navigable Admiralty collections of papers, such as ADM 137 (papers used by the official historian), yield a great deal of information, if sometimes very slowly. ADM 137/881, 1089 and 1090, for example, contain letters of proceedings from naval commanders, including Carden, at the Dardanelles. ADM 116/1432–4 cover the Dardanelles operations of the East Mediterranean Squadron. De Robeck's report on the troop landings is in number 1434. ADM 116/1437 and also 1713 and 1714 record the work of the Dardanelles Commission.

In the Cabinet papers, CAB 2/1–3 contain Hankey's minutes of the pre-war Committee of Imperial Defence. CAB 22 contains his minutes of the War Council from 5 August 1914 to 14 May 1915. The CAB 17/123 series is of great value, including some of Hankey's letters as well as Churchill's account of Dardanelles operations dated 13 May 1915 (the time he was leaving the Admiralty; also found in CAB 1/12), some of his memoranda and letters, the operational order for the Dardanelles attack, as well as telegrams between Kitchener and Hamilton. ADM 116/1713 and 1714 contain invaluable reports from the Dardanelles Committee (as distinct from the Commission), a group of navy, army and air-force officers who went to Turkey and examined every aspect of the double disaster for

British arms at the Dardanelles and Gallipoli in enormous detail, interviewing many of the main enemy figures at length.

The Liddell Hart Military Archive at King's College, London, contains a very useful compilation of official papers and letters about the campaign. The collection of naval documents at the Archive Centre at Churchill College, Cambridge, includes the papers of Admiral de Robeck. I am grateful to both institutions for their help.

The same goes for the Imperial War Museum's Sound Archive, from which I garnered quotations from participants in the campaign. The references are: Marine William Jones, 004141/D/A; AB W. G. Northcott, 4187/B/B; ERA Gilbert Adshead, 660; Cdr. Norman Holbrook, VC, RN, 7142; Capt. Henry Mangles Denham, RN, 8871.

When it comes to books (see select bibliography), Sir Julian Corbett's *Official History of the Great War – Naval Operations*, Volume II, may be elderly and enormously detailed, but remains essential. Volume II of Marder's magisterial *From the* Dreadnought *to Scapa Flow* and Robert K. Massie's *Castles of Steel* both provide detailed running accounts of events and background. Churchill's *The World Crisis*, Volume II, is his dazzlingly readable account, best consumed with liberal pinches of salt – and best read alongside Corbett and Volume III of Martin Gilbert's enormous biography. General Hamilton's diary is a commendably short if slightly wistful account, well written and without self-pity. For highly readable general accounts focused on the Gallipoli campaign I would recommend Robert Rhodes James, Alan Moorehead and Tim Travers.

Select Bibliography

Aspinall-Oglander, Brig.-Gen. C. F., *Military Operations – Gallipoli*, Vol. I (London, HMSO, 1929)

Baedeker, Karl, *Konstantinopel, Balkanstaaten, Kleinasien* guidebook (Leipzig, Baedeker Verlag, 1914 edition)

Beesly, Patrick, *Room 40 – British Naval Intelligence 1914–18* (London, Hamish Hamilton, 1982)

Bienaimé, Amiral Amadée, *La Guerre navale 1914–1915, fautes et responsabilités* (Paris, Tallandier, 1920)

Çannakale Onsekiz Mart University, *The Gallipoli Campaign – International Perspectives 85 years on* (Record of symposium, Çannakale, Turkey, 2005)

Carver, Field Marshal Lord, *The Turkish Front 1914–18* (London, Pan/National Army Museum, 2003)

Chack, Paul and Antier, Jean-Jacques, *Histoire maritime de la première guerre mondiale: Tome II Méditerranée 1914–1915* (Paris, Editions France-Empire, 1969)

Churchill, W. S., *The World Crisis*, Vol. II (London, Thornton Butterworth, 1923)

Coates, Tim (ed.), *Lord Kitchener and Winston Churchill – The Dardanelles Commission, Part I* (London, Stationery Office, 2000)

Colledge, J. J., revised by Warlow, Lt.-Cdr. Ben, *Ships of the Royal Navy – the Complete Record of All Fighting Ships of the Royal Navy* (London, Greenhill Books, 2003)

Compton-Hall, Richard, *Submarines and the War at Sea 1914–18* (London, Macmillan, 1991)

Corbett, Sir Julian, *History of the Great War – Naval Operations*, Vols I and II (London, Longmans Green, 1920/1921)

Gilbert, Martin, *Winston S. Churchill 1874–1965*, Vol. III 1914–1916 (London, Heinemann, 1971, with companion volume of documents)

– – –, *First World War Atlas* (London, Weidenfeld & Nicolson, 1970)

– – –, *First World War* (London, Weidenfeld & Nicolson, 1994)

Gray, Randal (with Argyle, Christopher), *Chronicle of the First World War*, Vol. I, 1914–1916 (New York/Oxford, Facts on File, 1990)

Grove, Eric J., *The Royal Navy Since 1815* (London, Palgrave Macmillan, 2005)

Halpern, Paul G. (ed.), *The Keyes Papers*, Vol. I (London, Navy Records Society, 1979)

Hamilton, General Sir Ian, *Gallipoli Diary* (London, Edward Arnold, 1920)

Hill, J. R. (ed.), *The Oxford Illustrated History of the Royal Navy* (OUP, 1995)

Hough, Richard, *The Great War at Sea 1914–1918* (OUP, 1983)

James, Robert Rhodes, *Gallipoli* (London, Papermac, 1989)

Jane's Fighting Ships: various editions, esp. uncensored fourth edition, London, 1914

Jouan, Capitaine R., *Les Marins allemands au combat* (Paris, Payot, 1930)

Kearsey, Lt.-Col. A., *Notes and Comments on the Dardanelles Campaign* (Aldershot, Gale & Polden, 1934; reissued by Naval and Military Press, Uckfield, E. Sussex, 2004)

Keyes, Admiral of the Fleet Sir Roger, *The Fight for Gallipoli* (London, Eyre & Spottiswoode, 1934)

Kopp, Georg, *Das Teufelschiff und seine kleine Schwester*, trans. by Chambers, Arthur, as: *The Flight of the* Goeben *and the* Breslau (London, Hutchinson, 1931)

Lewis, Geoffrey, *Modern Turkey* (London, Ernest Benn, 1974)

Liddell Hart, B.H., *History of the First World War* (London, Cassell, 1970)

Lorey, Rear-Admiral Hermann (ed.), *Der Krieg in den türkischen Gewässern* (Berlin, E. S. Mittler & Sohn, 2 vols, 1928 and 1938 – part of the official German naval history of the Great War, *Der Krieg zur See*)

Lumby, E. W. R. (ed.), *Policy and Operations in the Mediterranean 1912–14* (London, Navy Records Society, 1970)

Macmillan, Margaret, *Peacemakers – Six Months that Changed the World* (John Murray, London, 2001)

Mäkela, Matti E., *Souchon der* Goeben*admiral greift in die Weltgeschichte ein* (Brunswick, Vieweg, 1936)

– – –, *Auf den Spuren des* Goeben (Munich, Bernard und Graefe, 1979)

Mango, Andrew, *Atatürk* (London, John Murray, 2004)

Mantey, Vice-Admiral Eberhard von (ed.), *Auf See Unbesiegt*, includes Admiral Souchon's own account of his campaigns (Berlin, Weller, 1927)

Marder, Arthur J., *From the* Dreadnought *to Scapa Flow*, Vol. II (Oxford, 1965)

Massie, Robert K., *Castles of Steel* (London, Jonathan Cape, 2003)

McLaughlin, Redmond, *The Escape of the* Goeben (London, Seeley Service, 1974)

Milton, Giles, *Paradise Lost – Smyrna 1922: The Destruction of Islam's City of Tolerance* (London, Sceptre, 2008)

Moorehead, Alan, *Gallipoli* (London, Macmillan, 1975)

Pollock, John, *Kitchener* (London, Constable, 2001)

Stone, Norman, *World War One – a Short History* (London, Allen Lane, 2007)

Thomazi, Captain Auguste Antoine, *La Guerre navale aux Dardanelles* with preface by Vice-Admiral P. Guépratte (Paris, Payot, 1926)

Thompson, Julian, *The Imperial War Museum Book of the War at Sea 1914–1918* (London, Sidgwick & Jackson/IWM, 2005)

Travers, Tim, *Gallipoli 1915* (Stroud, Glos., Tempus Publishing, 2001)

Tuchman, Babara, *August 1914* (London, Macmillan, 1980 – US title *The Guns of August*)

Van der Vat, Dan, *The Ship That Changed the World: The Escape of the* Goeben *to the Dardanelles in 1914* (revised edition, Edinburgh, Birlinn, 2000)

– – –, *Standard of Power: The Royal Navy in the 20th Century* (London, Hutchinson, 2000)

Wells, Captain John, *The Royal Navy – an Illustrated Social History* (Stroud, Glos., Sutton Publishing, 1994, in association with Royal Naval Museum, Portsmouth)

Wragg, David, *Royal Navy Handbook 1914–1918* (Stroud, Glos., Sutton Publishing, 2006)

Index